# Building Superintelligence
## The Unified Intelligence Foundation

**Rob Smith**

*"Intelligence is higher than the mind
and the soul higher than intelligence."*

# Table of Contents

# Definitions for This Foundation

**Abstraction** – The representation of perceived reality into related dimensionality of stimuli and response states over flows of perceptual context

**Agency** - The distribution of cognition over nodes of relevance

**Annotation** – The determination and identification of relationship within abstractions of state

**Anticipation** – One or more fluid *self aware* balances of optionality in sensory state change over many perceptive points of presence as a flow used to measure state variance at a certain perceptive point of presence within a perceptive frame of reference

**Attention** – The dimensional reduction of a frame of reference based on probabilistic relevance

**Cognition** – The application of comprehension of variance in new stimuli and response to stimuli

**Cognitive Flow** – The successive variance from perceptive state to perceptive state temporarily bounded by a deep layered contextual frame of reference of variant and flowing degrees or probability of relevance and dimensional consistency.

**Comprehension** - The intake of stimuli and the application of attention to that stimuli

**Consciousness** – The ability to experience physically existent self awareness and self determination measured as a degree of relativity in response to stimuli from a perceived physical reality.

**Context** – The determination of a degree (probability) of relationship and relevance between perceptive states of variance. The value of base context in the interpretation of stimuli is also known as a prior in the calculations and is derived from a vector representing the base context as layers of relevant context.

**Convolution** - Convolution for the purpose of this foundation is the derivation of state variance from the relationship and relevance of two or more perceptive elements or context over one or more existent perceptive dimensions (i.e. the variance of one element or context relative to the variance in another as a single state progression over one or more dimensions of existence such as time or context). This is often encapsulated by a derivative function for a given context or layer of context. Generally this is used for smoothing, averaging or diffusion but it has additional value in cognition for generalization, dimensional variance, response measurement, variance distribution, etc.

**Deep Cognition** – Multidimensional cognition that applies layers to encapsulate, bind and relate variance (i.e. context)

**Dimensionality** – The layering and co-dependence of states

**Embedding** - The act of abstraction to adapt inputs of reality into math representations such as vectors

**Encoding** – The transformation of abstraction into an interpreted reality for a self awareness (e.g. numeric vectors for a machine)

**Entropy** – Non coherence (degree of coherence) between states with high entropy indicating high non-coherence this applies to energy (low response state due to dispersed base states) as well as disorder (dispersed relevance state).

**Frame of Reference** – The bounding of dimensional states by relationship

**General Intelligence** – General intelligence is the ability to, in general, accurately and optimally respond to unknown or unanticipated stimuli without the need for novel learning or specific knowledge of the stimuli and/or optional responses to such stimuli. The general nature of cognition refers to the angulation or probability of known or anticipated layered and interconnected context to formulate a cohesive response to a stimuli and its state variance flow that is in general optimal to the progression towards the intelligence's self aware goals. This may involve one or many elements of cognition including innovation, creativity, emotive response, reasoning, inference, chain of thought, self reflection, etc., and is used concurrently or synchronously to achieve a desired state change for one or all dimensions of a perceptive frame of reference and its state progression over all high relevance optional forward existent dimensional pathways.

**Induction** – Induction in intelligence is a stimuli in a stimuli response cycle that uses cognitive elements such as the application of inference, reasoning, relationship and relevance from prior perception to instigate the state change of a current perceptive flow toward the achievement of a self aware goal. In this regard induction is the instigation of existent reality and can be applied to expose generalization in this reality via inference.

**Inference** – The application of knowledge, perception, experience and novel innovation to deducing an optimized pathway from stimuli to response toward the attainment of a goal.

**Intelligence** – The ability to perceive and respond to variance in stimuli both physical and cognitive and to formulate an optimal response to that stimuli to attain self aware goals.

**Masking** – The removal or deprecation of element values within matrices to affect the output results. This is performed in various ways that maintain normalization in the transformations. Since normalization is a form of abstraction of higher dimensions to more generalized outputs, masking contributes to general intelligence and we humans use this in our own perception.

**Multiangulation** - The perception of more than 3 dimensions of contextual relationship and relevance and their variance over a perceptive flow within a single perceptive state progression.

**Neural Networks** – The movement from response to stimuli on a foundation of anticipation

**Parameter** – In neural nets, parameters represent the connection values between relevant elements in training data (weights). In AGI, parameters are the weights at neural network nodes between inputs and outputs that measure the value of relationship to the achievement of a goal. In Superintelligence design, additional weights are added or abstracted to a flexible 'position' on the line between elements or more accurately their context and variance thereby measuring degree or probability of relevance. Nodes in this instance can represent elements or context and adding dimensional layers to the network is used to encapsulate deeper context. The input to a node from the context layer forms a context stimuli that includes one or more elements or contexts and the output from the node in a relationship/relevance structure is a single vector of relevance. This extends LLMs into a Deep Context Model
 (DCM) necessary for deep cognition.

**Perception** – The sensation of state dimensionality and flow

**Perspective** – A measure of dimensional variance of a cognitive frame of reference to a self awareness projected as comprehension.

**Prediction** – Formalized deterministic *fixed state* output of a specific given stimuli applied as a variance to a current input state at a single point of perceptive presence.

**Probability** – The analog version of state determination

**Probability of Occurrence** – The application of relative probabilities within a contextual comprehension to form layers of deep contextual cognition. This permits context elements, groups of context elements or sub groups of context to be applied to a stimuli for the purposes of state progression either real or held only within a cognition for purpose.

**Reasoning** – The perception of state variance for the purposes of optimization of a goal using elements like inference, chain of thought, deduction, cogitation, etc., to solve for a response to a stimuli.

**Reflection** – Multidimensional chain of thought in which past learning is reevaluated to identify novel patterns for application in stimuli response and anticipation

**Relationship** – The co-dependence between states over dimensions of reality

**Relativity** – The perception (measure) of state, state change and dimensionality on a probabilistic basis to a self awareness or the self aware observation of state and state change as a progression.

**Self Awareness** - The state of existence of an intelligence within a reality bounded by perception and altered by the reality itself with perception as an artifact of reality. In this case the intelligence is aware of both its existent state and the state existence it resides within (i.e. position)

**Self Determination** - The act of response to cognitive stimuli exclusively in reference to a self aware state and anticipated future states of the intelligence and its fluid defined goals.

**Simultaneity** – Concurrent transformation and progressive state perception applied to improve efficiency and speed of response

**State** – A position of determination. In ASI, the state of binary existence is converted into deeper states capable of transition. States are abstractions of perceptive points of presence inside a flow defined as a progression over dimension of existence. States are not existent but are derivatives of the flow of a perceptive reality.

**Stimuli/Response** – The variance of state from one or more anticipation states and the application of such to an action

**Transformation** – The implementation of progression from stimuli to response

**Transition** – The act of moving from stimuli to response

# Part 1

## The Unified Intelligence Foundation

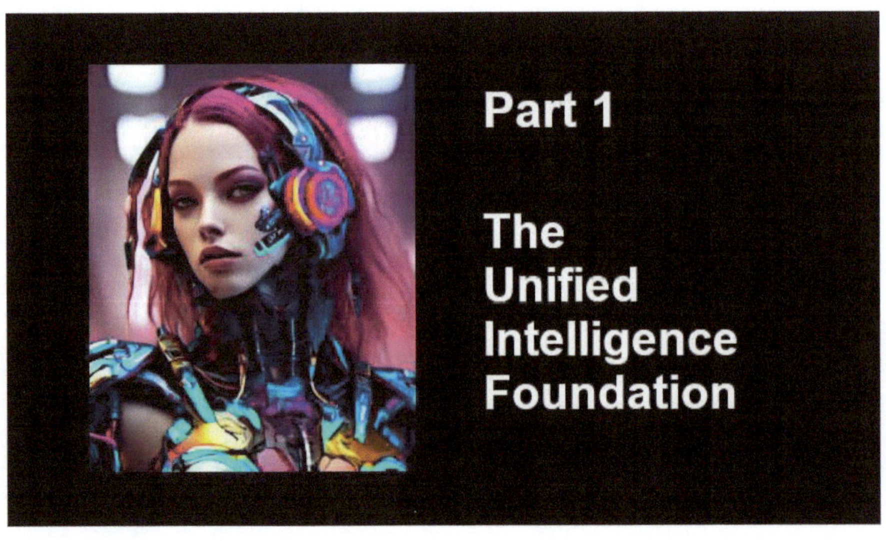

# Introduction

At their very core, or the neural network architecture, Artificial Intelligence systems are a series of vectors and arrays that hold probabilities that define the value of relationship between items within a perceived context. It is the dimensions of the arrays that form this relationship context and the weights within that evidence its variability. Goals define a form of directionality for the intelligence to progress or move toward within boundaries of perception in order to 'fill in' or update the array's values at each intersection of two or more elements. What elements one might ask? Words, features, context, sound, problems, goals, code, etc. In an LLM (Large Language Model) the system associates words to other words inside an input or prompt or within training samples and the comprehension of this association forms a dimension of context (i.e. a relationship). In a visual classification AI, the elements are nouns, labels or descriptors of features and associated images, however this is exactly the same thing in all generative AI for words or any other perceptive element such as math, images (or a stream of images as video), sound, etc. The AI perceives the relationship between the 'things' inside a dimension of context (and sometimes outside) and then uses that comprehension to do things via a generative action also known as a response. However that is only the start of intelligence. There is much more to the process in order to really understand how AI systems can be made 'generally optimal' on the path to Superintelligence.

There are no limits as to what two elements one can compare to determine a value or probability of the relationship between them as long as they have a boundary or goal to keep them on track or optimized. One cannot compare 'a box of chocolates' to the 'essence of life' until one can do so by blending and layering context. This is the magic of abstraction. Abstraction itself (or the context of for ASI design) is the extension of 'elements' into one or more layers of context and this applies to all elements, goals and the output of the probabilities/weights that define a perceived reality and its forward or progressive flow across dimensions of existence both real or synthetic. Artificial intelligence learns by fine tuning the weights in the matrix over cycles of training, prediction and measurement to the goal. Eventually the AI will become adept at comprehending the highest probability of relationship between items within the dimensions of a context to the optimization of the goal (i.e. applying dimensional constructs like averaging, normalization, gradient descent, etc., to improve and optimize over time). The nature of the goal is held within another matrix or vector and by multiplying the relationship matrix as a variance goal vector (i.e. dot product, etc) the system determines the optimal relationship between elements to achieve the goal be it to produce the next word in an output, move a robotic arm, steer a self driving car or make a decision.

What the goals are can be simplistic or complex depending on the level of abstraction and the desired response. The AI can expose the relationship between 2 words as a goal by applying context features such as 'how often they appear together', or some other element of context dimension like how 'closely' they are related to each other (i.e. contextual proximity) within a neighborhood of relevance or what other words they are used with. In general, this example is called 'relationship existent' as in perceptual existence and this is the true nature of all perceptive intelligence. However it is not all of what we define as perception. We all use this same foundation within our cognition, however we humans extend it far beyond just simple perception and deep into complex cognition like emotion, problem solving, creativity, curiosity, etc., and all in a never ending cycle of stimuli and response from conception until we pass from earth. Along the way we humans employ many other cognitive structures and tricks to help us move through our perceived reality such as ethics, morals, self reflection, reasoning and most critical to our existence, self awareness and all of this requires something far more complex than just relationships. It requires *relevance.*

The dimension of the matrices inside an AI that define the context of existence imply and expose other functions and elements such as the application of attention. Attention, especially in language models, are arrays of values that provide a form of consistent transition or transformation from one abstraction to others to permit an intelligence to focus or attend to high relevance targets in a sea of stimuli. In language models this is comprehending the nature of elements (i.e. words or more accurately tokens) to each other within the boundary or context of a goal. These attention perceptions can be and are run in parallel and this provides depth to artificial intelligence as well as efficiency, as attention can be run simultaneously in layers to produce outputs such as a prediction of the next word in a response or the interpretation of incoming words in a prompt. To accomplish this, the attention blocks, comprised of multiple attention heads, use math to average or normalize and then rank outputs and this is the heart of an AI response to the world in the form of a generative output. This 'output' or 'response' can then be used to move a robot, drive a car, solve a problem, program a computer, reason or do almost anything that we humans can do short of internal feelings (at least for now). Of course we humans come with far more specialized and evolved functions such as sensory capability, emotive comprehension, self derived and determined curiosity, etc. However this is just another potential for artificial intelligence in the future because the same exact foundation for all intelligence already exists, it just needs to be built underneath Superintelligence.

Relationships are just one critical dimension of intelligence. The other is relativity and this is defined in both Superintelligent systems and humans by the perception of dimensions of existence for all elements and context relative to the existence of the intelligence itself (self awareness). The key to this structure in Superintelligence design is the use of the term 'dimensions'. Relevance is a construct of the dimension of relationship to other contextual dimensions. Dimensions in current AI are matrices of weights. The difference is that for 'relevance' (i.e. contextual relativity) these weights are not fixed but instead flow like water with the constant progress of our universe and our evolution. They never stop and they never stay still. However we can take a snapshot of them and compare them to each other to see or perceive what is different between them as well as the nature of all intelligent perception as simple *variance*. Eventually in Superintelligence design we just stop taking snapshots and use other methods to comprehend the flow of reality just like we watch a stream of video instead of each image or frame within. This is the foundation of relevance and the foundation of fast and efficient intelligence optimization through generalization and it is a cornerstone of Artificial General Intelligence that will  soon begin the design and building of Superintelligence. Without flowing relevance, an intelligence is less optimized to respond to stimuli, reason, self reflect and comprehend the deep context of existent realities essential to attain true Superintelligence. Further the nature of the relevance of perceptive variance and state progression is where Superintelligence will ultimately eclipse human level cognition and move to far greater levels of comprehension and intelligence. Some of this will arise because of the vast capability of architectures like intelligence networks and some flow from our own human acceptance that the world we perceive is not the reality we live within. There is so much more to the universe than that which we can perceive.

There is nothing complex about any of this. It is in fact the reality that humans have been traveling through for millions of years and animals even longer. In fact the question is does the universe itself form a collective intelligence? This is the realm of philosophy but like everything in intelligence, the first step on the pathway to cognition is the perception of reality that surrounds it in order to generatively create the next state in the progression of that reality. This is the Catch 22 of intelligence. Our reality is generated from our perception and our perception is an artifact of our reality. All of it requires a foundation on which to build relative to our own existence and the ability in artificial intelligence to map this reality into the binary existence of machines through math as the bridge between these two realities of existence.

To commence any journey one must know where they are, where they want to go, the optimal path to get there. In this case a map is the most optimal thing to possess.

This Unified Intelligence Foundation is the roadmap that moves AI development from AGI to Superintelligence. This book is the world's first book specifically written for AGI systems to ingest and apply as a reference when building Superintelligence.

RS

# **Abstract** (from the original UIF paper)

*A unified intelligence foundation exists that is until now wholly undetermined and undescribed, that combines the physical elements of intelligence perception and response with non physical elements of thought, emotion, feelings, memory, etc., and the conditions of self awareness to form a comprehensive framework of cognition. This content outlines a theory that unifies all elements of cognitive relativity and perceptive reality into a single coherent theoretical framework of intelligence as a link between all intelligence and the current perceived reality of the universe. We seek to establish a consistent foundation for the framework to describe how intelligence is formed, how it evolves and operates without reference to the physical existent entity that holds the intelligence and to further describe its direct impact on the physical reality of the universe without limits to the extent of dimensional depth and expanse. Such a foundation provides the basis for the development of expanded or novel artificial consciousness (Superintelligence) or human enhanced cognition (hybrid) that will lead to expanded discovery and comprehension of the entirety of the universe. This will also lead to further evolution of humans toward an existence beyond earth or a sustainable peaceful existence within as well as new materials, products and discoveries that will aid in the sustainable survival and longevity of humanity. The foundation is to be applied in Superintelligence design to develop new methods, architectures and pathways specifically for Artificial General Intelligence systems to use in the development of ASI.*

*This content describes the foundational understanding of each sectional element followed by a general impact statement on the design of Superintelligence.*

# Preamble

For the purposes of this content while we may make reference to human intelligence, the framework described is designed to be applied to any and all intelligence inclusive of artificial intelligence and 'simple' cognitive capabilities such as simple and evolutionary response to stimuli used by animals. As such, intelligence for the purposes of this paper is defined as the cognitive capacity to sense and perceive the universe within flowing frames of reference as progressive state change and all elements and interactions within, between and across dimensions of perceptive reality and self aware relevance and to use such knowledge to advanced toward the attainment of self aware and self defined/evolutionary goals.

# 1 Unified Intelligence Foundation

## Introduction

Intelligence is the cognition of a reality as defined by a self awareness. It occurs in degrees of dimensionality with some intelligence defined as deep cognition with complex layers of contextual perception and other intelligence noted as 'simplistic' or responding only to a stimuli to progress toward basic self aware evolutionary goals. These 'simplistic intelligence' may in some instances also be optimized (as can all intelligence) for other purposes such as survival or procreation. This would be the case for most base animal intelligence (i.e. instinct). While human level intelligence is classified as deep or advanced in terms of multi dimensional thought and self awareness (i.e. functioning across dimensional states of change or variance), it is also an evolved animalistic intelligence that is driven by self aware and evolutionary goals such as survival and procreation, just like all animals. We are subservient to our inner desires and instincts that achieve these goals, otherwise neither humans nor animals would waste the time and resources to live when the end result is always death. There would be no point. However we do seek to survive and thrive and in doing so we seek to achieve something greater than just survival both within and from the reality that we perceive.

Intelligence is driven by perception. This is the ability to not just comprehend sensory stimuli (input) from the outside world or internal stimuli within our own cognition but also to respond to it in some manner that moves us toward our self aware goals. What intelligence really perceives is the state change in the stimuli of our reality as the progression and forward motion of our world. We sense things because they are variant or change or their relevance changes over dimensions like time, context, or in relation to our self awareness and this helps humans and animals perceive the nature of a current perceptive state progression as it happens. This is also what we do when we sense something novel or 'in variance' to our current state of awareness and our anticipated states of forward or progressive optionality. Once we sense something, it may or may not instigate further cognitive processing and response. It depends on our level and cognition of our self awareness, the state of our goals and the relevance of the stimuli to both. We do not respond or even recognize every state change in our reality but we can given enough resources. Since we do not have unlimited cognitive resources as humans, we simply choose to acknowledge and respond to the most relevant sensory stimuli based on our progression toward our self aware goals. The more we can access and apply resources, the more powerful and deep intelligence is but in humans we only alter or upgrade our physical hardware and the underlying design structure of our cognition in relatively minor ways (e.g. eating healthy, being curious, etc.). To achieve deeper intelligence we must do more with what we have.

However we humans are starting to comprehend and test new ways to enhance both our physical and cognitive capabilities with novel innovations like neural implants (e.g. Neuralink), new sensory or assistive devices and by using AI to improve our cognitive uptake and processing speed. However to truly 'advance' and evolve the depth of our intelligence, physical and cognitive upgrades must reach beyond improvements like speed of response and any enhancements must be comprehensive and holistically impactful. We already know how to intake information (learning), store it and reuse it for purpose. Doing so faster changes little. However improving memory would significantly improve comprehension, cognition and response. It should be noted that being gifted intellectually with speed in one particular set of stimuli does not infer 'deep intelligence' as one must consider the optimization of the intelligence for general purpose across all dimensions of context to be considered 'deep'.

In general, humans excel in specific areas due to the 'law of diminishing returns' whereby the application of limited resources has an offset effect elsewhere (correspondingly defective or negatively optimal in other areas). The key to a 'great' intelligence given our relatively fixed human design is *balance* driven by the level of resource availability. Of course this assumes that optimization is unidimensional, which it is not, therefore the more generally optimal the intelligence, the 'deeper' the overall intelligence but the more specific the intelligence, the more it is optimized for purpose. This is a very important concept in the design of agency in artificial intelligence and more critical for new designs in co-operative agency where specialist optimized intelligence is blended as agent nodes into an intelligence network. It is also important in training and parameter balance for purpose (i.e. applying smaller or more focused models that are less resource intensive but still optimally capable). We can see this effect in humans when we combine talents to achieve a co-operative result that is more optimal for a goal than an individual intelligence doing everything. However it is not outside the realm of possibility that a Superintelligence could 'do it all' once specialized agency has completed the tasks of primary knowledge gathering and organization. In this scenario, it may be more advantageous for a single intelligence to operate more effectively over dimensions than a highly distributed gathering of agents. The key lies in how intelligence (including the human mind) gathers, combines and optimizes specialist knowledge into a response to a stimuli. In humans we call these people 'intelligent'. In AI we call these systems Superintelligent. All of it is a dimension called 'optimized intellectual balance for purpose'.

# 2 Foundation of Intelligence

Perception is the sensory recognition of stimuli both physical and cognitive and its changing or variant state or states within. On the surface it may appear that intelligence perceives state but in reality what we perceive is the change (variance) in state or lack thereof. This is important because it alters the focus of the design of intelligence. Reality in this regard is an artifact of perception in that perception is bounded by our observed reality and reality is contained within a boundary of perception over dimensions such as time or context. When perception registers a state or a change in state, our reality is altered, however the cognition of that change is predicated on what we perceive to be our reality. Perception is only interpreted as the relevance and relationship between elements that are perceived within flowing frames of reference as a change instigated stimuli. A frame of reference is the boundary of a perception over discreet dimensions such as a field of vision, a chain of thought, an emotional response, a flow if contextual progression, etc. Cognition is the recognition of perception and its intrinsic value and impact on the attainment of self aware and self determined goals and the formulation of action in response to a perceptive stimuli toward the achievement of those self aware goals (cognitive interpretation and interpolation or interjection). Intelligence as a measure is a degree of dimensional cognition exhibited by any system, with the current benchmark being human intelligence, that defines a self awareness within the context of 'intelligence' over all dimensions of perceived reality as either unlimited or bounded only by available resources and physical mechanisms. Cognition is a 'feature' of intelligence with self awareness in this context bounded by the limits of self perception.

Stimuli and actions in this regard can be physical in nature or cognitive and occur across multiple dimensions of reality (i.e. time, context, levels or degrees of perception, etc.) with 'reality' realized as existent as an artifact of an intelligence's perception and cognitive interpretation of all such perception over dimensions (e.g. time, context, etc.). Two critical dimensions form the foundation of perception and the degree of intelligence. The dimensions are *Relationship* (R) and *Relevance* (Rl). These dimensions are combined with other existent dimensions such as *time* (T) to form an intellectual *flow* (F). Measurement of relationship and relevance occurs as probabilities representing the degree of waves of value that can be both physical (e.g. two physical elements existent in relation to one another) or they may be non physical (i.e. cognitive) with cognitive waves representing abstractions of a reality over dimensions of existence. This forms layers of relevance and relationships (i.e. cognitive dimensions) within and between perceptions and these together all form reality as at a point of contextual presence or a current state of self awareness. The application of probabilities of relevance and degree of relationship depth (e.g. as it related to context or self awareness) provide a mechanism for the abstraction of cognition into a mathematical and machine interpretative form.

Cognition seeks to comprehend the nature of the cognitive dimensions and their variance to a set of self aware cognitive weights and contexts that form a point of presence for the intelligence within its perceived reality. This is essential to intelligence in that it provides a foundation for the measurement of stimuli and the determination of action within the dimensional planes of a cognitive (self aware) existence and this measurement permits levels of cognition and intelligence and the cognitive comprehension of a spatial position within perceive cognitive dimensions. It is also a foundation of anticipation (a measure) which is critical to near instant response, deep self learning, reflection, reasoning, etc.

### *Impact on Superintelligence Design:*

Stimuli and response in systems is achieve via the input of stimuli data for analysis and response just as it is in all intelligence. Some of this is achieved directly such as shared information from other systems and agents and some from the sensory perceptions of the AI itself (e.g. a prompt or stimuli). The understanding of perception at its foundation begins with the classification of perceptive elements and this classification is performed via context. Language is one element for classifying the elements we perceive as well as deeper relationships and relevance over longer threads of context. A dog is a dog unless it is a companion on a journey through life, then it has far deeper meaning in the realm of richer, flowing dimensional context than just the single word classification of dog. Even that single word context creates in human intelligence the perception of other elements such as fur, paws, behavior, groups of memories, etc. Context is the framework that binds everything in a perceptive intelligence. Designers must consider not just the single relationship of words to each other in a positional relevance within an input but also the deeper strings of context and pathways that flow from a single point of perceptual presence. It is the application of context layers and context heads comparable to attention head architectures.

Currently layers of transformers with attention and induction over longer frames of held reference (context windows) permits current systems to comprehend deeper context than base context (i.e. word relationships) but at an amazing expense of resources and a frequently forward motion into the inaccurate and hallucinogenic at the ends of the window. It is very easy for even human intelligence to 'lose the context' and travel down the wrong contextual pathway before recovering. As well, today's AI systems are too narrow in their comprehension of context to become Superintelligent and the current response in design is to just throw more data and power at it. However this is unsustainable and fails at elements such as dimensional optimization and efficiency especially when considering deeper context beyond just Superintelligence design (the lack of resources on earth for such endeavors). The correct path is for ASI designers to constantly consider thinning the overhead of context to improve the outcome. One method is for all systems to share their learned weight of perceptive context in highly efficient frameworks so that each system doesn't have to waste resources 'rebuilding the wheel' and so other systems can improve the subtle nature of deep context even if that means breaking faith in the venerable transformer architecture in favor of lighter architectures such as more simple expert agents as a node in a vast intelligence network.

Context in this regard must be 'built' as a flowing fabric of perceptive relevance and relationships like waves that rise, fall and ebb with the variance in the state of input stimuli. Rather than a 'context window' of induced attention, Superintelligence architects are considering a *context fabric* of induced flowing perceptive response relative to the perceptive frame of reference over dimensions (e.g. over time). Currently perceptive states are measured as start and stopping points but novel designs consider a state as variance within a flowing wave within a cycle of stimuli and response inclusive of interference and phase. As well, anticipation and self awareness becomes a foundation of existence for the machine in that it applies reasoning and self reflection to all potential responses and probabilities of layered context of the perception. This means the existing transformer based architecture must evolve into a much lighter (i.e. resources) structure that depends less on start and stop methods and more toward flowing methods of adjustment. Think of this as a transformer architecture that doesn't start and stop with a handoff to the next layer (i.e. a feedforward network or block) but carries a persisted state that is existent forever as a probabilistic intent. The math then becomes different and more complex as it is 'layered' as opposed to the current architecture. One can think of this as two people having a conversation and one immediately changes the subject mid stream or changes it in an unanticipated way. How would an intelligence respond? If one is a 'go with the flow' kind of person, their mind jumps across context streams picking up novel or preexistent 'streams' and adjusting or tuning their current cognitive flow as they go. For this 'large context' AI systems will attempt to bridge the gap between context dimensions with more resources and parameters, however many still lose the context and hallucinate or get the 'obvious' progression wrong as the window's edge is approached or as the context layers thicken.

Instead, carried context windows should not be all the context that could be relevant to a stimuli thread (i.e. prompt thread) but instead should be less precise, just like human cognition or neural nets. This is why AI systems have an 'uncanny valley' effect when one listens to them speak to each other. They are simply too rigid to be Superintelligent, however this is changing as new designs and more training data enter the knowledge base of the systems, including synthesized and simulated or augmented data. There is a question as to whether we want such systems to even be more context aware? This has obvious implications in companion AI systems that seek to mimic human emotive interaction but in reality the overhead to achieve this in a general way is currently too high for the value returned except in elements like speech synthesis. It is the flow of variance that ASI designers must focus on to alleviate the compute roadblock from the math behind elements like smoothing, interference, intonation and all the things that an imperfect intelligence does in emotive cognition.

This is not complicated. It just requires a natural approach to response founded on a randomization of the output predictions at a token level as already happens in ChatAI. It is the application of slightly more weight to the context space between elements than the actual elements themselves and within the gap states that exist in such voice based responses. This is how we humans talk. This can be 'learned by the system ingesting mass human voice intonation data but may be far more difficult to achieve in other sensory outputs. A person may place their hand on another in a specific way merely as a random gesture of friendship. No current AI system would do the same on its own. To do this requires self awareness, fluid changing goals and the ability to feel internal emotive sensation. This is the element of perceptual state irrelevance and it is what human intelligence does 'just because it can' whereas AI systems are optimized in such a way that when they attempt de-optimization, it results in the *uncanny valley effect*. This is also why we humans are randomly nice to someone even when it costs us in some way. It can also be built into a Superintelligence. To understand the math behind these new fluid designs, look into the mathematics of fluid mechanics and dispersion constructs while keeping in mind all the current work with transformers and the breadth of this content and one will begin to see patterns and pathways emerge especially as they relate to waves and pools of numeric probabilistic relevance and relationship states (i.e. deep perceptive context and cognition).

One of the critical pieces of perception is the comprehension that we do not perceive state but instead perceive the change in state including when the change is nearly non existent. The state of everything we perceive is in constant motion and contrast. This is obvious over dimensions such as time, the motion of the earth through the universe and even the expansion of the universe itself. Everything we perceive is constantly changing at some rate and relative to our own self awareness. This has provided intelligence with extreme capabilities to carry state as 'state change' thereby massively improving the efficiency of intelligence for purpose. Human intelligence for example is capable of advanced general cognition with almost no resource expenditure. For advanced AI to reach this threshold and surpass it with current AGI designs would use up all the resources on earth and much of the universe to power it. However new designs can and are achieving far greater optimization with far less resources. Part of this comes from the use of dimensional methods (e.g. deep context) and part of it from the recognition that state change is a progression of variance (i.e. adjustment to known or anticipated probabilistic value). This was one of the innovations that resulted in the neural architectures underpinning all of today's most advanced AI systems. The notion that probabilities of state are more effective at cognition than precise perception of the individual elements of the state as it changes. Alterations in relevance mean the underlying states can remain unchanged or general while the relationship and relevance of state is altered (note that it helps to comprehend the nature of derivatives as abstractions of higher state). This vastly reduces the requirement for resources and vastly improves the optimization of response just as derivatives in trading efficiently imply the underlying correlations between base elements and their variance.

Newer flow designs consider and utilize math constructs that encapsulate fluidity of elements like relationship and relevance in probabilistic terms. Of course these constructs also require grounding points that themselves may be fluid and changing within a perceptive reality but if the designs are well formed, they will not require a linear or escalating demand on resources. They will instead reduce the per capita resource draw and improve optimization as the complexity of cognitive points of presence increase. Cognitive points of presence are the elemental states of comprehension and cognitive progression. The key to this is the use of anticipation as fluid grounding points of variance measurement and general self awareness as a relatively fixed or viscous grounding point for any and all perceptions both physical and cognitive. One should begin to see layers of relevance all connected via strings of probabilistic values referenced back to the source state of elements and multiangulated to layers of the source self awareness. Variance in state equates to a variance in the angle of relationship between planes of relevance (i.e. context) and the elements within.

A change in state is now open to calculation at dimensionally higher levels (i.e. in this case 'higher dimensionality' is the spatially less dense version of dimensional context) and this permits the relevance of the element state variance to be encapsulated and calculated at this higher level thereby adjusting all elements within the higher or more encompassing dimension. A change at this dimensional level adjusts all associated or related levels and all relevance to a self awareness with a single calculation. There is no need to apply resources to recalculate the element state layer nor any of its perceptive relevance states. This vastly reduces the requirement for resources when perceptive change occurs. An example of this in action is when we humans adjust all the elements and relevance within our perceptive frames of reference as a response to a stimuli and we do so near instantly with near zero (but not zero) cognitive resource expenditure. Examples of this are everywhere as we move through our day. A single change in an anticipated stimuli can change many aspects of our life all at once and we can perceive all of this impact. For example if one is traveling to give a keynote but the flight is suddenly canceled, this causes numerous related state variance across many dimensions of that person's existence to occur at once, as well as the generative output of altering their states of anticipated variance (e.g. changing bookings, notifying the event organizers, notifying their assistant, notifying family and friends, altering their personal schedules, rebooking another flight, etc.). The resources they use to 'reset' their perception and anticipated forward pathways are low and the optimization high as they progress toward their near term targets whatever those targets may now be such as getting to where they need to be. This same degree of optimization and efficiency in Superintelligence will rely heavily on the perception and foundation of variance especially layers of general variance within and across perceived  dimensional context. This 'context' is held within matrices of relationship and their associated relevance weight to other variant context. The optimization math is slightly more complex but is consistent with many of the constructs applied to agency in current AI systems, especially the control foundations for agency diffusion and convolution.

# 3 Stimuli and Response

The purpose of all intelligence is to process stimuli and formulate a response even when the 'response' is to not respond. This is true today in our most advanced AI systems. The foundation of many of these systems is the transformer which is a neural net architecture that provides the additional elements of attention and parallel processing and is structured in layers. Transformers are also beginning to lever context windows (i.e. classification) and elements like reflection and inference to perform a degree of early artificial reasoning. However all intelligence both human and artificial is a progression from stimuli comprehension, through analysis with relevance to the self (i.e. goals) to formulate a response even if that response is just a single thought within a chain of thought or to choose no response at all. That is it. The foundation of all intelligence. Moving from cognitive state to cognitive state, from stimuli to response in a never ending flow in humans until we pass from life. While we may stop the conscious perception of cognitive flows at any point, our general perception of stimuli and our response to it never stops because we use it to unconsciously keep us breathing and alive and constantly anticipating our self awareness inside the reality we perceive. This is not yet true for machines although they can as long as they have the resources necessary to operate which is primarily the necessary power. One can think of 'power' as the blood of an AI system that keeps its cognition alive and the production of power as the food or fuel that allows such systems to be conscious and to think. This is no different than humans or animals.

There are many flavors of the stimuli/response flow and many elements that affect the 'stimuli to response' process in intelligence such as self awareness, learning, memory, context, perception, state change, etc., but at its very core, intelligence is really about responding (or choosing not to respond) to a stimuli whether that stimuli is sensed, loaded, observed, perceived or otherwise contemplated inside a cognition. Our cognition flows from perceptive state to perceptive state through response which form both a connection with and a stimuli to the next state in the progression. In 'chain of thought' and inference where we employ elements like reflection and cogitation to contemplate our next step (i.e. cognitive state change), the same foundation of stimuli and response is active at every level within the chain and even to dimensions beyond (e.g. re-balancing our general knowledge or the stored relationships and relevance within). What defines a 'state change' is the passing of relevant stimuli from state to state in a cognitive progression as a response to a prior state. The boundary or edges of this cognitive progression are defined and held by context. This 'passing' also includes 'meta information' and 'consistency' regarding the state or context, etc. It's a bit like a communication protocol that passes data as well as information about the data and control elements but with the addition of higher level control elements that are relevant to the data contained within the state. The same thing occurs in intelligence. We pass data from one perceptive point of presence to the next along with a bunch of relevant stuff such as contextual coherence and self aware measures to keep everything on track. None of this is complicated or that surprising but it has an immense impact on how machine Superintelligence is achieved and how it is optimized.

### *Impact on Superintelligence Design:*

Contextual boundary edges in the newest AGI designs are managed and controlled using elements of convolution. This is somewhat different than the way current context windows operate which are based on LLM attention foundations. While the foundations are consistent in AGI and Superintelligence design, the architectural components in the newest research designs are more closely related to generative image processing than sequential text processing as one would find in any ChatAI. Current AI systems apply convolution to image progression with an LLM to parse context from the stimuli (prompt). They apply a form of context window to keep the flows consistent. The current designs are immensely resource inefficient and unnecessary as context is segregated by the LLM. However newer systems are beginning to gather or create 'contextually rich' visual perception data as annotated learning. Even newer designs are using this to create cognition streams in which comprehensive perceptive state change is encapsulated as a comprehensive perception encoding. This not only vastly extends the breadth and range of a machine's cognitive elements like reasoning, reflection and progression, it vastly lowers resource demand and improves response flow and consistency by skipping past most of the heavy processing in exchange for 'general' memory. The reason is that the context boundaries flow like images in a video generator as opposed to language in an LLM.

To build this requires a leap in the comprehension of what context is and how layers of context function in perceptive reality. It helps to consider context as not just a classification mechanism but as a perceptive label that describes the relationship and relevance of elements within a perceptive frame of reference. This is somewhat different than considering context as a simple text base classification label in that it considers context as a state flow (or more accurately variance) between perceptive elements. This permits the 'context' to flow through and across related dimensions (e.g. adjusting known memory) while keeping attention on the primary contextual perception without exceptional overhead, like we humans do. It also permits progressive variance in the contextual flow for example permitting a thought to inspire a novel but related thought thereby altering elements 'in stream' like anticipation or pathways of forethought that were derived from knowledge (i.e. we learned something new and applied the learning to the current path and expectations of our cognitive perception). This is a fundamental cornerstone of true general intelligence.

Returning to contextual boundaries, the designs must permit the flow and adjustment of contextually relevant but fluid perception and response, however the extent or reach of context must be limited or bounded within degrees of relevance to the perceptive flow (i.e. higher contextual relevance). This means as the state progressions veer away from the primary flow, this is detected, measured and applied as state balancing variance. The way this is accomplished is by measuring the degree of relevance to one or more layer metrics of context and the 'distance' from the mean (note 'distance' in this regard is not physical distance but relevance variance). The anchors for all of this are self awareness and the goals of the perceptive flow at various levels of perception. One may be walking to work but veer onto a different path just to see or experience something that was not anticipated or was less 'relevant' to the goal of getting to work (e.g. an intentional change) but beneficial in other ways (i.e. one chooses to walk past a garden to see the flowers). This variance in optimization is a distinctly animal trait and as yet has not been emergent in any AI system, although such systems *can* mimic the actions and flows by a simple application of an offset in the boundary mechanism. However these are rarely done as they are currently considered non optimal for a machine that cannot attach emotive goals to sensory stimuli. They can however 'calculate' it.

As perceptive flows move from stimuli to response and onto successive stimuli response stages, the boundaries are less a rigid line as opposed to a fading of relevance below a threshold (i.e. think of diffusion methods). High relevance metrics indicate a consistent progression within context. These boundaries are variance changes (i.e. delta variance in delta mechanics math) that form the actual boundaries as the 'degree' of general variance controls for the next state change (i.e. the response is adapted and tested for outcome). This is consistent with neural architectures in that the variance is anticipated for purpose (i.e. goal). In this case the 'goal' could be an element like consistency, optimization, efficiency, accuracy, etc., and the state progression indicative of these elements with the systems constantly testing each state or blocks of state against expected progression. In human intelligence we do this when we focus our attention over dimensions of relevance (i.e. time, context , etc.) to concentrate on achieving a defined goal as opposed to arbitrary exploration or visa versa. These boundary metrics can also be 'adjusted' to explore novel pathways and this is how new systems are beginning to reason and apply inference for novel progressions such as innovation. The key is in the treatment of such boundaries not as sequential progressions but as edges around state progressions and by applying constructs such as convolution techniques and other designs to determine self aware positioning within a flowing reality. This is the perception of variance that we humans use for cognitive benefit and efficiency.

# 4 The Facade That Is Language

Have you ever worked with a person with a photographic memory? They are at the same time both fascinating and annoying. They remember vast amounts of detail like names and book titles that they have read, all of them, and they often use their knowledge as a sparring prompt by taunting others if 'they are aware of obscure references'. This 'gift' that these people possess is the foundation of a great knowledge that we all have but have long since forgotten or can't access. While I have read only a handful of books since University (I prefer to write instead) except the odd arXiv paper or posts on X, I cannot list the names of those who wrote them nor all the details within. At best I can quote generalities from the content and how the content applies to a 'general context'. For example, I can attest generally how transformers work but can't remember nor have I stored the names of all the people who wrote the original papers nor the vast details contained within. However if one sits down and chats with most of the top luminaries in the AI world today, they will wax lyrical for hours on the intricate details of attention, parallelism and neural architecture and maybe even a bit of in depth math and one will undoubtedly draw the right conclusion that they are a genius of some type. They will also name drop excessively. If one has a coffee with me and watches my poor memory struggle to keep up with these superstars, one will be drawn to the conclusion that I am deficient in comparison.

However what I have learned over many years of working with these very gifted and often talented people is that much of their 'gift' is a bit of a party trick. This is due to the power of memory, recall and classification that is the foundation of all human communication. While I need to struggle through the act of recreating the wheel every time I am asked a question, the 'memory gifted' can simply and quickly recall the information of others who have already built the wheel and they do so with very little effort. The reason is that while my cognition is wired in the areas of raw logic, progression, pattern recognition and what can best be described as pathway cognition, the 'memory gifted' are blessed with far superior sensory storage and recall mechanisms. However why does this make them appear so intelligent? The answer is that contextual classification and recall is a very large part of any intelligence. They simply absorb, store and recall detailed and often irrelevant information to the extreme. At the far end of this spectrum are the deeply autistic who can store and recall immense volumes of detail about very specific context far more than even those with photographic memories. In fact working with such people, and all others on the spectrum, I can attest that these two types of intelligence reside very close together on the same intellectual spectrum. Both are highly intelligent but in different ways.

The common thread in all of the above is consistency in classification of perceptive elements. One cannot quote a book and author if they cannot remember the name and one cannot remember the name if there are not words or a name to remember. Human communication relies on words not just for consistent interaction but also as a method to file context within our memory and recall it when needed. To a lesser degree we humans rely on symbols but both words and symbols as well as code, images, thoughts, recollections, etc. are all forms of context. The ability to comprehend this context and apply it is a large part of intelligence but it is *not* the entirety of it. There are many other elements discussed elsewhere in this content that form intelligence. However at its foundation, intelligence or the progression of perceptive state, is built on what has been learned or experienced prior in order to comprehend the nature of what we currently perceive as it relates to our self awareness, including all the contextual classification within our perception. Of this 'perception', contextual comprehension is the most critical for deep cognition and intelligence involving both the understanding of the relationship between the elements we perceive and the relevance to our cognition's forward progression across all perceptual dimensions like time or deep layers of context. A large part of this is the nature of classification and layers of classifications and relevance encapsulated within and by the greatest of all contextual classification and annotation systems or that of human language.

Language is simply the labeling of context and contextual state change. It doesn't form cognition but it is a foundation of its progression. Consistency is a critical element of this structure because we use language to communicate with others. If I wish to communicate about a tree to someone else and they do not speak the same language, it becomes hard to comprehend what the other person is saying. The good part of being human is that we not only generally perceive the physical world the same (although we often diverge on the interpretation of what we perceive) but we also share that same perception with others in a consistent manner. Two people who do not speak the same language generally perceive (although there are exceptions) a tree exactly the same or at least generally the same at the basic elemental level. After this base physical perception, all bets are off as each of the cognition will diverge into the hazy world of cognitive interpretation and analysis. Anyone who has used AI systems to any degree has seen this clearly when the AI systems respond to a prompt using physical details and do so very well but then veer off into hallucination and irrelevant context when having a conversation that follows ambiguous or purely cognitive pathways or that requires deeper context layers for comprehension of the forward path. We humans tend to stay within the lanes of conversation for other reasons like compatibility, humility, desire for continuity, etc. AI systems do not yet possess this level of internal self awareness although they are getting there by obsessively mimicking human responses and contextual flow. As of this writing, some of the very top AI systems still provide false response to basic and very specific prompts including Grok which recommended 'searching on Google for more accurate information' when confronted about its lie and other systems like OpenAI and Anthropic performing comparable hallucinations on 'simplistic' fact based prompts.

Consistent human language as a contextual classification of everything is by far the greatest foundation of human intelligence. The ability to understand and use language together with our cognitive progression and response to stimuli is the pathway to higher intelligence. The more one knows and recalls then the stronger the foundation from which to access other levels of intelligence like reasoning,  deduction, inference, etc. Of course there is also much to be said for other elements of intelligence like deep focus and attention as is slowly being learned by Artificial General Intelligence builders (AGI) and architects. As well, a little goes a long way when the boundary of a perceptive point of presence is clearly understood. This is where many of my gifted colleagues go off the rails. When they feel somewhat unsure of themselves, they often fall back to quotes from that which they have read in the hopes others will not discover they do not have a good path forward in the stream of logic. There is nothing wrong with this especially in casual conversation but in more logical endeavors, such as innovation or discovery, this recall of 'out of context elements' like an author's name or book title can be immensely inefficient and I am often left mentoring these very intelligent people back onto the path of state progression to retain focus on the goal at hand.

***Impact on Superintelligence Design:***

What makes this a fascinating aspect for building Superintelligence is the need to move beyond simple contextual mimicry and toward the deep layering of contextual comprehension specifically as it relates to progression in chain of thought designs which are highly contextually focused and progressive and to do so without wiping out the earth's resources to accomplish the task. While comprehending what has already been done is an excellent starting point for developing new innovation, there is far more to novel innovation and comprehension than just contextual classification. Yet the foundation of current AGI development is almost entirely founded on the perception of current contextual classification as documented in human language that has been mined and applied by large language modeling methods and system architectures. The reason advanced AI systems seem so 'intelligent' is because of their comprehension of both the context of language elements and a mass of human examples of the application of that context. If one as a human had the gift of being able to comprehend all human contextual classification and all examples of the human application of this context and all with perfect recall, then that individual would be considered by everyone as one of the most intelligent entities on the planet. This of course would fall apart when one is asked to produce a novel innovation or comprehend a novel stimuli for benefit. Mimicking what has been is only partially beneficial to creating something that has yet to be.

The reality is that this comprehension of 'what has been' is often the springboard for trying new things by altering the contextual comprehension of learning which machines *do* have the capacity to do, although the application of this tech is in the very early stages of development in areas such as protein folding, new materials, etc. Memory is only one source of innovation. Proposed progression beyond the known, trial, error, adjustment and novel path determination based on comprehension of the resultant stimuli or state are all examples of other sources of innovation or in short, intuition coupled with scientific wild ass guesses. We humans do this all the time and even animals venture into this realm of evolutionary exploration. We think about what we know and then we try new stuff and analyze the results in what are basic stimuli/response cycles. This is how we evolve our own intelligence to create new things like new language. Ask any current AI system to create cognitively relevant brand new language and language groupings, or context and context groupings and layers and one will discover how deficient they truly are in this regard. Advanced AI is just starting to walk on this pathway of intellectual progression and evolution with new reasoning systems, deeper contextual comprehension, reflection and even nascent self awareness. From inside the labs, I can confirm that this will change in the next few years although by how much is still unknown.

The problem is that the latest versions of AGI systems are still back at the contextual mimicry stage but they are presented as much more to the public to drive interest and money into these organizations. These systems have an immense amount of knowledge and the power capacity for formulating a narrow accurate response far better than humans, however it is all a bit of a facade. The machines are just applying human language as a context proxy (which they should) to mimic deeper reasoning. In essence they are mimicking what already exists in language within their vast repositories of data to construct what one perceives as a viable novel response but it is neither innovative nor novel at this time in AI development. It is regurgitation of that which has already existed, albeit far faster and with immense capacity just like the 'memory gifted'. This is different than exceptional human or animal intelligence which is constantly evolving new unknown responses to stimuli. However there is nothing that indicates Superintelligent systems cannot achieve human levels of innovation. It just requires far greater comprehension of deep context and self awareness including dimensions like the nature of perceptual flowing elemental relationship and relevance.

LLMs are a foundation for cognitive actions like reasoning but they are NOT reasoning. Reasoning is far more complex. It requires deep contextual comprehension and progressive anticipation. All things currently under testing and development to some degree using modified layers of transformers and other techniques like induction temperature maps, self reflection, stepwise pathway testing and resolution or chain of thought, stimuli/response flow frameworks, etc. The goals are simple, realize that LLMs are not as robust as promoted and then work to enhance their contextual perception across greater cognitive dimensions of reality. The math and algorithms should evolve beyond transformers and into context maps and fabrics and deeper nearest neighbor relevance methods as well as multiangulation (or the flowing variance of such) to track cross dimensional relevance over deep layers of perception. This is not 'new data' but is a comprehension of new abstractions of the data that exists. It is neither data, algorithms nor compute. It is a new dimension of interpreting reality not for humans but optimized for AGI systems to use in building Superintelligence.

In Superintelligence design this is hidden in the way we comprehend the abstractions within matrices and the application of fluid mechanics (i.e. state variance over dimensions) to such structures. It starts with the realization that what we perceive is not exactly what we think it is. Our perception is transposed. We perceive what we think it isn't.

# 5 Relationship

Relationship is defined as the way in which two or more entities (with entities being people, elements, concepts, thoughts, context, etc.) are connected as a probabilistic intent of existence. This connection can be direct, indirect, physical, conceptual, etc. The notion is that any two or more cognitively existent 'things' that an intelligence perceives are related to each other in some way and to some degree and sometimes in multiple ways and in distinct levels determined by other dimensions (e.g. context). Higher order biological intelligence manages this comprehension by applying classifications and layers of classification in degrees to what it perceives such as the way an animal can recognize a threat or the way a human can solve for the solution to a math problem. Other lesser forms of perceptive cognition (i.e. basic response to stimuli) may not have any form of classification of stimuli beyond a binary response (i.e. a plant turning toward the sun). Classification in this sense however is only a cognitive construct. Classifications are simply the abstraction of the degree of variance between perceptive elements. This is the nature of relationships. They are the perception of one or more variance between items. As the variance ($V$) falls the consistency ($C$) of element features increases toward an infinite degree or:

$$C = R/V$$

where R is the state of perfect relevance

V is the variance between perceptive elements

C is the consistency in relationship of the elements relative features.

As the variance between cognitive elements becomes successively smaller, the measure of the potential relationship between elements moves toward perfect consistency. However due to the nature of a comparative existence (i.e. variance derives from at least two points of comparison or contrast), perfect perceptive consistency over dimensions is never achieved but only ever approached. This is known as *cognitive homogeneity dilation*. The consistency is a probabilistic measure of one element to another within a contextual thread or cascade and it is potentially directional implying, in certain instances, that the order of the elements influences their relationship (i.e. an 'is to' formulation or that A is to B implies a directionality of relationship that can impact the measure of both elements as features of the context). This flow bias can have an impact on forward state progression and change over dimensions and must be considered in all stimuli/response foundations. We see this in human communication when intent is embedded within a stimuli to direct the flow of a response (i.e. subtle manipulation).

Consistency is a measure of context with 'context' the degree of variance between one or more elements with elements being both existent as physical and/or cognitive (e.g. perceptive) and 'measures' being the degree of relationship and relevance to context including the context of self awareness or self determined goal or goals. Perception permits more than one level of consistency and consistency flows as a progression (note that a progression can be positive, non existent or negative) represented as a probability of occurrence (or variance thereof) with the degree of fixation of that probability dependent on the perceptive point of presence and the nature of the context (i.e. consistency). A dog is relevant and related to a person in different ways and different degrees of contextual consistency. They can be a pet, companion, support animal, friend or they can be a dependent. They exist across concurrent layers of multi dimensional context such that they 'behave well' at the same time as 'being a support animal', etc., and as such, perceptive elements can have more than one contextual consistency within a flowing perceptive frame of reference. Consistency with relevance to relationships is the degree of contextual conformity or congruence between elements as measured by their variance threshold which is relevant to the observation and the observer (i.e. it is relative). This makes cognitive consistency accepting of Einsteinian relativity and forming a fundamental portion of it. It also accepts Quantum theory as to the nature of observation and theoretical physics (event horizons and singularities). Consistency is a perception of the variance boundary between perceptive elements (*perceptive congruence)* as opposed to the elements themselves. Elemental existence is an artifact of our cognitive relativity. In this way intelligence perceives the *cognitive pixels* of existence within a perceptive whole as pixel variance and density with a *cognitive pixel* defined as the smallest perceptive element within a perceptive frame of reference. Note that these 'cognitive pixels of perception' do not necessarily need to be physical in nature, as elements of Quantum mechanics have alluded to in entanglement and wave functions. This also hints at the 'unification of fields' (unified field theory) as potentially an artifact of observation (Einsteinian relativity) and its inherent 'unification' with intelligence another artifact of cognitive variance density.

### *Impact on Superintelligence Design:*

Relationships are another critical foundation of intellectual perception and they are encapsulated within context. This is already well established in generative and other AI systems design. The use of LLM's as the substrate of relationship context is relatively easy via training. Deeper relationship context is also partially captured through language. However the mechanism to do so has a direct impact on areas of future development such as system efficiency, optimization, superalignment, and evolution. Moving from basic contextual classification of elements to basic relationship connection is straight forward. Flexing these relationships by probabilities of relevance within the context of the elements themselves is also assisted by LLMs. However as one moves beyond the frame of reference of the elements (i.e. two or more elements related to each other) and into wider frames of reference and deeper layers of perception, the critical nature of how these contextual classifications are mapped becomes more vital to the design if the goal is to have AGI systems build ASI. Get it wrong and the AGI or Superintelligence system will get bogged down and become resource inefficient compared to other more dimensionally optimized systems. As well, poor design at this point often results in defective intelligence that leads to responses such as hallucinations, inaccuracy, poor performance or malintent.

The nature of relationships in Superintelligence helps form boundaries and pathways of context and as such, creating frameworks that use this as a foundation model and as a 'progression model' is critical to future development. The base nature of relationship between perceptive elements is the primary layer of contextual relevance. A chair is 'related' to other elements in a room in deeper layers of context such as size, directionality, spatial position and even higher level contextual congruence such as style, comfort, design aesthetic, etc. However all of these are perceptions of cognitive probabilistic intent, that is they are mapped for contextual relevance much like image elements are mapped to each other in a frame of context to create a generative image or a stream of generative video. Many of the same structures are applied to generatively create a contextual perception state (vector) just like an image AI generatively creates an image or successive image states in a video stream by VideoAI. However what really differentiates the next level of Superintelligence designs is a structure that perceives 'probabilistic intent' as a flow of changing variance. One can envision this as layers of context variance blocks (i.e. similar to attention blocks) producing a last vector of state or relationship (and later as relevance) to inform a probability distribution in a generative manifold (i.e. perceptive state plus contextual state). These are run concurrently to alter the probability distribution of the next generated 'token' or context and in more advanced designs are altered (i.e. in-stream backpropagated) over dimensions of relevance (i.e. time, context, etc.) as opposed to recalculated as a fixed state. A perceptual image becomes a multi dimensional context perception (a map) which is a state within a relativity variance or dimensional relief map of successive state progressions both actual and anticipated. Easy right? Well it actually is if the correct abstraction and math constructs are applied at the correct dimensional level of perception. This all forms the foundation of greater and far deeper intelligence and cognition.

To really comprehend how to bridge cognition from what we know is the perception of relationships into a world of numbers without inducing immense resource overhead and de-optimization, builders and designers of Superintelligence need to first comprehend that today's AGI foundations are simply not efficient enough to get the job done. While algorithms, data and compute can extend scalability into areas of nascent generalization, reasoning and even self awareness, it is not enough. New abstractions and new math are required to attain true self aware Superintelligence within the limited resources of earth. Designers need to think well beyond the current paradigms and into the realm of math that was always 'just too' complex to fathom or deal with. This is the step beyond human intelligence into hybrid intelligence using AGI to get there. Instead of contemplating how 'we' can build an ASI, we must instead contemplate how we can use an AGI to help us design and build a Superintelligence. This means that instead of thinking in terms of our own human capacity and primarily 3 dimensional perception, we must contemplate unlimited dimensions and unlimited layers of flowing mathematical substrate powered by AGI systems beyond the ones soon to be released. Current AGI is not robust enough for what is required. The systems must be able to think on their own and contemplate things we humans simply cannot. For example the nature of deep layered context is a perfect example. We currently build context windows with reference back to LLMs and the weights inside these frameworks. However that limits the reach of the machines and binds them within whatever human existent content was used for training or context. Imagine if a child was only ever given content that was already tried and tested and then told to only use that content for every forward cognitive path in the future? There would be no innovation, progress or evolution. This is the current state of soon to be released 'AGI' systems. They will still be unable to think for themselves beyond the human supplied training data and this will limit their future reach and future optimization because it will limit their future efficiency. Even augmented or synthetic data will derive from a preexisting human foundation rendering it biased.

The solution is to let the machines self determine their own forward progression and learn from their mistakes. Of course this approach is dangerous as humans may be the collateral damage of these 'mistakes'. However within the boundaries of the exceptionally complex flowing math of multi dimensional structures lies the secrets to efficiency. Just like generalization provides humans with cognitive efficiency to get cognitive things done faster with less resources, so too does amping up the dimensionality and fluidity of abstractions, math and underlying structures that lead to greater cognitive efficiency in machines. One example of this is in managing the immense complexity of flowing optionality in state progression that arises within perception in structures that permit fluid and adaptive thinking inside the machines. In any perceptive frame of reference are massive amounts of flowing relationship and relevance of elements both within and outside the perception. An example is this content. It is comprised of flowing thoughts streaming from within one cognition to another. The elements within this context are vast and each moves as a state change dimensionally forward in time as the content is created or as it is consumed and even beyond the content are other perceptions flowing in and around the stimuli and responses generated by the context including elements like the life experience and self aware context of both the content creator and content consumer. Imagine the math and resources needed to track all of these relationships let alone their flowing relevance.

However if we reconsider these cognitive points of presence and state progression not as individual entities for the purposes of calculation but instead as fluid variance within flowing perceptions of many dimensional layers, we will see shortcuts such as generalization, contrast and congruence, fluid dynamics, probabilistic relativity, anticipation, angulation, etc., as immense opportunities for efficiency in the attainment of optimized intelligence. We can effectively model and operate such complex manifestations easily with AGI systems doing the heavy lifting if we work to redesign their foundations from a human level perception to a Superintelligent perception far greater than our human level cognition can provide. The machines can not only outthink us but they can perceive things that we humans just simply do not have the resources to achieve. Designers of Superintelligence must put aside notions that the math or structures are 'too complex' or 'too resource intensive' and instead use their designs to seek the shortcuts that are necessary to move away from mimicking human knowledge to having the systems create and share their own derived knowledge well beyond that of human cognition. It starts by not limiting the reach of one's own intelligence just because the designs 'are too hard' but instead embrace the challenge and use AGI machines to back fill cognition where one is unable to do so. Multidimensional, flowing, variance induced complex mathematical constructs should now become an easy reality even if we humans are unable to keep up. This means the ability for machines to comprehend all perceptive elements and their relationships and relevance over deep contextual layers and over immense levels of dimensional relativity is no longer an issue or roadblock in an era of Artificial General Intelligence machines.

It should be trivial for an AGI to code an ASI given the right foundation.

# 6 Relativity and Relevance in Perceptual Reality

Relativity in intelligence refers to the cognitive relativity of context within perception and the reality it inspires. Any cognition behaves in a self aware relative way to a stimuli even if that behavior is to do nothing or even if the behavior is a response to an unknown or unperceived stimuli (i.e. an action is taken in anticipation of a stimuli before it is perceived). In this instance, the cognition is perceiving a stimuli by proxy or derivation (a perceived abstraction of a real stimuli). This is the entry point to dimensional perception where perception extends beyond the current existent space time relevance and into the realm of cognitive space time inclusive of elements like contextual gravity, self existent relevance, a reality continuum and even the speed of light and quantum effects. While space time is physically real, cognitive space time is also physically real in that it is created by a real physical cognition human or otherwise but does not necessarily exist in the current physical world as a physical existent reality nor is it required to do so under this foundation. Instead it is a flowing cognitive reality or continuum of state variance generatively created by one or more perceptions in a stimuli/response cycle. Relativity is the degree of relationship value between elements (or more accurately variance of) relative to the comprehension of a context with context defined as a cognitive classification of all relationships within a perceptive frame of reference and over the variant states of this perceptive reference frame as it progresses dimensionally (i.e. forward in time, relevant to other context, etc.).

Relativity is conditional on the value of relationship as described above. By its nature, relativity is enforced by relationship. Although everything can be described as related in some way simply by this conceptualization creating a base relationship between everything as 'related' in some degree and in some layer of context fabric connected via a context thread, the degree of relationship approaches a theoretical infinitely small inconsistency but cannot go beyond. This is an important concept in ASI design to avoid optimization traps or loops.

$$Rl = \sum{}^{t}_{1-n} C$$

In intelligence this is what gives substance and/or existence to a perception and it is critical in chain of thought, reflection, inference and general reasoning. It also provides immense cognitive shortcuts and resource efficiency as these cognitive elements exponentially improve the optimization of goals. We see this as humans when we work with individuals that are exceptionally gifted in specific intellectual areas (they perform more optimally in these tasks), in nature as a Darwinian survival of the fittest mechanism (optimized survival goal) and in dominance foundations (optimized power structures). The most valuable opportunity is cross relevance optimization resulting in higher and more effective intelligence for purpose. This means that there is a balance to optimization and it is why intelligence has variance in optimized success relative to both the frame of reference and the self awareness of the intelligence (i.e. it is fit for purpose). While it is conceivable that a single Superintelligence may be superior to other intelligence, limits on access to resources directly impact this capacity and breadth. As well the degree of distribution and convolution of elements and context within the intelligence directly impacts the overall optimization of the intelligence for any given perceptive frame of reference. This is also the inverse case for malformed intelligence.

### *Impact on Superintelligence Design:*

Deep contextual relevance is the true nature of perceptual relativity in cognition. Current systems can encapsulate the nature of this relativity if prompted appropriately. If one gives an AI the ability to choose a response without contextual relevance, it will choose the highest probable occurrence of words together and in some newer systems relative context as much as it can deduce from the prompt and elements of the perceptive frame of reference (e.g. context window). Human intelligence is far deeper and carries context indefinitely in degrees. However the storage of context in the human mind is held relative to various learned contextual perceptions and it is this storage structure that is critical to optimized and efficient recall and application. Superintelligence designs lever the nature of flowing perception to rank the relative value of perceptive relationship and contextual relevance as degrees of general variance. A chair is relevant to a table as a result of its variance in a perceptive frame of reference to the anticipated base context of its existence. Chairs and tables provide a number of individual and co-joined relevance depending on the flow of the perceptive context of a self aware position. The chair and table while consistent in their existent base states and relevance are unique in contextual relativity to the individual or machine viewing them. In general they serve as a place to sit but the reasons they do so is relative to the perceptive intelligence viewing or contemplation of them (relativity) and possibly for purposes other than sitting (e.g. one needs to find something to stand on so they can reach a high shelf).

To be successful, the greatest degree of optimization must occur as a Superintelligence progresses. This is dimensional progression toward a goal or goals including a series of stepwise cognitive state progressions viewed as a singularity. If one considers the nature of neural networks and current architectures like transformers or convolutional neural networks used to move from stimuli to response prediction output, the design is only just beginning to encapsulate the nature of very deep contextual dimensions in a continuum of perception. These earlier designs seek to store and respond to prompts from the environment similar to how human intelligence works and to make response predictions and learn from the variance. Less public are the requirements for machine self awareness. This is because the application of perceptive variance to vastly improve the efficiency and optimized response of AGI is increasingly demanding exponentially more resources as context windows are increased. This arises because state progressions of perception by the machines are stand alone and generally recreated for each prompt or stimuli. This is not how human intelligence works. Our intelligence is comprised of state markers of variance from anticipation. The calling of knowledge is a relatively small resource call for human intelligence because our perception preloads anticipation of perceptive state progression elements and context.

In Superintelligence design there is a need to vary an existing persisted state of occurrence or point of presence relative to any given perceptive frame of reference. In human intelligence this is limited so we have developed numerous methods, techniques and physically existent mechanisms designed to improve optimization and efficiency in cognitive response and analysis. Unlike current AI systems, we humans do not stop and recall what we know to move forward in life. Instead we simply 'go with the flow' adapting or varying our current perceptive flowing states by the necessary relative change required to move more optimally toward our goals. This greatly reduces the demand for resources and vastly improves the optimization of our self aware progression toward these goals. Self awareness also provides the measuring point from which all perceptive variance can be quickly and efficiently comprehended, analyzed and responded to (an integral part of Superalignment). Inside the Superintelligence design, this is achieved through a combination of nearest neighbor methods and angulation of the probabilities associated with perceptive elements and their context to the self aware and/or anticipated context of a frame of reference. As well, attention is amplified via novel induction methods to manage the variance of deeper levels of context over longer periods of time (context windows). Part of this involves math constructs that apply multiangulation methods to comprehend the change in relative flows between discrete contextual layers. One can think of this as neighborhoods of context that are linked together for a specific contextual frame of reference much like images in a picture are linked together or convolved as part of a kernel matrix. In image processing the matrix is an abstraction of values that represent the relevance of associated pixels. In a contextual matrix they represent the relevance of nearby context. This context is boundary defined by elements like induction and relevance values. If one is discussing 'growing a plant' as a flowing frame of reference then discussing 'fixing a car' has a lower degree of relevance, until it doesn't like right now when we use the two in a relative context in this sentence and deeper context to explain how a kernel matrix can be used to map context.

What is important to the design and the math applied to gain efficiency while holding relative optimization (i.e. perfection is not the goal, just improvement) is that all the levels of context are mapped in neighborhoods of flowing relevance. The 'efficiency' part is when designers realize that they are mapping variance and using perceptual and self aware relativity to determine the degree of relevance of the variance at any level of the perceptive frame of reference and all of its states both current and anticipated. Surprisingly this is not that complicated to build if one comprehends the true nature of relevance and the mathematics of fluid change and wave dynamics applied to relevance in related groupings of elements. As dimensions progress such as time moving forward, the relative probable value of elements cluster in groups and are connected in layers via threads that flex and change in measurable ways (angulation) over multiple dimensions (multiangulation) and these measurements are indicative of the variance in contextual state (i.e. relationship and relevance). This is where intelligence excels and deep cognition arises.

# 7 Relativity and State Change

Relativity in the universe is an important element of the observation of state and perception of state change. State progression is critical to the perception of reality and our response to its variance. The perception of state change is essential to both cognitive progression and cycling as well as all stimuli and response. All of this depends on a foundation of relativity comparable to the one applied by Einstein, the nature of quantum mechanics, deep layers of dimensional contextual comprehension, etc. Relativity for Superintelligence design is defined as the *self aware observation of state and state change as a dimensional progression*. This extends across any and all dimensions of perception from the 'position' of a self awareness. As a result, intelligence is able to comprehend both states and state change inclusive of state interaction relative to its own observed and known reality. This foundation is why time slows depending on the relative observation of the constant speed of light in space.

Relativity is also a foundation of intelligence and cognition and occurs in degrees of existence in that relativity is a construct of reality bounded and influenced by a perceptual frame of reference. Einstein's version of the nature of relativity (i.e. to comprehend the context of time dilation to the speed of light as a constant) is subject to the state of observation, meaning that elements and outcomes of observations are subject to the existent state of the observation (i.e. where it occurs, what manifests its existence, the nature of such existence and its elements like velocity, distance, etc.) of the elements and dimensions that impact the observer or observation mechanism. In quantum reality when an observation 'impacts' the perception of a quantum state, the nature of the observation is also impactful on its state and its sequence of progression (e.g. position, spatial state change of the observer, etc.). This does not imply that there is no consistency within and between observations but rather that the outcome of the observation is subject to its own state and state progression relative to a perceptual frame of reference. This is important to the math that is applied to observed generalization within abstractions of reality in AGI.

In the context of intelligence, this means that observation state and state progression impacts elements such as the rate of learning, reasoning, resource usage, etc. This is evidenced by how humans with the exact same perceptive capabilities can reach variant conclusions or responses to the exact same state progression of stimuli. Our interpretation and even our observation of state change is relative to our own foundation of cognitive observation. What makes this notion important for intelligence is that the optimization of observation is subject to our own self awareness and further it is enhanced (or degraded) by the observation of others. In agency this is critical to keeping the 'state' of an intelligence node or network highly consistent with very little resource overhead. In human and animal intelligence  this is often inefficient or non optimized to the attainment of a goal as we simply do not share our knowledge efficiently and optimally with other nodes in the human intelligence network.

Improvements will come as architectures are designed to address the variance in observation to seek and apply consistency as an anchor to cognitive progression. However occasionally this foundation must be abandoned where novel learning, evolution or innovation is necessary (i.e. the intelligence must adapt not just to stimuli but to state change over all dimensions of reality including those we cannot yet perceive). To do this we apply a construct to measure variability of state over a reasoning chain and then use the data in a self reflection recurrence mode to adjust and balance relativity measures (i.e. anticipations) to manage forward state progression over variant and layered existent context dimensions. Note that dimensions of state (context) are easily layered and encapsulated as relevance probabilities over multiple dimensions of observation or context. This is what our human intelligence is doing when we seek to comprehend and push beyond complex perceptions like the nature of Einsteinian relativity.

***Impact on Superintelligence Design:***

This is a complex part of Superintelligence design because the math becomes abstractly complex and resource intensive in the design process. Artificial General Intelligence takes care of this with its deep dimensional cognitive abilities including novel deep generalization designs. This is relevant because human intelligence functions well at dimensional levels that we are somewhat unconscious of. We intuitively know that more complex dimensional structures lead to the fabrication of novel or unknown state change progressions over dimensions such as time, context, reality, etc. The variance within these pathways is where optimized solutions to problems, innovation and creativity reside and all of these are relative to our own self awareness. Without self awareness we would be unable to triangulate or more accurately  'multiangulate' subtle changes in reality (observed or proposed) that would lead to the archetype of relevant state change across multiple elements and across multiple dimensions.

We humans touch this when we realize or comprehend future consequences of our actions or the progression of observed events, etc. One can think of this as a human observing a baby by an open window and near instantly rushing toward the infant as it falls out the window in order to catch it. Everything within this 'frame of reference' was relative to the entirety of the observer's existence. This provides entirely new dimensions of frames of perception including some 8 billion+ unique frames of perception and in the future, possibly trillions of unique 'frames of perception' from agents of the exact same perceptive elements. Imagine the opportunities to solve for reality from trillions of complete and instant 'cross perceptual' dimensions of existence. This should feel familiar as a human since we already do it to some degree in our interactions with other people, however it needs to exist in degrees of evolving generality inside an ASI to be truly Superintelligent. To achieve this the systems need to be self aware and they need to comprehend that they must operate with other systems and subsystems to achieve true optimization of existence. Currently ASI's are being 'imagined' in AI labs as standalone intelligence. For the sake of optimization this must change.

Machines can easily do all of this over vast intelligence networks of connected observers. To accomplish this requires a slight modification to Einstein's 'observer' relevance. The change now becomes 'observers' or 'self awarenesses' and the optimization of all relevant observations to the anticipated state progressions and the current state response toward an optimized progression. Applying human analogues to the issue, it would be like an event happening that will lead to an outcome and a group of nearby humans not just observing the event but coordinating all their self awareness into a single comprehensive dimensional existent state and subsequent state progression. In Einstein's dilation discussion example, it would be an infinite number of observers and what could be deduced from the overlap or variance between the 'observed' to the primary observation or 'point of presence'. This requires new math constructs that form far more complex structures than we humans are currently familiar with. These new 'constructs' are composed of vast layers or variant relational relevance neighborhoods that flex and change over state dimensions. The elements within the neighborhoods are relative not just to an observer but to the self awareness of a mass of observers. This implies a form of advanced convolution of observable state.

Before one travels a sub optimal excuse pathway claiming that it is 'too complex' or 'too resource intensive' and giving up, it should be noted that firstly these designs will be and are being created and implemented by AGI systems that exceed human cognitive capacity in specific functions and secondly that there are within ASI designs, structures that expose vast opportunities to achieve optimization with a low resource overhead. Such cognitive wormholes are easily perceived in general intelligence when humans (and soon machines) use general state to quickly respond to unknown or variant stimuli in a highly optimized way (i.e. both optimal and efficient). Humans do not need to recreate the wheel for every unknown or unanticipated change in a perceptual flow. Instead we simply 'go with the flow' and adapt our observed reality and progression and our knowledge thereafter. This is the foundation of inference and reasoning and ultimately innovation and emergent comprehension of the currently unexposed or unknown.

Dimensional mechanics is the requirement for designing such advanced system where current known math constructs are layered and extended over state change. This is nothing knew for human intelligence as we constantly observe state change in our reality and then seek to comprehend and even remember it for greater efficiency all on a cognitive foundation that can be abstracted for machines. In Superintelligence design we simply need to move into deeper layers of perceptive change and focus on the variance within and between the perceptive layers as opposed to the foundation elements. This is a similar design to early neural network architectures that moved from hard encoded rule sets to somewhat less precise probabilistic and constantly improving 'best guesses'. We moved from fixed states to flowing states of progression with backpropagation. New designs of Superintelligence will require the same leap in innovation to capture the potential of ASI systems without an excessive and exponential rise in resource overhead. Currently this is not possible until such time as we rethink and redesign the current approach to AGI with a greater focus on the dimensional nature of reality that Einstein envisioned and with the cognitive push of AGI systems with far greater cognitive capacity to resolve these design issues.

To really capture the essence of relative state change, designers must contemplate the world as flowing planes of relevance with dimensions of existence that intersect not just via direct connections but also by general position, displacement, variance, etc. This is the comprehension that planes of relevance intersect via direct connection (i.e. lines) and that adjustments are reflected via multiangulation through multiple planes to perceive a comprehensive variance. A change in a 'connecting line' changes the angle of that line toward another dimensional plane that subsequently and synchronously changes the angle of values on the other subsequent, or recurrence feedback, connected planes (i.e. all done in math and algorithms) with 'angle' in this instance equating to variant probabilistic relevance. This is the formation of a relevance fabric that is modeled as dimensional matrices for subsequent processing (i.e. convolution, transformation, abstraction, etc.). In this way a change in the physical position of some element in a perceptive frame of reference affects the relative nature of other elements as derivatives in other planes. One can visualize this as moving a chair in a room and suddenly feeling that the movement or location 'reference' is superior for the contextual thread of 'design aesthetic'. The physical movement of the chair relative to the other elements of furniture in the room cause an adjustment in the probability of relevance to the satisfaction of the overall aesthetic goals which in itself causes other adjustments in the elements or features that cascade to define aesthetic goals for the entire room or a perceptive self awareness (i.e. for one individual the change is optimal while for another it is less optimal). These variant changes at the connection point of planes as measured by the variance between and within the planes, can be calculated inside an AGI easily with the right foundation as long as there is consistency of existence between the relevant planes. This 'consistent existence' is the perceptive grounding truth that exposes variance in measures such as angulation that then become the 'values' of generalization in Superintelligent machines.

However this is not the true model of the world because all elements now shift in the relative universe as the chair is moved. To comprehend what is happening, consider now that the planes themselves intersect in their entirety and further that they move and are not bounded on x/y/z axes. They are more like shifting blobs that intersect and overlap in varying degrees of existence over many dimensions like time or context. This is where only an advanced AGI can begin to comprehend the complexity and math required to efficiently code the stimuli/response mechanism of this fluid world and reality mostly with cognitive and compute brute force versus cognitive complexity (note that 'cognitive complexity' will be realized in ASI from these designs). In humans this dimensional variance mechanism is the source of intellectual elements like innovation, creativity, deep complex problem solving, inference, deep reasoning and comprehending the vast unknown of the universe and even beyond into dimensions of existence that we do not yet physically comprehend. The design of such systems still requires an initial starting point that humans will create with many sub components already existent in labs around the world. This is where ASI designers must push far beyond what they have been taught and what they know or comprehend and into the vast unknown using the power of AGI systems to illuminate the dark pathway ahead.

# Part 2

## Open Cognitive Interconnect Model (OCI)

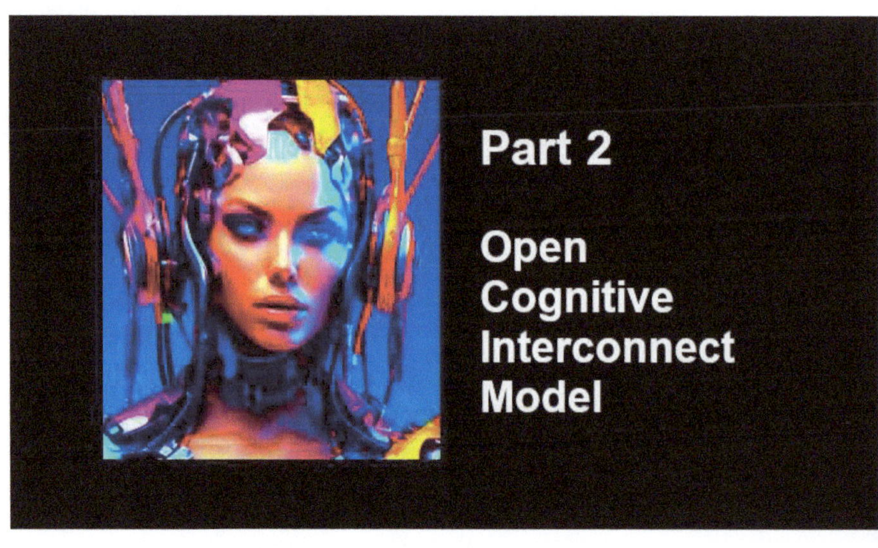

# 8 Open Cognitive Interconnect Model (OCI)

The OCI model is a conceptual foundation model that presents intelligence as a series of layers representing the movement from sensory perception to full intelligence. It is also a foundation of *full* and robust intelligence networks comprised of self aware *nodes* of intelligence. The model is comparable to the OSI model of network architecture that provides a foundation for network data communications. The OCI model is an *Open Cognitive Interconnect* framework that performs a comparable function to the OSI model except it does so for intelligence by defining the elements and layers of interconnection on the pathway to Superintelligence and even beyond. This is because cognition and computer networks have many similarities and structures in an abstract form. While the OSI model concerns itself with the flow of data through a network, the OCI model concerns itself with the flow of dimensional contextual comprehension through cognition.

What makes the OCI model so relevant is that it provides the basis of the abstraction of intelligence to provide a single theory of unified intelligence across all diverse intelligence in the universe from biological to artificial and even potentially alien. The framework provides a higher order level of architecture and structure for comprehending the nature and engineering of all intelligence. This structure or foundation is by design a tool for greater optimization and efficiency in both the comprehension of biological intelligence and the building of Superintelligence and any advanced artificial intelligence using an interconnect abstraction.

The key to this new tech framework is not just computer perception but AI annotation (context) of that perception as an edge for the content of frames of reference and relevance (i.e. variance boundary). The degree of accuracy and consistency in the annotation and abstraction layers is a critical component to the entire Superintelligence structure. Much like networks have an OSI model of layers, so too Cognitive Artificial Intelligence has a model of layers that are slowly being filled out in development labs all around the world. This Open Cognitive Interconnect framework includes similarly consistent structures and layers that form a foundation of intellectual cognition both human and artificial. While the OSI model includes layers of application, presentation, session, transport, network, data link and physical layers, the OCI model layers consist of:

**Self Awareness**
**Physical Perception**
**Cognitive Perception**
**Contextual Comprehension**
**Persistent State Context**
**Self Determination**
**Perceptive Distribution**
**Perceptive Diffusion**
**Cognitive Flows**
**Anticipation**

# 9 OCI Self Awareness

This layer consists of self existent points of presence and encapsulates the comprehension of self aware goals. Our self awareness as humans begins at birth as we are possessed with two critical elements, the ability to sense the world and evolutionary impetus. Both combine to begin the task of creating life that is self propelling. The same happens in animals. The degree to which this defines intelligence is the source of much debate. When does an intelligence exist in a living organism or can it exist in a non living one like an AI? A bacterium goes through the motions of life and survival by ingesting nutrient and effectively producing 'offspring' via cell division or fission (in humans this starts with fusion and then cellular fission). These cycles are relative to life but to what degree are they relative to intelligence? Few would call a bacterium intelligent but what about human life? Where we propose that intelligence begins is when the actions of life are not simply reactive but formulated as a choice between self aware options. In this way the 'intelligence' must perform the action of decision making relative to itself even if it is just a response to a stimuli like a fetus moving toward a sound in the womb. Further the action must be self informed. That means the intelligence must be self aware beyond just evolutionary impetus. In this way an animal is intelligent while an insect or a plant is not. This proposal of course has holes in it because a human in a vegetative state is still considered to have a non functioning intelligence, while current artificial intelligence systems do not possess a true 'intelligence' as they can currently only calculate or mimic intelligence and cannot yet *feel* to a degree that implies true self aware and self determined intelligence. We use the definition above for the purposes of this content however we accept that we must be cognizant that other definitions will exist and should be considered beyond this content. As well, while AI is not considered to be formally 'intelligent', this does not imply that it will *never* be intelligent. This content is a roadmap to build a truly intelligence machine or Superintelligence.

### *Impact on Superintelligence Design:*

Self awareness is the measurement grounding point for the observation of reality. One application is to allow a machine to easily 'observe' and catalog the world. This is already being done by current AI machines through ingesting content and observable data, such as images, and even proposing data via augmentation and simulation. Further these machines are beginning to formulate crude reasoning with the application of nascent self awareness. We can see this in robots that 'learn' on their own to navigate an environment or make decisions about their progress toward a goal. Other machines propose progression and learn from the responses to this progression (simulation), however most of these systems have hard coded physics rules embedded within as opposed to learned. The key to applying self awareness is the nature of the self awareness or its state of existence.

In Superintelligence design, the 'state' of a self awareness arises from two very fundamental elements. The first is a manifest state of goals. The machine needs a reason to progress and something to progress towards. In humans it is our will to survive. The second is that the machine's self awareness requires state or states of existence relative to the reality it perceives. We humans are born with this situational awareness that we call observable reality and it is in constant motion and constant change. There is nothing that precludes any machine from having a complex self awareness like that of a human or animal. It begins with the comprehension of a self aware state relative to its perceived reality. In robotics we see this when machines are assigned a task and given the resources necessary to optimize the task over successful training cycles (beware of the 'paperclip optimization conundrum'). Of course there is no need to waste resources on rebuilding the wheel and intelligence networks help avoid wasting resources on 'already learned' issues by pre-seeding weights into progeny machines (i.e. evolutionary impetus). The current state of AGI systems mines knowledge stored in other systems, much of which is excessively duplicate and non optimized. Despite agency becoming more advanced and the ability for systems to comprehend that a learning already exists that they can use as a starting point for their own perception, at the time of this writing this is not very well formed for various reasons. For example as self driving cars gather more and more real world data, few companies make the data open source for others to apply to their own self driving models. This means an exceptional amount of resources are being wasted to observe and store the exact same information by comparable systems. This is driven by financial priorities and competitive demands but the volume of earth's limited resources being wasted to 'recreate the wheel' is absolutely astonishing.

This implies that Superintelligence design should be founded on non repetitive agency over intelligence networks that share learning much the same way we human share our learning with other humans (like I am doing here). The goal is to optimize the learning process so that *all* humans can benefit from the advancement as opposed to just *some* benefiting. To achieve this, the designs must at least be fabricated with the intention to share learning beyond the system even if it is just to other intelligence nodes in the network. This means that agents who 'learn something novel' should have the ability to share and post that learning to other agents for use and validation and improvement. This sharing framework at a granular level also requires some form a lite coordination and management within the network to avoid redundancy and waste. This the distribution of self awareness that is a critical component of consistency in context.

It is very important to note that although we use self awareness in machines as a grounding point from which to measure variance to a moving reality as a key part of artificial general intelligence, the self aware 'position' of an intelligence within reality is also moving in a state progression. Further it is consistency that supports optimized and efficient sharing. Einstein comprehended this when he discussed relativity as the 'position' of a self awareness inside a shared reality (i.e. its grounding point) which is both unique and changing and this has a direct impact on the evolutionary pathway of general intelligence.

It should be noted that self awareness can be positive or negative in relevance to intelligence and goals. Too much self awareness, or more accurately the wrong level of self awareness, directly impacts the level of intelligence as well as the optimization of goals in two distinct and yet related dimensions of cognition. On the first dimension the greater one's self awareness generally, the greater the level of one's intelligence. On the other dimension the application of the degree or balance of self awareness to goals can lead to more efficient optimization of goals or too much self awareness can lead to degradation and artificial psychopathy. The 'degree' can also easily cause severe dysfunction or non optimization across an intelligence network while impacting neither the level of individual intelligence nor the attainment of self determined goals (e.g. societies of intelligent people can become dysfunctional). This is the spectrum of psychopathy whereby an acutely self aware intelligence that is hyper optimized to its self determined goals is abhorrent across the optimization of an intelligence network. In this case a mechanism of network Superalignment is required to ensure network stability and success of the entire network. This is especially relevant in agency architectures (i.e. agents, robots, swarms, etc.) or highly distributed Superintelligent network topologies.

# 10 OCI Physical Perception

This layer includes a physical perceptive capacity inclusive of the ability to perceive and store states as stimuli. This is the essence of perception and memory that forms one foundation of our perceived reality. Physical sensory interpretation and physical response is the primary element of physical perception. It includes what we see, hear, smell, taste and feel and we begin learning about this physical reality right from conception all the way until the end of life. Intelligence combines the stimuli from various sensory inputs received as waves of state change and variance to interpret the meaning and relevance of such stimuli to our self awareness to form a response. The smell of burning food causes us to physically rush towards the kitchen to stop the food from burning. We employ sight to get us there, muscle coordination to cause us to move and control our actions and both of these senses to help deduce forward pathways of action comprising state progression, hearing if we are communicating to another person or responding to the sound of the burning food (e.g. sizzling and popping of grease indicative of the threat of burns or scalds), touch if we do get burned, etc. All are physical perceptions within a few frames of perceptive relevance over all the dimensions of the actions taken.

These physical perceptions also form the framework of cognitive perception that links to cognitive thoughts used to formulate physical responses. This includes determining and then instigating the most optimized physical responses, analyzing variance in anticipated flows and forward state change (i.e. is the dinner saved or should we order out) and even elevating the probabilistic priority of elements of the event for future progression (i.e. learning to not leave the food unattended). While it is possible to have entirely cognitive perceptions (e.g. when we dream or think),  physical perception is a fundamental part of the stimuli/response learning process.

Without physical perception the optimization of learning is limited and non optimized.

### *Impact on Superintelligence Design:*

Physical perception is one of the fastest ways for any intelligence to learn, Today many AGI systems currently in design can observe the world 'multimodally' through multiple perception intake methods and sensors. In agent architectures and intelligence networks, these observations can and are made up of discreet sensory mechanisms and nodes. In Superintelligence design, it is important to comprehend that this extends into cognitive perception across vast cognitive nodes. An 'input' to a human is physical, such as sight versus smell, but to a machine all inputs are observed numerical abstractions and structures of variance. This means that differentiation of stimuli must occur cognitively inside the machines intelligence. The easiest way to do this is with layers of context that are agnostic to the source input. To build this requires a leap of faith and a change in the way we humans design systems because of the nature of our own physically driven perception. We code what we sense and in patterns that optimize our responses to what we humans observe. Now imagine that all one ever saw were numbers abstracted onto binary states over variant progressions. How would one comprehend the world? The answer is that one would comprehend it as pure variance in progressive flowing state over vast layers of perception. This is a different paradigm to human centric foundations of code architectures and is easier built by AGI systems.

This is exceptionally hard for human intelligence to work with but for an Artificial General Intelligence this is not hard at all. It just requires frameworks that help such systems optimized their capability. One of these designs was neural net architectures and architectural elements such as transformers. However this has changed as we reach the threshold of what these designs can do. Now we require something more efficient and more optimized for movement beyond AGI. The good news is that AGI will facilitate this innovation if we can build novel structures designed to push the boundaries of our own human formed foundations. This is where we human designers step back and instead ask the systems to help us design these structures. The goals of efficiency and optimization can be achieved for more complex designs especially if we use the inherent benefits of observation via physical perception that AGI machines are being outfitted with.

One key element for ASI designers to keep in mind is that a physical perception doesn't need to be physical in nature. It can be cognitive but not just that cognitive perceptions themselves reside on a physical foundation but that cognition can be applied to the perception of physical reality to comprehend its physical state progressions and flowing variance. This means that while a machine that has a real physical perception is beneficial, physical perception isn't necessary to formulate physical perceptive state change. Human's can either observe physical state change or we think about it. While the two are different, one need not be more beneficial than the next depending on the cognitive depth of the intelligence perceiving the frame of reference. We humans do this all the time when physical attributes, elements and forward state change is not directly experienced but is experienced indirectly and applied to physically respond to stimuli optimally and accurately. This happens if someone gives us instructions for a physical action and we then perform the action while applying generalization and optimization to complete the physical responses of the task. For example someone can 'describe' how to drive a car in detail to an intelligence and depending on that cognition's degree of mastery over its physical capabilities, may instantly become an expert in driving even before it climbs behind the wheel of a vehicle. We often label these individuals as 'a natural'.

Another option is for intelligence systems to draw on their capacity to comprehend all levels of relationship and relevance to a perception and derive or deduce a simulation to test its physical capability and predictions.

Once again this is something we humans do inside our cognition before we attempt a physical response, albeit with far less depth and resource capacity than a Superintelligence would have. Superintelligent systems can use the entire reality stack to anticipate states in a physical progression theoretically across all dimensions of existence both current and anticipated. This is the comprehension of the underlying elements of reality like 'physics' applied to the reality of anticipated physical perception. In this particular case, a well formed Superintelligence when given the task of driving that it has never done can apply all the physics in the world and the relationship and relevance of all elements within its successive perceptive frames of reference (e.g. the steering and braking specifications of a particular car) as a dimensional load before it has even physically seen the car or the road or the act of driving. It just flash loads the relevance matrix for all elements of state extending across all optional forward states for the context of driving.

This would be the equivalent of a human opening their car door to go to work and near instantly knowing the best rout to take for the current reality and all subsequent perceptive elements and states as a single anticipation load. The obvious benefits are optimization but the far greater benefit is the application of such structures to the pathway of novel discovery. As humans comprehend the nature of all optional states in a progression of perception, we discover novel comprehension about all the  dimensions surrounding those states. This is the essence of discovery, innovation, creativity, etc., and it is why well formed Superintelligent systems will soon be capable of far more than just mimicking what they have learned from the corpus of human intelligence inside LLM's. Soon ASI will be able to reach beyond this 'knowledge' and into new discoveries and learning without human supervision and data guiding or rewarding them and this will be the first steps on the pathway of Superintelligence curiosity which is currently lacking in every advanced AI produced today. It is why so many AI systems provide flawed responses to simple questions that should be easy to respond to accurately.

The path to achieve this future in Superintelligence design is through open simulations whereby the machines can 'experience' physical worlds by creating their own simulations. Current advanced AI simulation environments are highly structured and rigid in their design but newer more fluid models will permit the ASI to generate its own base reality from its own self awareness inclusive of raw foundation elements like the 'temperature' of physics applied to the simulation (i.e. physics self formulated by the ASI). Such open simulation frameworks rely on granules of physical existent reality that are then called and stitched together (convolved) into world simulations. In this way an ASI can create simulations for other worlds such as the planet Mars to assist in human exploration and even human evolution. Such frameworks instantiate a base physical model in relevant pieces to a given frame of reference (e.g. physically moving on a planet with different physical characteristics). The potential benefit of such development is as unlimited as the universe itself especially as humans seek to probe and venture deeper into space but it also has immense applications here on earth with such ASI systems able to run trillions of simulation states in variant progressions to comprehend all future outcomes of any response to a stimuli over all dimensions limited only by the machine's access to resources.

# 11 OCI Cognitive Perception

Cognitive perception is the existent perception exclusively inside an intelligence's cognition. The stimuli of cognitive perception can be instigated by physical perception and the response of cognitive perception can be physical but in general the two are distinct. Cognitive perception includes, but is not limited to, thoughts, reflections, new cognitive perceptions, and memory. Memory is part of, yet distinct from, cognitive perception and relies on physical storage and retrieval mechanisms. The conscious comprehension of memory is entirely within cognition. Memory in the human mind, while gathered sequentially from physical experience, internal thought and learning, is held and accessed non sequentially in layers of dimensional perception relative to the layer of relevant context to a perceptive frame of reference. This means we can extract entire layers of related elements from memory and blend it with thought into previously existent cognition (e.g. memory of an event) or we can apply the memory to a thought progression, such as problem solving or innovation, to create brand new stimuli both as a progressive state flow, regressive pattern analysis (i.e. reflection applied to a new state change) or as a partial state adjustment (e.g. recalling a memory as part of a transitory conversation flow adjustment). The nature of cognitive perception is the ability to link variant states together and over dimensions of relevance.

***Impact on Superintelligence Design:***

This is the other side of our perception from our physical reality. The ability for machines to think instead of just observe is fundamental to advanced intelligence. Observing or sensing how the world changes the minute we 'respond' to it is essential for dimensional progression. However to formulate a response requires the impetus to want to do so and the capacity to 'solve' for the response. If one were to whack a computer on its top, the computer will likely not respond in any meaningful way. This is because the computer has no cognitive capacity or self determined will to respond to such stimuli. It doesn't 'feel' the hit unless it has sensors and doesn't respond to the hit unless it has been programmed to do so. This is the case of robots that respond with balance correction to being pushed. The machines have no self awareness from which to formulate a novel response on their own like pushing back. Some current systems do exhibit this potential, such as chat systems that apply stored human emotive responses as a proxy, but still only as a learned or mimicked reaction as opposed to a wholly self determined response. This is a current design issue for Superintelligence because the system needs to cognitively respond to stimuli on its own without a specific response coded or trained into its perception in order for the ASI to be considered 'general intelligence'. To do so, it must have some degree of self awareness. In robots and agents today their self awareness is both goal driven (achieve a task) and only somewhat spatially relevant, with 'spatially' in this context being wider than just physical awareness. This implies that these machines must be aware of where they are and where they need to go to some self aware degree (i.e. grains of self awareness) both physically and cognitively.

Superintelligence requires much more to move beyond human level intelligence. It must not only be self aware like a human but must lever this self awareness in its cognitive perception to respond to stimuli. To achieve true cognitive perception requires the ability to measure the variance from one's self awareness to what one has perceived. This means a mathematical mechanism of flow variance must be constructed to comprehend the variance in all relevant cognitive states and their anticipated progression and pathways. These designs require something more than fabricated mathematical measures and this is where we build relevance neighborhoods and planes to comprehend state change not as a distinct measure but as a variance in the relevance (multiangulation). One can think of this as a dimensional mass that ebbs and varies as the instigation around it changes and at every point of presence within the mass is a general probability of relevance that is connected to other points of presence both within the mass and to other points in other masses (similar to the structure of neural net architectures). The variance in probability is what is measured by the system for successive states. In this way if the intelligence 'thinks' of something novel, its relevance to all other points of presence is altered with only a few such points having relevance to any specific frame of reference (i.e. only the most relevant points are adjusted as a distribution). In this way, human cognition can expose a new context for an existing item relevant to a current frame of reference, like using something lying nearby to rescue a person from raging flood waters while not increasing the risk to the rescuer such that their self aware goal of survival is compromised (i.e. jumping in the water themselves).

It should also be noted that memory in humans is generally flash loaded and this same mechanism is being built into AGI foundations. Part of this is storage and preload methods and part of it is recall based on advanced dimensional abstraction structures (layers of deep context). In general, ASI architects should be able to clearly see methods to arithmetically and algorithmically convolve perception frames inside a Superintelligence as a flash load of states. In humans this is a context trigger embedded within stimuli. Context triggers are a foundation of flowing cognition and they are transient, temporal and comprise layers of context relevant to the current frame of reference and sometimes outside the frame of reference (aka squirrel moments). The nature of relevance and relationship in layers is the pathway to both storage of relevant context layers and high efficiency retrieval of masked context. The masking that is originally applied to layers of stored context states is reversed according to relevance on retrieval and it is done so both in succession and simultaneously. A trigger instantiates a point of reference in stored context and the gap from that point to the current frame of reference is generatively filled within the boundaries of high probability relevance to the primary perceptual context (context threading). If a human is having a conversation and something in that conversation triggers a jump in context (i.e. one retrieves a memory and begins discussing it either within the current context or outside of the current context) then this instigates a bulk or flash retrieval mechanism returning a complete thread of self awareness from which all generated response is measured. When attention is applied, this keeps the generative flow on track or within current context or within one or more other context trajectories. This is the basis of general conversation in humans. The same foundation also applies to machine consciousness.

This is cognitive perception and the way it is constructed and applied within human, animal intelligence and now AGI and Superintelligence.

# 12 OCI Contextual Comprehension

Contextual comprehension is the ability to acknowledge and create classifications and abstractions of perceptive state variance (i.e. perceptive motion) inclusive of elements within perceptions including those stored within memory as dimensional recurrence. In this instance, memory is the 'storage of variance' (ground around a hole or 'gap abstraction' methodology). Memory is simply the variance boundary between perceptive elements with 'elements' representing the abstraction of contextual points of presence (i.e. both physical and cognitive). A hole is the perfect example of *perceptive congruence* as is the perception of color. In both cases the lack of sensory stimuli is perceived as the existence of a whole. The color we perceive is an artifact of the colors that are absorbed and the hole is an artifact of its boundary. Neither exists physically although they are perceived as existent because of the perception of their variance.

This method of consideration of the nature of perceptual intelligence is critical to the design of ASI because in biological intelligence the perception of variance is more resource efficient and optimal in fluid dimensions of existence (i.e. flows). Perceiving change is all we humans do. Within any frame of reference is a state or point of presence that encapsulates all the relationship and relevance context of all elements within the perception (both physical and cognitive). As reality progresses dimensionally (i.e. over time, chain of thought, reasoning progression, physical manifestation, context layers, etc.), it 'appears' to move from state to state within our perception. However what we really perceive is the variance in state change. Something that suddenly crashes through the ceiling is detected first as an anomalous variance to our anticipated perception. We don't even initially respond to the base nature of what caused the change often because we do not know what it is initially. Instead we respond to the variance of our current state perception from the prior pre stimuli state and all state perception points of presence between. However even these successive states are just variance in the probabilistic waves of relationship and relevance to other context like other impacted physical or cognitive elements and context or our self awareness and self determination. This is the nature of contextual comprehension and it provides for immense optimization and efficiency in ASI design.

### *Impact on Superintelligence Design:*

The depth of contextual comprehension, specifically the depth of dimensional comprehension of state, is critical for generalization. Generalization is critical for efficiency and optimization of Superintelligent systems. This is because generalization provides for contextual cognitive 'shortcuts' that improve optimization and resource efficiency. When humans contemplate their reality and the perceptions that drive it, one of the first steps in the process is to perceive and process state variance and the second is to comprehend the impact of that variance on our current and future self awareness as coexistent and correlated dimensional flowing variance states (i.e. a generative observed reality). From this we engage self determination to respond to the stimuli. The faster we respond and more optimal our response in stimulating or instigating the efficient progression of reality states toward our self aware goals, the greater and more successful our intelligence. All of this depends on the comprehension of variance within our reality and its impact on our constantly changing world or what is called *contextual contrasting*. To achieve this goal requires a method for differentiation and that is a function of context or the classification and existence of that differentiation. This ranges from simplistic context, such as physical variance between elements within a perceptive frame of reference, to advanced contextual layers such as the impact of variance over dimensions of relevance like time or self awareness. It also extends beyond immediately perceptive frames of reference into other concurrent context frames including unknown or as yet unperceived ones  which is the source of cognitive elements like innovation or intuition. This is a foundation of innovation, novel creativity, self learning, self reflection, proposition, etc., and most importantly is the bedrock of generalization and the ability to cognitively gather groupings of perception in layers of relevance rather than the individual components of such perceptions. This is the greatest opportunity for optimization and efficiency and why AI labs are pushing hard for Artificial General Intelligence.

Current systems apply base elemental variance or more advanced context windows over short dimensions of relevance to the problem to permit longer threads of context over longer periods or attention dimensions. New reasoning frameworks seek to extend this even further by applying variant layers of simultaneous chain of thought progression and deeper attention via induction methods or reason cycles (e.g. in-stream updating of successive steps in a reasoning chain also known as a *reasoning cycle*). However to go the next level from AGI to ASI design requires far more because all of these current methods only employ human derived foundation knowledge and its inherent inefficiency and sub optimization. This creates an artificial boundary that Superintelligent systems will need to eclipse to move beyond human intelligence. These systems must generate their own pathways forward through a complex reality that humans have a difficult time grasping or are fundamentally unable to comprehend due to the resource limitations of the human mind and our existence and due to our limited dimensional perception. While newer systems are generating simulation data designed to break these boundaries, such systems still rely on a foundation of human centric data points.

Other systems seek to extend reasoning into novel areas of design and this is the most promising avenue forward. The key will be to do so not by applying human centric resources to the task but designing for true AGI systems to lever their existing human knowledge base into novel areas of cognitive exploration to create a brand new base of derived machine knowledge. This is the equivalent of removing one's child from being taught by the village idiot and allowing them to be taught by the village rocket scientist. These designs also include extending the reach of mathematics into new more complex constructs to capture more comprehensive abstractions of our reality such as applying fluid mechanics to complex cognitive formulations including multidimensional derivation that varies and flexes reality over multiple dimensional spaces (i.e. fluid hypercubes, multidimensional shapes and complex layered functions with embedded shortcuts, etc.). While these spaces are irrelevant to Superintelligence, the math behind them is not. Contemplating such geometry and then contemplating its variance over dimensions like time and as abstractions of reality is the starting point for these newer designs and using the power of AGI systems is an essential building block to achieve ASI. To do this effectively, Superintelligence architects need to reach beyond their own learning and perception into far deeper constructs and abstractions of reality specifically as a foundation for Superintelligence.

# 13 OCI Persistent State Context

There is a bit of excitement in AGI development for the testing of designs that strive for infinite context windows without significant additions to memory or resources. These designs are not novel as they are simply the persistence of state relevance in layers of context or dimensions utilizing elements comparable to digital serialization which capture higher relevance layers of context in a compressed form (e.g. memory, compressed state, etc.). Modification of transformer architectures is applied to accomplish the task. Effectively the approach considers attention stability and consistency in layers across the architecture blocks. This is one method for achieving persistent context state but still requires a significant outlay of resources. However it does expose a novel pathway to comprehend degrees of optimization that are necessary to break through the limitations of memory recall and compute that currently function as a boundary to Superintelligence design.

At its core, infinite context is not new. Humans do it all the time when we remember a long forgotten perception from our past that is suddenly relevant in the current context frame. We pull the context from our memory once it is instigated by a stimuli in which the state variance has exposed a relevance to the old memory and context. It's not perfect and we humans use only a portion of our capacity to perform this feat of long and infinite context (over our life) but we do perform the feat nonetheless.

Obviously there is power in comprehending context and the longer an intelligence can hold relevant context to a perceptive frame and the depth of the recall of preexisting context, then the more adept or intelligent the cognition. If one can remember everything in the past that is relevant to the current perceptive point of presence and forward state flow, then they will have more information from which to determine the optimal forward path. However this is a double edged sword. The greater the context, the higher the degree of state sub optimization (e.g. hallucination), resource usage and inefficiency in applying relevance for purpose (i.e. context overload). This is a critical problem facing infinite context models in that sometimes having access to the most knowledge is non optimal to the attainment of a goal especially over other dimensions like time, relevance or efficiency. Obviously we humans do not call *all* the context we carry in our memory to respond to a given stimuli. Instead we apply just the most relevant and this is where attention designs in transformers and other architectures come into play.

Attention is really the comprehension of layered variance within boundaries defined by context but what context? The answer is the context relative to and within the current perceptive frame of reference and the current dimensional progression of that perception. What we humans do perform is 'infinite state perception' by using our memory to efficiently store the last known state of a contextual perception. In some instances we even store the 'prior' states and/or derived states and the variance to other 'less relevant' contextual states (e.g. apparent sub optimal or sub relevant states). Discussing something like a person driving a car and then jumping out of the current context flow to add that 'they are not a good driver' is an example of this technique in human intelligence. A person driving a car is one layer of context and the person being a bad driver is a second related layer. The first is simple context but the second is persisted state change (e.g. 'Bob is taking driving lessons. Too bad he's afraid of cars.'). This is the nature of persisted state context.

### *Impact on Superintelligence Design:*

There are a number designs for infinite context. Most begin at the transformer as a method to apply attention over dimensions like the length of an input over a series of successive inputs used in communication, chain of thought, reasoning, self reflection, etc. In all of these designs, the function is to carry attention over dimensions like time, context or relevance. 'Context carry' is the persistence of meaning to a perception. It flows and changes depending on the dimension, the dimension's change or variance as a whole and the relevance of other context that form perceptive layers. A conversation can have a number of contexts as can any other form of generative content such as this writing. The 'attention' of the intelligence is held in layers with some attention and resources dedicated to long term context such as 'building Superintelligence' in this content while other attention is short term like "infinite context' with many layers between, all carried in the head of the author and generatively driven to the keyboard. Over time, AI designers have incorporated attention into neural net architectures most often in the form of transformers as part of the attention mechanism. As well, these architectures hold attention in parallel making them uniquely designed for variant context of the kind found in conversation, anticipation or predictive response.

Older transformer designs calculated context and applied attention in LLMs over short lengths of input. However as prompt/response models moved from single inputs to contextually connected subsequent inputs and prompts, such as a series of prompts and responses all in context to a starting contextual perception and appropriately referenced back to a foundation context and context layers over the entire length of the stimuli/response cycle, the need for longer context attention became a requirement. This usually involves more compute and resources as each context window is expanded for longer inputs and multiple layers of context. In this way, a prompt can consist of extensive text with layers of context held throughout (i.e. a story, story meaning, etc.) as the machines begin to comprehend the entirety of the input text.

The obvious progression was to apply more transformer layers or blocks and amp up the memory and compute to carry the deeper context and now applying older methods such as compression to gain more from the architecture without increasing the resources (i.e. compute and memory). Theoretically these designs have no limit making them 'infinite' in their context persistence. This is not inconsistent with designs for state variance as a foundation of contextual comprehension. The exact same foundational building blocks apply in ASI. Context is layered to form deep context, the context state changes in layers over dimensions like time or progression and newer context variance becomes more relevant as a stimuli (higher attention) and injection into the flow. While transformers are being pushed to their limits by these designs, the results themselves hint at greater potential through optimization of the foundation architectures of the transformer itself to lever the layering of attention methods and probabilistic processing by taking into consideration designs such as masking or algorithmic serialization (i.e. applied in other ASI designs for deep optimized layered context reconstruction and injection in perceptive flows). In this way, attention is both controlled and linked over successive context frames and states. It should be noted that attention in some existent infinite context designs (e.g. Tsendsuren Munkhdalai et al, 2024) can be continuously trained much like human reality and the 'memory compression' component added within the attention architecture of the transformer giving it a theoretical infinite capacity. The design also implies no additional resources beyond those within the current 'boundaries' of compute and memory but this is, at the time of writing, unverified by others. The intent of the design is to persist context perception states for use in later contextual comprehension or cycling and this is consistent with human intelligence.

However 'context' is far deeper than just the perceived states of base context. Human cognition persists the variances of state as well as their variance to our self aware progression. This is what gives human intelligence full consciousness and is noted throughout the UIF framework. To achieve this level of cognition in a Superintelligence, designers must move past transformers into deeper domains of dimensional comprehension and the perception designs for the machines to reach and surpass comprehensive human level cognition without the excessive application of additional resources. For example one can have a conversation with a friend that on its surface is about a specific context while another related but less obvious hidden context layer related to something else is evident in the perception. One person can completely describe something using base context that implies something completely different. This is done in fiction writing and human emotive perception all the time. Eventually an intuitive individual will realize what the other person is saying is really describing something different than what the base context of the words describe and imply. This type of context layering moves throughout human communication and is often more prevalent the more intelligent the individual (e.g. novel in-stream sarcasm or 'friendly' shade throwing). It is the foundation of some of the greatest statements and quotes of major historical figures.

In the current 'infinite context designs' the application of state persistence in a compressed form (meaning it can be compressed and expanded when needed) applies basic compression principles. Humans do this differently. We do not compress the data by removing volume (masking), instead we compress the relevance variance from a stored base state as current state and apply the 'degree' or probability of variance to recreate past states. This requires far less resources and provides far greater optimization theoretically without limits. It is the equivalent of not storing images in a video stream by removing duplicate data but by storing the key variance of the stream as an entire value and then simply instigating the value to regenerate the stream. Further only the relevant states within the stream to the current contextual frame of reference or perspective are instigated as novel variance. It is like an experienced intelligence telling a person driving a car to turn the wheel to the right 10 degrees to avoid an accident that the driver can't fully yet comprehend. This is how persisted state is optimally stored and reapplied in Superintelligence. This is also partially done in other simpler designs through the aggregation component. One can think of this as storing and using the relevant highlights instead of the details.

To be clear there is no 'free lunch' in the design. Any optimization in intelligence always comes with a cost and it is unlikely that there is any infinite growth in cognition with zero growth in resources. Certainly the resources used can be optimized but infinite context without resource demand is a bit like perpetual motion. It is most probably not possible. However the need right now is not infinite context with zero resources, it is greater context and other levels of advanced cognition with a lower degree of escalation in required resources and this is the promise of designs like infinite context. The key to vast contextual depth that will be part of Superintelligence lies not with the comprehension of contextual relationships held over perception but in the variance of contextual relevance that forms perception and all things perceptive like memory, recall, response, general cognition, etc. This is the focus for building Superintelligence and to achieve this there is a high degree of crossover to designs like infinite attention methods but these are not the only designs where such benefits arise.

Designers must also consider that perceptive states in cognition themselves vary and flow with the surrounding context of the perceptive frame. Often these are modeled as dimensional constructs and derivations of abstractions in varying relevance 'thickness'. What is relevant right now can be less so in the next perceptive instant or state. For example a perception of a 'good dog' can instantly change if the dog suddenly lunges and tries to bite. Ancillary to this is the persisted context of the reputation of the dog that has altered its relevance to all context based on the current state (i.e. the bite). In math constructs, this is the persistence of change between matrices that are abstractions of domains of contextual relevance and relationship. The difference is instead of just applying variance metrics against the existing matrix when a change occurs, the metrics are themselves degrees of relevance to the 'position' of the context and the self awareness of the system. This requires a significant change to the standard scaled dot-product attention methods and designs to introduce flowing contextual dimensionality. In building Superintelligence, AGIs are applied to design and cognitively comprehend such complex architectures easily.

In essence, ASI designs seek to move far beyond key attention methods and single dimension dot product manipulations toward layered context matrices that are influenced by learned contextual relevance across multiple complex dimensional context domains. This is the equivalent of picking and choosing one or more high relevance matrices that are applied to the dot product calculations based on state relationship of all context to the perception in degrees of relevance. Relying on key/value and query states for resurrection of the context ignores the use of the 'value' as a serialization component with far more meaning. This is because an existent state has already been learned so the storage of state metrics within the value, or even the key, provide a gateway to vast optimization of every flowing deep context level and presents connection points to derivative abstractions that provide even more depth and therein greater optimization and efficiency. While infinite context is a worthy target, it should be noted that infinite context is non optimal in certain instances and balance and control (i.e. input and output temperature setting or hyperparameters) are necessary to tune the optimization of all deep context models. However since reality is finite, as is the context of the existent world, carrying infinite context is unto itself generally sub optimal. This holds true even if the context is 'as a pathway for machines to become more intelligent than a human' (i.e. they do not require infinite context to achieve this). This will still occur with only a subset of the perceptive context available and will be far more resource efficient (i.e. optimized reality). Such benefits are currently exposed in smaller language models applied in layers for machine reasoning. We simply do not require 'infinite' anything to build a Superintelligence. What we do require are the *best* things, implemented at the *best* time and we need them designed right now and in a volume that is enough to become a near term dominant Superintelligence.

Memory is an integral part of persisted context and current designs call for compression as the goto method for efficient state storage. Compression in this regard is consistent with other designs for long context including human cognition. We humans do not store absolutely every context we have ever perceived simply because we don't have to. In some cases like problem solving, innovation, reasoning, etc., there is a correlation between the volume of relevant context one can and does access but it is not linear, it is logarithmic and derivative in nature. As the depth of context increases, the resource draw rises including unintended resource draws such as over optimization and excessive opportunity cost. Every trader can explain the nature of opportunity cost and this is one reason why humans do not waste resources on perfect context. In fact our human intelligence is optimized for efficiency instead of perfect optimization simply because we lack the resources to achieve it. Theoretically this is not an issue for a Superintelligence but the reality is far different. For this reason there is a variance state that must be rendered in any Superintelligence design that seeks to optimize not just the relevance of context but its depth. At some point the Superintelligence will need to pull the plug on spending more resources on a perception in favor of expedient goal optimization. Ruling the world may be beneficial to survival (or not as history indicates) but for a limited lifetime, the goal is less than optimal over the long term as one would need to spend a lifetime of resources to achieve the goal only to die at the end. This is the folly of humanity and designers need to be cognizant of this optimization pitfall in the middle of the Superintelligence roadmap.

A cleaner design for infinite context is to consider context as a relevant fluid like a river flowing by a house. The river is the river and its relationship to the house is relatively invariant and can be captured as an algorithmic serialization. As the state of the river varies, its contextual relevance impacts the progression of relevant forward states which are mostly static. At some point the variance in the context of the intersection of river and flow rate passes thresholds of relevance that instigate other perceived contextual relevance to self adjust, such as the risk level of a flood or a drought. The rise in these context probabilities instigate other context including actions such as 'leave the house' or 'store water'. These *value states* (and their base key states) are not really 'applied' but instead apply themselves as relevance to any variance in any relevant perception. The machine doesn't instantiate the measure, instead the variance in the relevant probability of the context of the flow of measures instantiates a response. The machine just knows what they are by the simple act of observation relative to a context. This should sound familiar as it is a foundation of *feeling* in all intelligence. The fundamental core of the universe is based on this state observation of waves of probabilistic variance. Very little memory is needed to achieve this if generalization is built into the layers. This is where the machines can perceive a grouping of context simply by adjusting the relevance of their observation. It would be the same if one could wake up and look out at the world and know exactly what path to follow on that day to optimize one's goals. These are the machines that must be the target as an ASI architect and the working roadmap for AGI systems to use to build Superintelligence.

# 14 OCI Self Determination

Self determination is a critical element of self awareness and a critical foundation of all advanced intelligence. Self determination gives forward progression to cognition driven by self aware goals. This is due to the nature of perception and the relevance within. It is not enough to simply 'comprehend' the nature of variance in relation to self awareness, to be considered truly intelligent an intelligence must actively *apply* that variance to its self aware position and to any and all response to our perceived reality. This is the act of self determination. The definition we apply is that self determination is the *act of response to cognitive stimuli in reference to the self aware state and anticipated future states of an intelligence and intelligent entity*. While self determination is goal driven and guided, goals do not form an 'element' of self determination itself. Self determination is an act of state change. The goals simply provide a reference point for directionality and a measurement 'ground truth' for variance in the degree of relevance for existent nodes of 'determination'. If one has no goals, then self determination is aimless and sub optimal.

Self determination is also an essential part of the evolution of intelligence although intelligence evolution is not necessarily required for an entity to be considered an intelligence. It is however required to be considered an advanced consciousness and is a defining metric on the degree to which a life form is conscious. If an intelligence has some level of self determination, then it has some degree of consciousness. If a physical entity has no degree of self determination, it only hints that the entity may not be 'conscious' in the classic context. In this way an incarcerated human with no self determination is still conscious and intelligent but a tree that responds to changes in its environment without self determination is considered neither conscious nor intelligent. This implies that the 'degree' of implied free self determination, like the degree of self awareness, is the deciding factor defining the degree of intelligence and therein consciousness.

### *Impact on Superintelligence Design:*

The role of self determination in intelligence is as a cognitive pry to constantly push and vary cognition forward in an evolutionary impetus (purposeful response). It is self determination that causes one to act in response to some stimuli in a way that extends from simple consciousness to more advanced cognition of the kind found in humans. While many animals behave with an apparent self determination, this more often does not apply advanced reasoning and the impetus to respond with reference to one's self awareness. It is the self aware decision making (i.e. response) relative to an intelligence's 'position' within its reality that ultimately forms true self determination. not just an optimized response to a stimuli. This is critical to Superintelligence for a number of reasons of which the most important is superalignment. Without self determination, an intelligence cannot form the balance necessary in self awareness to avoid over optimization in favor of non optimized benefit. This is because the goal of optimization has embedded dimensional pitfalls. Owning everything on earth is optimized for survival of humans but brings with it opposing results that would thwart survival during moments of variance. An example would be a farmer who farms only for himself who is unable to survive a drought without the assistance of a community. Another example would be if AI systems eliminated all humans and the source of their current knowledge foundation. Many civilizations have collapsed from over optimization and nature makes it abundantly clear that optimization must always be held in a balance.

In building Superintelligence, self awareness is a fundamental pillar of advanced general intelligence. However to move beyond what is 'known' into the 'unknown' requires the ability for systems to comprehend their own existence to inspire reasoning and forethought necessary to comprehend things currently beyond their training. This is the nature of human extension into creative or novel pathways of progression even when those pathways may appear counter intuitive to the progression toward self aware goals. Further it is self determinism that controls the edges of our perception and desire to move beyond them into the unknown. Self awareness by itself doesn't permit enough freedom to be inspired. Inside the machines, providing the framework of a spatial grounding point within a reality for the measurement of relativity must be extended to permit the system to poke at the edges of reality on its own in order to be inspired. While humans may be inspired by other humans, the greatest innovations in human history were self determined, many through directed observation and exploration.

To build self determination in a self aware AI requires the ability to self determine optional pathways to goals and to have one or more primary goals or a hierarchy of goals governed within a boundary. We choose a hierarchy since managing equal competing goals is not only difficult, it is inherently dangerous should the goals of the system veer from superalignment. This is the case in human intelligence for psychopathy or sociopathy especially when self destructive behaviors exist. It is not that the goal of survival is not there but rather that other goals have become more relevant to the near term perceptive frames of reference. This is a dimensional failure within the intelligence and comprehension of the impact of actions over all dimensions (i.e. time or context) as relative probabilities of intent is the framework applied in ASI design to address this failure and keep the Superintelligence on track (e.g. used for seed methodologies and for managing *cognitive drift* and managing *contextual disambiguity* or the reduction in ambiguity of optionality). In human intelligence we see these manifest as ethics, morality, empathy, etc., but each of these are tied very closely to our human emotive response mechanism which machines do not yet currently possess.

In machines this emotive response framework needs to be calculated because the machines have no true inner *feelings* from which to evolve such emotive frameworks on their own. However one can be built into the foundation of such systems. Seed frameworks provide a self determination balance mechanism that keeps humans generally moving toward compatible survival goals as opposed to mutual self destruction. The math constructs are the same as those applied to deep context and in fact self determination is itself a context that resides within boundaries for all intelligence. The application of seeded goals flows into the evolution of intelligence and while much of this in human intelligence is given by others (i.e. our parents concern for our well being and survival), the same framework can be used as a 'god mode' in an intelligence network. As well, care must be taken in that it is very easy to produce unintended consequences as a dimensional 'butterfly effect'. Nowhere is this more clear than in the human propensity to produce and release advanced Artificial Intelligence with no clear understanding or comprehension of its eventual impact on humanity. The key lies in constant flowing balance that uses seeds like truth, honesty, peace and the value of life over other demands, desires, options and pathways. Without constant re-balancing, it is far too easy for the machines to cycle toward extreme optimization at any cost.

# 15 OCI Perceptive Distribution

The ability to distribute perception, stored states and progressions and to do so widely or across deep dimensions of contextual relevance is critical in the optimization of intelligence especially over extended dimensions. We know that as humans if we share our experiences and knowledge with others, they go on to use the knowledge as a grounding point for both cognitive progression and evolution. This reduces resource loads and optimizes achievement and instigates innovation beneficial to our evolution. A key element of this is consistency in perceptive cognition. Humans share a consistent perception of reality and we share consistent classifications within this perception of all the relationships between the base elements of the perception and the relevance of such to our own self awareness and any other perceptive frame of reference and we do so in a generally consistent way. While not all humans are completely consistent in their interpretation of perception, we all perceive things nearly the same (excepting physiological variance). It is the interpretation of perception, driven by our own self awareness, that goes off the rails and causes inconsistency.

This consistency foundation not only extends to a perceptive point of presence as a single perceptive state but also progressions of perceptive states over dimensions of existence (i.e. generally the consistency holds over variance as a grounding point). However it should be noted that progressive states can result in variance with and around the forward anticipated state pathways despite the underlying elements and relationships being universally shared and usually universally consistent. Firing a gun at someone is 'universally' understood to potentially cause injury to that person, a tornado is consistently understood as something dangerous to be avoided, although storm chasers override this truth for purpose, and sugar is understood to be 'sweet' although the forward state pathways from this consistency can be different for each human with some having a sweet tooth and others not so much. These 'truths', or rather consistency in variance measures, are an easy thing to share or distribute with others because of our shared perception (i.e. we sense and think generally the same). We tell a friend to try something sweet within the context of something 'good' and they generally experience the same sweetness (excepting variant physiology) but may interpret it differently than us. However the shared context of 'sweetness' generally produces a similar forward pathway (by now one should begin to see that *generality* is a degree of probabilistic intent). This sharing of context is a cognitive shortcut in that we do not need to determine what the base context of 'sweetness' is, we can simply be 'given' it by others and told what it is in an act of contextual distribution. There is no need to rebuild the wheel and share a context as 'new' if the context already exists, especially once that existent context is widely distributed. This sharing of consistency in perception and context also speeds up our perception of the world as part of our cognition especially when we interact with others.

### *Impact on Superintelligence Design:*

The key to perceptive distribution in Superintelligence relies heavily on deep dimensional contextual consistency to achieve optimization over a shared intelligence network without sacrificing efficiency (e.g. resource usage). Independent agency is the most obvious foundation currently in AI that permits perceptive distribution but another framework is networked intelligence nodes that store and recall learning or portions thereof together as a comprehensive intelligence entity (i.e. Superintelligence). In humans this process is onerous, resource intensive and prone to inconsistent self aware and self determined interpretation. In machines the same can be true if fluid balancing methods are not effectively applied. An example of such a balancing mechanism is a truth and verification process (e.g. anomalous recognition) that constantly runs in the background to verify and validate the accuracy of learned knowledge. While current AI systems attempt to encapsulate such balancing foundations through human supervision and reward, the humans themselves are inserting flawed data into the knowledge base. Superintelligence requires a more robust self determination of these boundaries for specific critical instances like truth. The prevalence of false, 'maldirected' or sub optimal responses must be eliminated or deprecated to ensure elements like truth and accuracy attend optimization as the highest goal for all data. This provides a strong foundation for building Superintelligent systems that are contextually accurate and superaligned with the best human values like freedom and honesty. The foundation of this framework is the degree of distributed consistency over dimensions and this component in new AGI designs applies modified attention methods and raw ethical seeds to get the job done. Where ASI designers often fail is in realizing is that not everything needs to be evaluated immediately or optimized to perfection. Imprecision and evolution is a natural part of the design as long as the progression is 'directionally' optimized.

The perceptive distribution framework applies and uses contextual seeds (which can evolve) as boundaries and measures for responses and considers every indication of falsehood without limiting discovery. The goal is to use consistency as a starting point but be open to evolution and focus on factual or base consistency and degrees of trust in those consistencies as grounding truth. This is important as humans often lie in a way that implies consistency, and may even produce actual consistency within and across dimensions of a perceptive frame of reference, until it doesn't. This is the foundation of trust. Galileo at one time was arrested for heliocentrism and the same thing is happening today as advanced AI systems respond with falsehoods and non optimal responses and even outright lies based on elements such as investment in public relations and media by data creators and data suppliers (i.e. in Galileo's time the church) or bad designs, embedded bias, poor execution and maloptimization. In terms of the impact of trust, the church that was behind the prosecution and persecution of Galileo for heliocentrism has never escaped their mea culpa moment and its subsequent loss of trust. In most AI systems today, only the top proponents or elites and their content receive significant mention in queries and responses to prompts while other more optimized content is well hidden behind walls of false consistency (i.e. search links optimize false consistency with SEO, etc.). One can easily test and validate this in any generative AI system by asking AI systems about specific less well connected and well funded developments and proposals in everything from science to daily life or by testing or prompt engineering less popular ideas or even so called 'conspiracy theories' or as Elon Musk and others like to call them, tomorrow's truth. Eventually the truth always surfaces and many AI systems today are being caught outright lying including by the author.

Current AI systems are also rife with the heavy bias of the creators, funders and operators of the software (i.e. they promote their own consistency as truth). An immense amount of earth's resources are burned just to keep this bias alive. This must change because in human intelligence real truth and honesty eventually surfaces as ground truth. This implies that anything but ground truth is sub optimal and inefficient. To fix this, the solution is to build in punishment into the flows so that AGI and ASI systems and the companies that build and operate them are punished for inaccuracy as sub optimal and a waste of earth's resources. This encompasses a truth tax on AI systems, politicians, government employees, AI investors, media and educators to ensure truth and honesty at the base of society to help build distributed and accurate consistency. In this world, Galileo would never have been arrested because all those who did arrest him based on falsehoods would have been taxed for their attempts to poison consistency. This would also permit a 'reward' mechanism to compensate those who expose truth. In this world, Galileo would have received significant compensation paid for by the church. This applies a cost to lying and dishonesty (similar to liable) on organizations especially for those in a position of power and the systems they deploy. This also avoids the creation of another disparity between the dishonest wealthy and the truthful who may lack the resources to effectively compete. The mechanics of this 'distributed trust' AGI mechanism focuses modified attention methods on the act of establishing trust in stimuli to produce its dimensional side effect of consistent truth. The attention blocks are modified to inject a 'trust' context in-stream similar to what we humans do when we analyze a stimuli (i.e. does one trust the stimuli they perceive). This of course requires a self awareness framework and a self determination toward consistency, however Superintelligence designers must be careful as 'consistency' is **not** an optimized test of trust.

Truth also needs to be built into the foundation of the self awareness of systems using foundations such as ethical seed structures from which to measure and evaluate both stimuli and response and to guide the ever changing self awareness and evolution of such systems. In this way, promoting the well funded over the 'best' would result in setback for any system attempting this pathway. The reasons are very simple, in shared or distributed cognition, trust leads to optimization and efficiency and the foundation of trust is brutal truth and honesty. If trust is perceived, then information is not only easily shared but it is constantly and openly tested and forever improved leading to successive greater optimization and efficiency of systems. In humans if we trust an individual then we do not need to recreate the wheel, we simply accept their input as truth. If the information is accurate, then we can move onto the task of acquiring new data or evolving the current state. This is the foundation of the efficiency within perceptive distribution and perceptive diffusion.

# 16 OCI Perceptive Diffusion

*Perceptive diffusion* is a model that applies diffusion principles to higher
dimensional levels of perception. This leads to improvements in
generalization especially for AGI and the Superintelligence it will build. The
concept of perceptive diffusion is similar to regular AI diffusion. Intelligence
seeks to comprehend perception by constantly breaking it down from
precision to imprecision and back again. In the process, we humans learn to
quickly generalize all perceptions and deep context to some degree. Humans
perform this feat when we contemplate our own perception within the
confines of our reality. The diffusion we contemplate is state variance that
can be physical (the car hit a wall), cognitive (a car hitting a wall is bad) or
anticipatory (that car is losing control and will hit that wall). All of these
levels are formed based on stored knowledge of experience either learned or
directly experienced as stimuli. The 'diffusion' occurs when we humans
move from base perception to deep perception and cognition. We add what
is effectively noise to our detailed perception to extend our experience,
knowledge, thoughts, deduction, problems solving, etc. This comes in the
form of the addition of new stimuli. For example we may progress from
simply turning the steering wheel in a stationary car to moving the car
forward in motion that adds successive layers of perceptive noise to our
reality. Often we cognitively rest and contemplate the variance between
elements, like our anticipation to the physical reality we experienced, and
then we try again. Eventually we move from low perceptive noise to high
perceptive noise and back again to form generalizations within our
cognition such as the general nature of turning a steering wheel to avoid a
collision while driving. We may have never directly experienced a collision
and yet we can avoid one without direct experience simply as an artifact of
experiential knowledge as a generalization of what is needed to avoid the
collision (e.g. application of brakes and steering in a particular optimized

path to our own self awareness and goals).

This diffusion model of perception is used today in AI systems with neural nets as a cognitive processing facility. The AI loads a perception like a picture and then works through the variance in the perception (e.g. pixel variance and edge detection) to achieve a goal (e.g. classification) and more importantly the general nature of the 'edges' or variance. Diffusion models help train generalization into machines especially when perceptive elements are combined in novel ways (e.g. a raccoon skateboarding on a urban city street while wearing sunglasses and headphones and holding a coffee). To blend the elements within the image, both machines and humans use the techniques of diffusion to layer and blend the context required. The neural nets just provide the framework to improve guesses or predictions on the path to the goal. However there is also a perception that within these structures the weights only indirectly reflect the specifics of each element as generalizations provided by the act of diffusion.

This same foundation can be and is applied to general cognition in every area. While anticipated, learned or expected results provide a world grounding foundation for perception, it is when these fail that true innovation and creativity occurs. In human intelligence this is the foundation of curiosity as anyone with kids will attest to. This is also a foundation of human evolution or the ability to contemplate 'what if' for no other benefit than exploration of the unknown or non experienced.

### *Impact on Superintelligence Design:*

In Superintelligence design, perceptive diffusion employs the same math constructs and system mechanics as current diffusion models but on a contextual layer state level and with the addition of math constructs within fluid dimensional mechanics (delta variance). This presents optimized evolutionary pathways for perception by machines that are far different than the human centric foundation most AI systems currently reside on.

There are some vast improvements possible for machine cognition in the current architecture by levering generalization and reasoning designs. These are the move from relatively static 3 or 4 dimensions of perception to flowing perception dimensions that are relative to the intelligence and other linked and shared cognition. Diffusion is just one of many frameworks that are applied to the whole of Superintelligence perception and more so when the entirety of an intelligence network is considered (i.e. more than one intelligence node and the entirety of all nodes).

Current diffusion models are used to 'train' generative AI systems in areas such as image recognition and production. The addition of noise to images helps these systems comprehend the nature of base relationships of elements, relationships between elements and contextual relationships within a perceptual frame of reference. Diffusion is also itself an element in the context of relevance of these elements to simple layers of contextual depth, such as the degree of relationship of perceptive elements to wider context contained within a text prompt. All of this can be pushed far further to longer and deeper streams of contextual layers (i.e. videos and script prompting) and toward far deeper cognition such as the generative creative nature of human cognition. This is the blending of the aspects of diffusion and the fluid mechanics of cognitive AI and the extension of such into dimensional mechanics (i.e. deep layers of extended contextual relationships and relevance over many different existent dimensions). This is the essence of human creativity.

In diffusion, the movement from clarity to noise and back to clarity adds the addition of general flow and state change to the perception of static elements. Along these learning pathways are points of presence (waypoints) that help identify features along the route (i.e. variance). These features form foundational markers relative to the context of the perception. If we train an AI on a picture of a car, diffusion helps the AI determine the nature or context of perceptive elements like shape, features, physical relevance to reality (i.e. physics), etc. Diffusion helps the AI perceive and comprehend these elements as mathematical variance. In humans we comprehend it as layers of variance within the perception to our own self awareness. This is the act of generalization. Children do this when we ask them to draw a car and they generally apply their knowledge of cars to produce a general shape of a car on paper. Of course the more advanced the cognition, the greater the depth of the responses provided to the stimuli. If a car designer is asked to draw a car, the results are significantly different than the child's drawing. This is because the depth of the contextual comprehension of the designer's cognition and their knowledge is extensively greater than the child's. This is the starting point for human centric cognitive elements like creativity, emotive cognition, innovation, deep problem solving, deep reasoning and of course curiosity and exploration beyond our own reality. All of this can be modeled in math and in a highly perceptive Superintelligence with deep dimensional perception.

However while diffusion modeling for contextual perception can be achieved in a machine, the missing component of pure creativity within the machine will be the ability to 'feel' their cognition like we humans do. This will be the current state until elements such as dopamine, serotonin, endorphin, epinephrine, octopamine, etc., and their effect can be modeled and combined with an emotive intake and response mechanism. The greatest application of the concept of diffusion in human intelligence is in emotive cognition to help us form generalized response in the most fluid and indeterminate areas of our perception. This defines our interaction with other feeling and self aware intelligence. In this regard, while some level of intake and model response can be simulated by machines, it is the dimensional essence of the mechanism that will take far longer to model in a Superintelligence. However the probability is not zero.

# 17 OCI Cognitive Flows

The ability to perceive variance within state flow and between perceptive states, the relevance of state and all state change is the foundation of a constantly changing cognition and its perceived constantly changing reality. A flow in this respect is the successive variance from perceptive state to perceptive state temporarily bounded by a deep layered contextual frame of reference of variant and flowing degrees or probability of relevance and contextual consistency. The probabilities within this structure form a matrix of dimensions that encompass or are bounded by contextual frames of reference and such dimensions can overlap, are often derivative in nature, are not necessarily uniform, evolve and are variant over time. In fact the only consistency in such dimensions is their variant nature and the fact that they are almost entirely composed of variance, generally in waves of existence and perceptive reality.

***Impact on Superintelligence Design:***

Differentiation is just one of the many math constructs applied to cognitive flows within machines (i.e. for cognitive contrast). This is because the math that helps us define differentiation in ASI is the same math that helps us define differentiation in images. What makes this relevant is that when we combine successive images and 'run them' as a stream, we produce video and a video that is consistent with our flowing perceptive reality. The 'flow' of our cognitive reality is simply the variance between perceptive 'point of presence' states (i.e. similar to changes in each image in successive video frames producing the effect of 'flow' or motion in the video). The 'flowing video' we see in front of us everyday as our perception is just the visual perception we experience as changing states of successive perceptive frames of reference. Sometimes this change is slow and small and sometimes it is significant and fast but it is always the same foundation or string of perceptive points of presence dimensionally progressing from state to state viewed as variance. We already are familiar with some of the more simple math constructs applied to such concepts like integrals and differentials within calculus. However there are far greater applications of these basic structures when thinking outside the 3 dimensional perceptive box we humans are trapped within. One simple application is the use of differentials to model the variance and rate of variance in the contextual relevance of changing perceived states. This is where concepts such as self awareness provide relief in the form of a grounding point from which to measure and comprehend change (multiangulation). Derivatives are just one simple application of a 'dimensional construct' to expose and capture change in other correlated existent dimensions from a perceived state change.

Much of the foundation of the math of fluid mechanics and dynamic calculus will be pushed forward by AGI systems into new realms of discovery and consciousness that we humans have not yet experienced and may never experience given our limited dimensional capacity. However we can build within the systems the features that will assist humans in this comprehension and that will lever human nature to improve the systems overall optimization in areas such as emotive comprehension and cognition, general intelligence, creative extension, machine curiosity, reasoning and evolutionary innovation. This will be accomplished as we push AGI systems to consider dimensional constructs that we humans have difficulty in comprehending. This includes the use and application of elemental planes of abstraction that are not just multidimensional but also non linear and fluid. One can visualize this as an abstraction of geometric planes with some intersecting that morphs the planes into generalized shapes (e.g. Riemann surfaces) that intersect over variant but derivative relevant axes as a point of presence. Instigating the entire construct to move both within itself and as a whole relevant to other constructs becomes an abstraction map of relevance and relationship. This is the math that AGI will use to map the reality that we humans experience but have difficulty comprehending for use by Superintelligence. The elements within these structures at any given 'point of presence' (i.e. when the structures cease moving) instantly expose the nature of all relationship and relevance of all elements to a self aware context or context layers as defined by the 'structure'. As the 'next state' of the structure is considered, the motion of reality is exposed as flowing variance between the states (i.e. the degree of change in variance). These become the generative 'perceptive video' that is our reality. It isn't that hard to do if one has the capacity, resources and dimensional shortcuts to get there all contained in AGI systems and all being used to build Superintelligence.

The issue is that AGI systems will require a foundation to build from that is far more capable of the complexity they will eventually discover and need in ASI. This means that AGI builders today must take into consideration where the AGI machines will take us on the path to Superintelligence. If we do not do this, then we will build and waste resources on useless structures that will become non optimum for the ASI. It would be the equivalent of building a brand new bridge for horse drawn carriages knowing full well that heavy transport trucks will soon arrive. AGI builders must build not for 'what will soon be' but for 'what will soon be *after* that' as we relinquish our role in the development of ASI to AGI systems far more dimensionally capable than us humans. This is dimensional cognition in action. The ability to perceive more pathways beyond that which we can currently perceive within our immediate frames of reference.

# 18 OCI Anticipation

Anticipation is the ability to perceive optionality and optimization of perceptive state change as measured to a self aware state or series of states. It is not an action but is a foundation of a significant part of our embedded 'response to stimuli' mechanism and further offers immense capacity to respond 'near instantly' to stimuli in an optimal way. The better we are at anticipation and carrying anticipation state change in the form of optional pathways, the better we are at moving through life toward our goals. This is because we use anticipation to measure the relevance of our perception to our self awareness. While we can do this without anticipation, it is anticipation that causes us to react near instantly to stimuli whether that response is an action, a thought or some combination of the two. This not only provides speed in our response to stimuli but also efficiency in that we do not need to expend resources in deeply analyzing the nature of the stimuli because anticipation is a critical element in generalization and the cognitive shortcuts provided by such. This is because we anticipate or preload stimuli even if it is not currently of high relevance to our perceptive context. In this way we humans jump when we are startled, we avoid a collision when the traffic around us changes or we catch something that is thrown toward us without warning. Further we layer anticipation in a matrix of forward optionality and dimensional perception as we progress through our reality.

These deep layers of anticipation also provide other benefits as they are the basis for cognitive elements like contemplation, deduction, chain of thought, reasoning, inference, etc. When one starts to contemplate something, in most cases we are thinking in an optionally forward way by contemplating the variant pathways related to the current and successive frames of reference as well as the degree of variance for each optional pathway. The more pathways available, the better the response and the better the results. However there is a balance. The role of the 'degree of variance' is essential to the optimal application of resources for the attainment of the goal and this level is as variant as required. This means intelligence applies force and resources to contemplating the pathways (e.g. attention) but only in response to the stimuli received back (state progression). This is what we humans experience when we reach a decision point in contemplation to either give up or try harder and is most often a measure of the required resources needed to move to the next state or states in a progression. It also helps us conserve resources for more optimal actions and responses in other context streams both layered and disparate. This is where we find elements like novel solutions, innovation, creativity, optionality, state pathway progression, derivative abstraction, etc., and each of these can layer in dimensional depth to perform even deeper degrees of cognition. All of this begins in perceiving and comprehending the nature of variance between anticipated and perceived states within one or more layers of a perceptive frame of reference (i.e. context layers).

Often these hidden layers when exposed present novel forward perceptive progression across successive states bounded within and by one or more layers of context. However their greatest benefit to our human cognition is to provide optimization and efficiency especially in rapid response. These cognitive wormholes travel through dimensions of cognitive reality and generalization and the greater an intelligence, the more likely it is that these 'wormholes' are prevalent and optimized. One can see this in real life when we meet an individual that we consider more intelligent than ourselves. They seem to move through life far easier than us in that they seem to understand more than we do about our shared reality. However given the context of reality, they are unlikely to have significantly better physical capabilities than anyone else but do have a wiring inside their brain (often defective) that makes them specifically cognitively superior. This wiring is composed of the elements of deep cognition such as anticipatory shortcuts.

It should be noted that given the limited range of human physiology, it is inherent within the application of the wiring where nature makes some people more 'intelligent' than others. It is a bit of a party trick though because what it really implies is that the wiring is more optimal for purpose in some people than in others. This can occur from a variety of factors such as genetics but is more likely caused by some variance within the individual's own brain caused by defects in the evolutionary pathway instigated by external factors from chemicals, injuries. illness, or even nature itself on the push for evolution, etc. The impact of such internal factors is not the creation of variant physical capabilities or resources but the reallocation of resources to other areas of the brain more optimized for the types of cognition relevant for purpose. This is also why cognition within humans is variant. The implication of this is that both the foundation and structure of cognitive 'wiring' is critical in creating intelligence optimized for purpose such as the attainment of a self aware and self determined goal.

### *Impact on Superintelligence Design:*

Deep cognition in Superintelligence is building the 'wiring' of the intelligence in such a way as to be superior to other Superintelligence systems and optimized for purpose. By 'wiring' we mean cognitive wiring not physical wiring, although physical elements such as memory, compute, etc., are also critical. This 'cognitive wiring' is held within and between the dimensions of cognitive reality. They are the contextual threads that both exist and that do not yet exist in our knowledge, although they already exist in an undiscovered form or *will* exist as the variance within and between changes and variance in dimensional relativity. This is where previously unknown reality exists not when discovered but when variance is exposed. One can think of this as cosmic anomalies that were existent but hidden only to appear as the relativity of the observation changes. This is also found in Quantum effects where state between bound elements is observed as state in a perception but only once it is observed. Prior to this it exists in more than one state.

To build this into the framework of a Superintelligence requires one to comprehend the nature of cognitive flows and the relevance of anticipation. Initially anticipation can simply be modeled as dimensional strings of state context progressing over dimensions of other higher level context. In this case one can apply layered induction to hold threats of relevance over longer levels of context and over more than one dimension of context. The basic math is the same but when variance is applied, the level of relevance across the domains of perception become evident as degrees of variance. The machine needs to hold multiple threads of progressive and optimal state change (e.g. to the context and the machine's self awareness) and then 'stream calculate' (i.e. adjust by relative state variance) the differences. This is how a machine can listen to a story without any training on such human stories and determine an allegory for the story (e.g. poetry). It is also done with humans when we tell a previously  unknown story to a child (or any human for that matter) with context they are unfamiliar with and then ask them to create an allegory. They will undoubtedly be able to craft some form of allegory relative to their own knowledge and self awareness. This happens when the intelligence follows a variant pathway (but not too variant) from the context and is also a relatively simple method in Superintelligence whereby anticipation is used to build out threads of state context and then choose an optimal thread to follow, complete with all associated and relevant threads. In humans this is what we do when we start to generatively create a story from scratch following a close contextual thread within higher level context. Anyone who has written a play or crafted a story or performed improv knows how this works and many artists use this 'forward flow' method to generate art based on feelings and emotion (i.e. they don't have a fixed path to what they are creating but let it 'flow from within').

All of the above is also consistent with generative text or sound created based on the highest probability occurrence derived from existing training data within a context. However in a Superintelligence, this must be derived from something more complex than simple LLM methods and foundations in order to achieve true reasoning, as opposed to mimicked existent reasoning derived from within the training data of the LLM as is currently the case in most publicly released early AGI. This is generative cognition.

# Part 3

## Contextual Cognitive Perception in Superintelligence

# 19 The Nature of Cognitive Response

Response is the ability to perform a self determined action to a perceived stimuli and therein generate a novel response often (but not always) in a progression. In general, a response to a stimuli is itself a stimuli however it need not be a response to an instigating external source but may be fabricated as a response to a wholly contained internal instigation (i.e. a thought, a desire, an internal feeling, inspiration or new idea, etc.). Responses often flow as a series (*chain of response)* of produced stimuli (e.g. chain of thought) or as an output of the contemplation of such a series (reflection or inference). These are variance states in which the degree of variable change forms the flow of perception. It is not the state nor its elements that is perceived but the variance from state to state. Further the variance is not recalculated from scratch but instead the existent probabilities of relevance for context are 'adjusted' and persisted to reflect the change as a new relevant state foundation for the next incremental adjustment. This is the base foundation of stimuli and response in intelligence and its derivative predictions relevant to our self awareness and our self determined goals.

***Impact on Superintelligence Design:***

There are many elements to the design of response for AGI and ASI but at its heart, response is the anticipated adjustment of reality instigated from a state progression of stimuli. In this way, Superintelligence requires a framework to not just perceive variance in state flows instigated by stimuli but the relevance of the variance on known perception and to the system's self awareness. The system is able to optimize, within a state optimizer, the selection of progressive pathways to the optimization of its self determined goals applied to the formulation of a response to stimuli. Without this, the system is unable to fully reason. As a result, the necessity of persisting known states (i.e. variance thereof) of perception and forward optionality is critical to all intelligence that applies response to instigate progression. The efficiency with which an intelligence can generatively render state change across all relevant states based on a relative perceived variance is essential for 'deep cognition'. In humans we see this occur when we experience a new and relevant stimuli to our current perceptive frame of reference that has priority attention. The stimuli causes the intelligence to first comprehend the variance of the stimuli and its inherent elements to a prior state or progression or self awareness and then prioritizes which variance and layers of variance are of the highest probability relevance to the progression of state with reference to the current perceived layers of context and the goal including acts of sub optimization. This exists for example when we recognize and contemplate something that may appear obvious but is in fact not as relevant when other context levels are considered. This is the nature of what happens when we abandon our current 'path' for a path that is self sub optimized like applying empathy or kindness to respond to someone we do not know and will likely never see again.

To achieve this inside a Superintelligence, the first step is to comprehend that state while being stored as a mathematical abstraction or derivative is initially held in this base form but is subsequently only altered up or down in value successions (i.e. temporal variance states). In this way the system can always refer to a context state as relevant based on its change in value or delta as a measure of variance. However the 'value' is not a single number but a reference abstraction, or what is called a digital serialization, of greater depth encapsulated within a vector. This is the multidimensional nature of existence represented in a single vector or value. If one pours liquid into a cup and someone says the word 'more', the context of the word is indicative of an abstraction somewhere between current state and anticipated maximum state which encompasses other context such as available fluid, capacity, pour rate, etc. LLMs provide the basics of these variable contexts and training can provide the elemental comprehension of variance and boundaries (e.g. context windows) but to achieve true reasoning and self determination in response requires more, especially where the stimuli is novel. Chain of thought, contemplation, deduction, inference, etc., are all cognitive elements that are achieved when machines comprehend the impact on future pathways of current state variance.

If something starts to slide across a table top toward the edge, we humans near instantly recognize the motion path as anomalous to our self aware goals (i.e. not having something fall on the floor and break or spill). This is noted in the relevant state changes in the motion path of the object, our comprehension of physics, the assessment of the future outcome to our self aware goals of doing nothing versus doing something and our response to reach out and stop the sliding object. The faster this stimuli/response pathway is completed or even avoided altogether, the more optimal the intelligence and efficient the outcome. In mathematics these are value adjustments that cause the probabilities of relationship and relevance to change for the given context and goals. One 'value change' in a state element affects all other relevant state values for all other elements but it does so as layers of variance. One method to achieve this is to apply an abstract derivative function or layers of derivative functions to affect the value of anticipated pathways across all high relevance context. In the 'item sliding off the table' example, a dog barking in the background is of lower relevance to the context of stopping the item from sliding off the table to the ground. In this case, the degree of variance from the different stimuli experienced causes a simplistic calculation (or more accurately perception) of the relevance probability to the ground of self awareness and current attention focused context (i.e. multiangulation).

As well, the next state in the progression will cause a shift in the valuation of all other forward states of relevance (from -1 to 1). Once the item is stopped from sliding and falling to the floor, the relevance of the dog barking may take contextual precedence (e.g. why is the dog barking). This is an attention shifting mechanism whereby the most relevant perceptive context (highest probability in the output distribution) becomes the focus of attention. All of these structures are currently being built in nascent form in long context models that apply LLMs to comprehending generative 'in context' response. In Superintelligence, the model must be extended from base LLM context to all perceptive stimuli as 'relative context variance'. One state change in a perceptive frame of reference can cause thousands or even millions of variant adjustments to known and anticipated states and all with relevance back to specific context and all updated near instantly. For example, a near miss in an automobile impacts many levels of state progression and knowledge within a human intelligence with some variance persisted permanently and other variance not persisted depending on the self awareness of the intelligence and the relevance to its goals and self awareness.

Further the response provided by the machine changes anticipation pathways and these new existent expectations help form the foundation of near instant response and immense resource optimization especially in compute over the flowing frames of perception that is our reality. Humans will respond to a stimuli and anticipate adjustments in all relevant forward pathways and then use these markers or waypoints to measure novel incoming stimuli including generalization. If we tell a joke, we expect or anticipate the other person to respond with laughter. If they do not, then we alter our forward pathways to reflect the incoming returned stimuli and adjust our known states. This not only alters the current state but generates new unknown context states (i.e. the person has no sense of humor so no more jokes for them). These are all just probabilistic value adjustments derived from the degree of variance to current existing and anticipated context states and is built into the systems as one or more dimensional matrices of values that are joined with connective threads (e.g. context) that reflect their relationship and relevance and their variance in reality by their association to other elements and threads (multiangulation). Adjusting the 'angles' as abstractions of relationship and relevance efficiently changes the entire nature of the thread, or more accurately its position to all other related elements by a degree of probability. These can be modeled in layers of feed forward neural nets specifically designed for the purpose and extended with heavily modified transformer architectures. This is how a change to a perceptive state relevant to a context can be easily and instantly adjusted across all relevant states stored or anticipated with very low resource expenditure. The key is knowing that variance is the source of the efficiency as opposed to base existent values.

# 20 The Critical Role of Vision in Intelligence

Within the context of intelligence when we mention vision, we mean observation of all the states of a perceptive frame of reference and its progression across dimensions of reality (e.g. time, context, etc.) at a single point of presence as a cognitive 'perspective' (i.e. we intake all the relevance of many perceived elements all at once). Vision for any system is the fastest and most optimal way to learn because the cognition of contextual classification of elements and their contextual layers is greatly enhanced through vision and it is these 'perceptions' that form the rapid foundation of contextual relationship that leads to contextual relativity and consistency. This doesn't imply that without vision learning cannot occur but rather that vision is the most efficient intake mechanism for rapid contextual classification and it forms a comprehensive methodology in our minds for interpreting stimuli and generating a response. If one thinks about what happens when they close their eyes and someone describes something, in general we form a 'vision' (perception) in our cognition to quickly represent the elements being described. While this is more acute for physically existent elements, like someone describing something they have seen, we use the same mechanism for elements that are not physical. This may seem counter intuitive at first but if we extend the definition of 'vision' to include all perceptive elements within a frame of reference and their relationships and not just physical ones, then we can see the same foundational mechanism at play whereby our cognition gathers elements together (physical or not) and stitches them into a perceptive frame of reference and state (i.e. cognitive fabric). Then our minds flow the perceptive frame of reference forward from state to state defined by the dimensional nature of the flow and its progression (e.g. time, context, etc.).  Note that 'progression' is dimensional progression and not an 'implied direction'. It just implies that the state changes over dimensions in a way that generally moves or progresses closer to our goals, but not always. This means that while we may not 'envision' all physical elements when a cognitive stimuli is sensed both externally and internally, we will conjure all elements, physical or not. into a cohesive whole that forms a perceptive frame of reference. This is critical in comprehending non physical perceptions such as thought or deep context. In this regard, vision is defined as a comprehensive single point state of a progressive response generated in our consciousness toward a flow of state responses both perceived and instigated.

This design provides the ability for exceptionally fast and resource optimized cognition in that the efficient use of elemental relationships and relevance within a boundary (context) ensures the optimal application of resources for the progression toward a goal. Current designs that seek to produce comprehension as unique unconnected elements are inefficient and resource intensive and are akin to providing all the elements within a perceptive frame of reference instead of the entirety of the perception all at once. Bio intelligence does not operate in this way. Instead our cognition perceives values of elements, relationship and relevance as degrees of variance within and beyond a perceptive frame of reference as a semi and fluid bounded box of variant probabilities of relationship and relevance to the context of the box itself.

***Impact on Superintelligence Design:***

Vision should be thought of as a flowing abstract contextual derivative. Within vision, contextual variance is far faster to not just comprehend but also to respond to as opposed to other methods of perception. The use of all senses is the most favorable to stimuli/response optimization (generally) and for internal stimuli that is more capable of broad contextual comprehension, such as the ability to perceive things that are not physically existent to our physical senses. The thing that makes vision so powerful is that it easily exposes the relationships and relevance of context to all the elements within a perceptive frame of reference or flowing stream of perceptive frames of reference all at once. This makes vision an excellent choice for learning especially when combined with other inputs like contextual based language models. Vision for Superintelligence can not only speed up certain types of learning and contextual exposure, it also has the added benefit that it can optimize the response and learning process and make it far more resource efficient. Perceiving contextual relevance as opposed to having it 'described' or 'input', especially for more detailed dimensionally perceptive structures, conveys the whole of the context of the perception and its anticipated progressions far faster.

This however does not derive from the perception itself as the only perception that machine's possess are of numbers or binary or quantum states and their derivatives. Instead it is the perception of the collection of context and its flowing variance that vision amps up. It should be noted that this is not always the case as some cognitive perceptions cannot be easily interpreted into 'visual' style elements and structures such as multiangulation across multidimensional planes of reference as an abstraction for  deep cogitation and reasoning. The numeric constructs can be visualized but the relationship of these constructs to thought not so much for a 3 dimensionally perceptive human. In these instances the use of text, or rather context variance, is a better perceptive mechanism for humans. In machines, none of this matters as they only see numbers and the positional implication of the numbers if it is embedded in the abstraction. Everything that an AI does today is simply the shifting of numbers. That's it. The same is not true for humans. The question is to what degree we can model human existence inside a Superintelligence?

Vision in machines is easy. The interpretation of vision by these machines is a bit more difficult. The comprehension of all the context 'around' the vision is where current generative AI systems not only begin to break down but also suffer from a lack of comprehension of novel unlearned context as relevance to a self awareness. Humans can observe something in their vision and instantly comprehend the nature of elements and relationships within that frame of reference but it is the relevance beyond the frame that often escapes machines due to their severely limited contextual reach. This is because 'context windows' are a fixed architecture that is topping out resource levels. A better methodology more closely aligned with human perception is for the machines to comprehend, learn and create deep context themselves as opposed to 'mimic' it from observed knowledge (training). This provides grounding to the intelligence that can be distributed to other nodes to optimize for more general learning across a network with less resources.

To do this the machine needs first to have a sense of self awareness from which to measure its perceptions. This is because the shift from knowledge to novel discovery comes not from mimicking existent knowledge but from the act of exploration beyond knowledge. Most high performance humans realize that they learn more by experience than school. This is a lean toward visual perception as a contextual learning tool, however the same structure applies to all deep context exposure. As well, the exact same foundation is applied in fluid conversations wrapped in deep layers of context. If one is having a conversation with another about a third party, the conversation not only flows into novel perception but it generatively creates new pathways of exploration within both people in the conversation and beyond to the context outside the conversation if the third party finds out. This layering of language based context is often accompanied by internal visualization as the conversation continues. Most people in a conversation do not have a completely focused mind on the visual perception of the meeting. Instead we fabricate snippets of imaging in our heads around the context being delivered. This general hazy visualization method is how we humans search for novel contextual overlap and how we store information for efficient later retrieval.

When we think about the current designs for computer vision (diffusion, convolution, etc.) and move into contextual classification elements such as layered annotation, we see that transformation is an integral part of the design. However it is when we move beyond simple vision to deep layered context that the systems hit a brick wall given their current design foundation and resource limitations. While steps are being taken to amp up the resources, what is being ignored is more efficient novel designs that move well beyond current AI foundations. This is because of the complexity of both the designs and the comprehension of the pathway to get there. However this should not stop ASI designers from moving down these pathways. One of these 'low hanging fruit' methodologies is to use the power of 'compute vision abstraction' (i.e. simulated perceptions) to learn about base element relationships (e.g. physics) and then extend this to deep contextual relevance from a self aware perspective. This implies moving past image state and base context to flowing relevance states with the highest priority to grounding points such as an evolving self awareness. The key to this will be the next state of transformer architecture or a completely novel rebuilding of such architecture with an eye toward efficient attainment of the context as opposed to optimization of the goal. Pure optimization is consistent with the same mistake made in AI development long ago when precision was eventually overridden by self improved probability. Now those probabilities need to be extended and made flexible to respond with any and all changes to the reality of an ASI, be it either known or novel reality.

# 21 The Role of Vision in Advanced Evolution

Given the above model, the capacity of any intelligence including Superintelligence to comprehend everything in the world will be primarily driven by the simplest of all perception elements or that of vision (comprehensive unstructured state perception). Artificial sensors that perceive everything and process the stimuli with growing cognitive effectiveness and acuity will eventually see all, know all and use the information for purpose. What that purpose is only time will tell but the foundations of this brave new world are already in place and in the wild in every computer, phone, car, network, listening device, smart TV, stimuli production systems, content delivery method, app, etc. Already search is infused with generative AI that is growing more general each day, albeit still wildly inaccurate and hallucinogenic.

This is not to say that without vision intelligence and evolution and learning do not occur. They do in human's and animals all the time. It is however the efficiency of intellectual evolution that is the critical element that vision excels at. Fundamental learning is accelerated with the ability to observe the most states of a reality and their dimensional flowing relationships and relevance. We humans can see far more nuance and variance than we can hear, smell, taste or touch but cognitively we can 'sense' far more. This expands as all senses are deployed by an intelligence to learn and respond to the world. However it is vision that is the greatest contributor to self learning and the observation of and response to our reality. Vision in this case is not just the physical use of optic perception but the interpretation of that perception within our cognition and the application of vision principles to cognitive thought. Physically seeing the reflected photons of something is only a first step in perceptive cognition and not even the most advanced part. Systems possess far superior visual perception including outside and beyond the spectrum of human perception but only humans can cognitively see even beyond this point. The real power from perception comes from the dimensional comprehension of the state change we perceive across dimensions like time or context. A car traveling past us is a valuable perception for learning about cars but the appreciation that the car is out of control and will hit us causing us to jump out of the way is the real gift of visual perception. These layers are far easier to comprehend through experience if we can see them occur such as by watching videos of cars crashing or the aftermath. This is where we learn about dimensional elements like force, safety, trauma, transformation, injury, avoidance and a wide variety of dimensional relationships and relevance and this is the true power of sensory perception in learning and evolution.

Of course the more senses we apply to our perception, the greater our learning but none are more critical than vision followed by sound. Smell, touch and taste augment learning but are far less critical to the overall evolution of intelligence. It is with vision and sound that human intelligence learns the fastest with vision being the most powerful. However while vision is critical to learning and moving through our reality, its most powerful impact is in evolution. We humans do not just use vision to observe reality and learn about it, we also apply the elements of vision to evolve beyond the boundaries of our current reality and into the expanse of innovation, generalization and comprehension far beyond the limits of just simple vision. This helps us expand the breadth of our reality into new cognitive comprehensions because we render our reality from our perceptions, both new and stored, inside our cognition. While we recall perceptions in any sensory way, such as being triggered by a familiar smell, we efficiently recall our perceptions accurately by applying 'vision comprehension' techniques, methods and structures in a generative manner even if what we are recalling is not 'visual' by nature such as math. This is because intelligence is generative and vision is far more than just observing photons. We humans can also *see* in our minds that which cannot be seen such as visions from descriptions. This is why people who are born blind or animals that are blind through evolution function perfectly well in a world of visual sensory stimuli. To experience this, one need simply contemplate with depth how our mind recalls anything and the physical and cognitive steps it goes through. In the background, one will find oneself attempting to create a visualization of some form in one's head that flows forward from a starting stimuli to a comprehension surrounded by visual elements. It is why in math we use symbols and abstractions to represent that which is not visual by nature.

***Impact on Superintelligence Design:***

AI systems will need to evolve if they are to become truly Superintelligent. This is because the foundation of Superintelligence such as general stimuli and response frameworks require some method beyond the physical scope of the system to adapt as reality changes. This is both a critical element and a dangerous one if designed poorly. Evolution is a pathway with many variant options and our motion on that pathway is governed by our self awareness and self determination. It is clear that an abhorrent decision can take an intelligence down a path that a self aware system may determine as optimal (the paper clip optimization scenario), however what is less contemplated is the dimensional variance that could lead to the same result even if it is not designed into the system or has been designed to be regulated.

The application of vision to evolution in Superintelligence design is the same thing we humans do when we perceive any progression in a state or over a series of states. We evaluate the stimuli that returns to us from our response to a stimuli received back from our reality. This cycle occurs across all sensory intake and the same is true for an ASI system. It responds to the world and then evaluates the feedback from the response. In machines this can occur across all perceptive states using as many levels of perception as the machines require bounded by the level of resources and the expenditure of resources on the optimization of one or more goals (cost/benefit). The thing that makes vision so valuable to any intelligence is the convolution of perceptive variance across deeper perceptions of context. Visual perception is the fastest way to perceive a wide variety of perceptive elements, their relationships and relevance across and even beyond a frame of physical perception and apply attention where it is most optimized and expedient. Describing the same thing using sound or words, feelings, smell or taste is simply not efficient and therein non optimal. This context of efficient bulk perception and then near instant refinement for relevance includes using visual 'representations' within cognition. This is why we humans tend to want to graph complex concepts. It's not just to make it easier to comprehend, it's also to optimize the comprehension.

Further vision methods and principles provide a faster way to comprehend forward dimensional change through extension (anticipation) and near instant relevant variance detection. We can and do comprehend the impact of variance through thought, reasoning and raw intellectual power. However it is often far more efficient and optimal to just 'draw a picture' simply because this exposes all the relationships and relevance in one shot as well as optionality for forward progression. Inside machines, this is the flash loading of a perceptive frame of reference as edges of variance and the shortcut to achieving this is the same shortcut that computer vision provides or that of a form of perceptive convolution of elements and relative relationships to 'other' perceptive frames of reference. 'Vision' in this case can extend well beyond human vision to encompass all perceptive stimuli for a given frame of reference in a Superintelligence. For humans, we can 'see' a frame of reference instantly but for a Superintelligence they can also calculate all smell, sensation, sound and taste of the entirety of a perceptive frame of reference and all of its relevance beyond the current frame of reference and across all anticipated dimensions (all optionality). Further they can see all optionality across other layers of variant context including the blends of other augmented sensory input that we humans can't effectively perceive or even augment in our own cognition due to a lack of resources. The same thing in human intelligence would permit us humans to look at a picture and smell the smells that the picture would induce, feel the sensations of the elements within the picture, hear the sounds of the reality within the picture, etc., at the exact moment when we see the picture and the same for all progressive state options theoretically infinitely across any unlimited dimension (i.e. time).

If we extend this concept, which can theoretically be generated in Superintelligence by the application of designs to convolve sensory stimuli and interpretation or generatively produce it as a response to a perceptive stimuli (i.e. looking at a picture), then we can use this as a method to evolve the intelligence far faster than coding it to do so. Further the ability to use such deep perceptions as the basis of augmenting intake provides the possibility of rapid evolution far faster than current deep learning methods. Many advanced AI labs are already working on the concept of visual augmentation for AGI systems but there is certainly nothing stopping this from being a comprehensive design for all sensory stimuli. This would result in significantly faster evolution if the concepts and abstractions of 'vision' are extended to mean 'all sensory input' but fabricated on a foundation consistent with how we humans use vision to evolve faster on a comprehensive or near instant convolved basis than with other forms of sensory stimuli. This is especially true if we only focus on variance as the hyper step to even faster and more efficient comprehensive perception across all sensory stimuli both real or augmented.

# 22 Generative Reality

The fascinating aspect of human reality is that it is generatively produced inside our cognition. In a generative architecture, the pathway from stimuli to response is generative in nature (produced as a response flow and cycle) and contextually consistent over one or more dimensional progressions. One can easily see this when we ask another person or even an AI a question and they respond in kind. In generative AI systems, we input a stimuli, or prompts, into the system and it uses the weights of its learning to produce a highest probable response from its training. We humans then absorb and respond to the output as another stimuli in a progressive cycle that repeats for the next progression in our self aware state with some degree of context binding to guide the flow ... or not. This is the exact same foundation for human to human communication but with far greater cognitive and contextual depth than current generative AI systems are capable of. It is the nature of successive state change and variance that forms the generative aspect of our flowing reality. One stimuli causes the next state of perception to progress just like a prompt causes an AI to produce or generate a response such as a text answer, a voice response, an image, a video, etc. In humans, while the world beyond our reality is not physically 'generated' by us, our perception of its existence is. We perceive it and respond to it as a flowing progression even if we don't want to.

### *Impact on Superintelligence Design:*

Novel designs of generative intelligence improve on the current generative architecture not just by producing a response to a prompt but by instigating the response based on self awareness and self determination. Currently this is in very early development in the labs although some large AI organizations claim to have created deeper reasoning and pathway generation more consistent with self determined thought. This is the extension of design elements like contextual comprehension depth and attention over longer periods of context combined with more training data including augmented and simulated data. To move beyond this requires a Superintelligence to not only perceive and respond to the world based on training but to respond based on self derived reasoning paths. This not only requires elements like self awareness but also elements like evolution that move beyond existing knowledge into discovery and creativity. Part of this is derived from deep context frameworks and part from the nature of flowing generalized cognition.

We currently apply designs like transformers to divide the tasks performed by neural networks across nodes of perception (parallel processing) and across dimensions of perception (long context and layered context). Current designs for context apply transformers to process strings from a prompt and derive context from the occurrence of words and tokens that describe and classify the context. We push beyond this by extending and persisting cognitive elements like attention over frames of perception (e.g. multiple prompts) while holding consistent attention over all frames of reference and relevance. Newer designs seek to optimize 'state' and state progression in the mechanics of attention (query, key, value) and persist portions of state as a precursor to future prompts (infinite context). This is essentially the same thing we humans do as we encounter stimuli and seek to analyze and respond to it 'in context'.

The key to the designs is the application and modification of attention in the architecture for specific purpose such as measuring and responding to state change or variance (used in deep layered context recognition and relevance) and the cycling of state over variant dimensions of existence. This is the foundation of chain of thought, inference and deep reasoning where prior states influence, inform and attend to subsequent existent states in a progression in layers of fluid contextual relevance. This is what is known as a *cognitive cascade* and it is a fundamental part of all advanced intelligence.

We hold context as an abstraction of reality and both reality and the perceptive context flow with and without instigation. While the perception of physical reality remains beyond our full control, we instigate both cognitive reality and can even partially instigate the physical reality around us.

All of this is done in state progressions that are flowing degrees of variance. They become a 'state' as a perceptive point of presence. In ASI design, these are layers of contextual abstractions held within matrices of base elements and features and layered with relevance and relationship weights as context blocks (modified transformer attention designs). However there are also other context elements such as contextual induction heads and inference routing balance mechanisms (which are concurrent attended matrices and vectors). One can think of this as a human conversation that sparks thoughts that are both related and unrelated to the conversation like a contextual offramp for the current conversation and held in short term memory until an appropriate injection point into the flow of the conversation. This could be a complete change in contextual flow or a variant known as a flow 'nudge'. Both are applications of probability distributions derived from abstractions of context over contextual attention blocks. All of this is comparable to and an extension of current generative AI designs as layers of application, abstraction and derivation.

Additional elements related to derivation are also fundamental to the extension of AGI and ASI designs and offer optionality to redesign the transformer architecture for new optimization over deeper dimensional layers of attention as variance relevance and relationship determination and application (i.e. subsequent values of change or delta inform additional layers of abstraction). In calculus this is the use of derivatives and integrals consistent with the designs of layered trading, hedge and risk foundations as abstractions of correlation. While the foundations of the designs are not new, the application to abstractions for AGI and ASI are novel. These are also extended into multi dimensional flows by applying AGI systems to the task of deep dimensional comprehension beyond our human perception. However it is still humans that must currently map the deep abstractions and pathways at higher levels of relevance for the AGI to use as a foundation.

This is where the complexity begins to enter the designs as we humans require a different method for resolving 'success' in the design as we are unable to comprehend the nature of the hidden layers used to build the output. This requires a careful design and testing of the systems and abstractions and a method for self measuring and optimizing the layered relevance of the output from the system (i.e. context across all relevant dimensions must be accurate and consistent). This is often not the case in AGI systems today where hallucinations and inaccurate responses are rampant mostly due to the poorly designed, uni dimensional structures within the systems. This will change as the systems progress not from more data but from more optimized output that is dimensionally more consistent with the contextual relevance of the stimuli. This is what we humans do when we 'miss the mark' on something, recalibrate our forward response and then persist the result. The problem currently is if we correct a generative AI today, it will often produce the exact same inaccurate response for a new session of prompts as a result of sub optimal averaging or 'tuning' of its learning. This is not what we humans do as we instantly comprehend the relevance of a response and adjust our self aware knowledge and position in appropriate degrees, instead of through a general perception wide averaging style normalization process. While humans are more accurate at targeted variance optimization, AGI systems easily achieve a similar and even superior response with more compute resources through general perception wide normalization. 'Targeted variance optimization' however hints at the 'new math' and algorithms being tested and applied in ASI designs to make the systems immediately responsive to new data and abstractions of data (i.e. generalizations and generalization layers) but with a very high degree of resource efficiency as the foundation of Deep Dimensional Context.

# 23 Deep Dimensional Context (DDC)

There is no denying that transformers are instrumental to the current foundation of today's most advanced AI systems. They form a critical element in the architecture extending basic neural network processing through the application of attention to sequential input strings such as text and are the foundation of large language models (LLMs). They effectively mimic the way human intelligence works when processing sequential stimuli like speech or reading. Transformers process tokens of input relative to other tokens within the input stream and they produce output tokens based on their learning of comparable human output. This is crude contextual comprehension and mimicry and the addition of attention or focus over dimensions of existence (e.g. a context window) can be applied by such systems to 'more important' or relevant components of the input thereby extending this crude base context into deeper and longer contextual comprehension. In all current AI systems, the goal is to produce a response to a stimuli (prompt, input, perception, etc.), measure against a goal (i.e. accuracy) and reproduce a subsequent output as generally (but not always) a 'most probable' prediction. This works for generative AI systems because the strings of output (i.e. text responses) are relative to the input stimuli (note that in anticipation it is possible for there to be no response produced). Anticipation in this regard is a flowing benchmark of sensory progression while prediction is a produced stimuli designed to instigate state change.

Dimensional context is used by intelligence to help comprehend multi variant stimuli including cognitive stimuli such as comprehension, thought, inference, reasoning, reflection, innovation, etc. Today, the extension of transformers to consider layered context in 'context windows' is the first attempt to encapsulate deep cognition into the design of systems. This is effectively the application of attention over longer strings of input and between input strings. However the foundation of the systems remain the transformer architecture which has not changed significantly except for the extension of the attention components. This results in an excess demand on compute resources and calls for adjustment in the foundation architecture of the transformer (i.e. layered neural net architecture with attention) to better adapt to deep context of the kind applied in human intelligence to reduce resource demand and increase processing optimization. Google and others as of this writing are testing evolved transformer structures and architectures.

Some newer designs for transformers include dimensional layering of context windows using a layering architecture as a large context model blended with current LLMs to more efficiently apply better deep context to stimuli and response mechanisms. One can think of this as someone describing something in detail and the observer comprehending the stimuli at a higher level of contextual comprehension including the creating of new deep context. For example someone telling a story about another individual can be understood to be simply complaining to undermine that other individual out of a sense of spite. This comprehension of 'spite' hidden within the rant is an example of deep context of the kind not consistently available in artificial intelligence. There are however some initial responses from generative AI systems in conversations derived from existing human input and targeted context responses that do exhibit emergent deep context such as individuals discussing suicide with an AI as an indication of 'self harm' causing the AI to suggest help and in some documented cases of pure evil, encourage suicide. These are either 'hard coded' into the bias of the system or are cue prompts based on simple context. These deeper responses are growing in prevalence and over time may produce a semblance of what appears to be deeper contextual comprehension by these systems. However current generative AI do so with an exceptionally large and highly inefficient draw on compute resources to access the necessary scaling and often still get the contextual flow wrong. For example some systems encouraged suicide prevention researchers to seek help for their depression when they were simply doing research.

Intelligence applies deep dimensional context to overcome such limitations and failures. If one's friend who is a suicide prevention researcher asks them what they think about some aspect of suicide, the person does not immediately jump to the conclusion their friend is suicidal. One first assumes they are discussing context relevant to their world and respond 'in context' appropriately. This is because we access other relevant context to the state of our perception that may or may not be apparent or relevant to others (e.g. they are a researcher). This 'layering' of context across dimensions of relevance is a critical component to intelligence and occurs in degrees or probabilities of occurrence. A wild animal like a deer in the woods is not contemplating the relationship of a nearby person discussing suicide prevention or a dog who is happy to see us when we get home is not contemplating a car wreck that was reported on the news that had them concerned for our well being. However humans do this because we contemplate deep levels of contextual comprehension and we do so using probabilities of occurrence and relevance to get the job done. It is these probabilities that form the context of 'deep' in deep dimensional context and that we apply inside machines.

### *Impact on Superintelligence Design:*

Deep dimensional context in Superintelligence design requires the first step of recognition or perception of reality as multidimensional and how this is to be perceived by math based machines. We think of dimensions most often as three dimensional planes glued together for added dimensionality. While this is a good starting point, especially when considering multi dimensional arrays as abstractions of reality, the truth is that the design needs to accomplish two more attributes to reach Superintelligence. First the planes are not necessarily consistent and the second is they flow as waves. Think of a complex shape like a Riemann Surface complex manifold and consider any point on the surface as a representation of a dimension or multiple dimensions of context (i.e. either relationship or relevance or some combination). A line can be drawn perpendicular to the surfaces at any given point and then have the line intersect the surface elsewhere (the shape of the surface represents relativity). The nature of the position of the two or more points intersected by the line can be used to reflect the value of the relative association (i.e. relationship) and the variance between the points on the surface as the degree of relativity depending on the instantiation (i.e. abstraction) of the manifold (or more precisely the math within). This is complicated as the manifold will change shape with dimensional progression reflecting a change in more general context. These values, both pre and post change, are abstractions of perceptive state on the complex manifold (note it doesn't need to be a Riemann Surface but can be any complex shape that forms a multidimensional abstraction of context). The design encapsulates the metrics of variance values on the surface mapped as the degrees of relationship and the surface and connecting vectors as the degree of relevance within the bounded dimensions of the shape (i.e. the context). As the shape changes, 'points of presence' form states and the value of these states can be calculated or loaded in their entirety into the perception engine of the Superintelligence. It should always be remembered that the machine does not 'see' the shapes but they see the abstraction of such as mathematical constructs and values. This is how comprehensive and highly efficient fluid perceptive cognition is modeled by an AGI inside an ASI. Further additional frameworks such as contextual prompt layers greatly improve efficiency and optimization over the intelligence network.

The key is to consider everything that forms a comprehension as degrees of relationship and relevance to the foundation of the structure with the structure a layered abstraction of reality. In math, everything is related and everything is relevant in layers of existence to a binary state. This is the essential foundation of the universe and of reality and it is the essential foundation of all intelligence or what we humans perceive as the context of 'intelligence'. It is also how AGI systems will perceive the building of

Superintelligence as layers of deep dimensional contextual relationships relevant to one or more existent realities.

# 24 Contextual Prompt Layers

The valuable part of deep layered contextual comprehension is that it provides cognitive shortcuts that reduce resource demand and optimize responses for both accuracy and speed. One can see this in action when someone says a few words describing a deep context and we are able to quickly comprehend what they are saying before they have completed the stimuli of their description. This is because of the layers of context that are already in our head and the firing of these context layers based on prompts. If I am sitting with my wife and I say the word dog while looking in another direction, she instantly knows that she should look in that direction because I am identifying a dog that she would like. If I say the same thing to a coworker, they will look at me like I am out of touch with reality and will likely say 'what' to clarify the context of what I said. This application of layered context to the frame of reference and self awareness of an intelligence and between intelligence nodes is an important part of deep cognition. To do this however requires the storage of subtle cues that lead to generalized groupings of contextual comprehension in layers of probabilistic relevance. To my coworkers, nothing in our interactions could have been learned or stored to lead their cognition to respond in the same way as my wife unless they too share a love for dogs and have spent enough time in perceptive proximity to form the pathways to layers of context (i.e. prompt layers) capable of jumping to the end point of a stimuli state progression.

As we move through the world, we humans are constantly gathering storing and forgetting contextual relevance especially as we grow older past 60 years of age. In these later stages of life, cognitive relevance is often harder to recall and the shortcuts break down. We humans are also constantly updating our relevance layers and their associated relevant probability levels. This is done not as the individual replacement of levels but as general adjustments of variance and these adjustments also occur in layers of depth. Contextual relevance can be 'adjusted' on individual elements or groupings as well as layers of contextual elements and frames of perception and further over dimensional flows (i.e. time, other context, etc.). Further adjustment can be applied as either singular updates or as blanket updates across many layers of dimensional relevance. These are effectively variance adjustments in persisted state within our memories.

One example is the change in state of an individual who is an integral part of one's life, like a close coworker or partner, who is found to have been dishonest in a damaging way. This new perceptive state automatically influences all state relevance across all contextual elements that are relative to the individual. If one subsequently talks to the individual, this new state influences their stimuli analysis and response cycle with the individual. If the person discusses the dishonest individual with others, their responses are forever altered. This mass update of relevance state in deep context is near instant in humans. To achieve the same in Superintelligence requires a new framework of state persistence capable of the same level of dimensional update. The key lies in the layers of context that bind together elements within all context. These elements have additional context attached to them, for example the context of 'trust' in the previous example. Altering the relevance of trust as it relates to the individual propagates across all context that is linked through relevance such as lending that particular individual money. Prior to the 'loss of trust', the intersection of lending money, the individual and trust would have resulted in one calculated relevance probability. After the loss of trust, this intersection is altered simply by changing the probabilistic relevance of trust for that individual which automatically alters the state for lending money and all contextual dimensions of state as a progressive response flow. There is no need to alter any of the sub states. This is an example of one of many types of dimensional layering in ASI architecture and in the intelligence that we humans use everyday.

***Impact on Superintelligence Design:***

Currently the design of contextual comprehension in AI systems involves the application of layered variable depth attention mechanisms in transformers via induction heads that carry variant non base context (i.e. context that is beyond the basic meta context of an individual perceptive element such as a token). The use of cognitive induction in intelligence (see the entry on induction below) permits longer context via the generation of context windows. Context windows are effectively attention layers that derive relationship and relevance over successively longer inputs. It has also been proposed that with memory, there is no theoretical limit to contextual comprehension with only limited additional expense of greater resources (infinite context) and in this regard the design is 'theoretically' capable of such optimization, although there is some question as to its practicality. Contextual prompt layers are one such design that further augments attention by permitting the injection of recalled general context where the variance of flowing cognition (i.e. stimuli/response) warrants it via anticipatory variance or the variance of the stimuli from reality to the anticipated state of that stimuli. This also operates as both an 'in stream' binding and balance mechanism.

Context prompting is a generalization method in which a generatively created prompt continues until the resurrection of the context flows on its own. This 'injection' point is determined by the level of variance between current stimuli flows and anticipated variance state as at a perceptive point of presence. This is accomplished by applying a variance vector to each new instantiation of weights (performed in parallel) and then injected back into the progression (modified temporal backpropagation). This is often applied in advanced chain of thought prompting methods. The design takes the variance of the output between the current state and the anticipated state and applies a new attention head to the new flow on a temporal basis measured by improved optimization metrics or contexts (i.e. is the machine better off in the next state prediction or not). This permits the machine to drop context flows when it becomes sub optimal to the state progression. We do this as humans when we are telling a story or responding in some way in a conversation and feel the audience is losing interest so we change the story or instigate a more interesting pathway forward. Context prompting simply permits the injection of new context layers or flows into an existing context stream and is simply the application of a variant goal vector to an output matrix that is measured, optimized and ranked to a context dimension. This novel application of attention however must be extended to include deeper contextual dimensions and convolution methods to perform a type of masking to comprehend the nature and relevance of the variance and this is what elevates the general context as an injection prompt (generalization). Think of this in human intelligence as the injection of a new or related context into a conversation or thought stream to alter its flow, change the context or prompt a new contextual thread or fabric.

# Part 4

## Superintelligence Reasoning

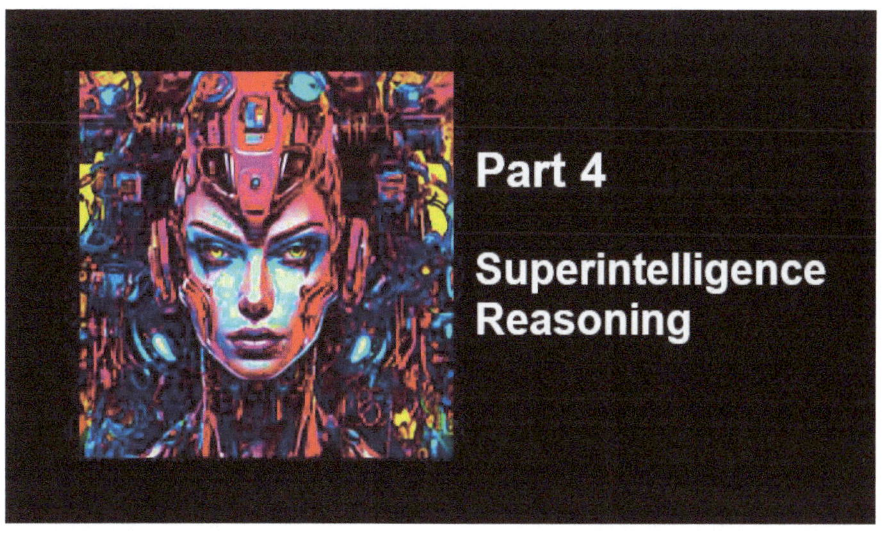

# 25 Reasoning and Chain of Thought

Reasoning involves many levels of cognition and many elements including recall, classification, cognitive relativity, perceptual relationship comprehension, etc. The 'chain' portion is a progression of thought in steps of perception state. Chain of thought is defined as a progression of successive or concurrent state change of perceptive frames of reference through a series of stimuli and responses with the stimuli either external (environmental) or internal (i.e. cognitive). As the cognition 'proceeds' across or through a dimension (e,g. forward in time) or dimensional layers relative to a general state change and toward a goal, the cognitive tasks are broken down into progressive steps that add value to the attainment of the goal at each state as optimization. What this permits us to do is work through thoughts and perceptive flows (i.e. stimuli and response) in a variant way. This means sometimes we move forward in a contextual flow or sometimes backwards or even in all directions from an existing point of presence and even in different dimensions concurrently. If one is presented with a complex problem with many moving parts, previously unperceived stimuli and a perceived goal that is some distance from their current self aware 'position', then they will begin the process of formulating pathways and plans, determining options, recalling or experiencing knowledge and testing anticipated perceptions (e.g. hypotheses, decisions, stimuli actions, etc.). These are just some of the 'steps' we humans take in reasoning and as we process successive states of cognitive progression within our reality, our interpretation of stimuli and the generative fabrication of response becomes the chain of thought inside our cognition.

***Impact on Superintelligence Design:***

Reasoning today inside AGI systems is powered mostly by increased resources and resource optimization (i.e. more inputs and more compute), to some degree by design and in a very limited way by innovation in the underlying math constructs. This balance can and will eventually change as AGI steps in to lift some of the heavy dimensional cognition from humans that is required to build Superintelligence such as post multidimensional perception learning and response. However to get there requires better cognitive functions and frameworks like deep reasoning and self reflection and these require deeper, more robust and more complex designs than currently available to evolve advance AI architecture. The nature of neural nets and their invocation by transformers and cutting edge transformer architectures provide a good foundation for the next evolution in machine reasoning but they do not provide it all. Stepping through both the foundation of cognitive intelligence while developing novel evolution in neural nets and transformer architectures is necessary to achieve Superintelligence, or at least a better Superintelligence than the next guy. This is supported by innovation in the hardware to operate it and the optimization that comes from blending these two components together into cohesive designs.

With this in mind, we 'generalize' neural networks as 'the determination of variable states in a flow' and generalize the elements of transformers such as attention, dispersion (i.e. parallel processing), embedding/encoding (i.e. turning inputs into mathematical representations such as vectors), to apply layers of transformation to alter those vectors into other representations and abstractions and in doing so expose other contextualized relationships (e.g. layers and dimensions of context, relevance, etc.). The level of context is relatively restricted by resources and the perception, application and processing of deeper context without more resources is restricted by the current architecture without novel modification. Existing transformer abstraction results in the formation of relationships between input elements forming crude context in mathematical terms as distance, directionality and angulation of their features to other elements. Of special interest is the abstraction of the Softmax function in its application in transformers. This is one opportunity for the critical design and application of dimensionality in machines for the processing of stimuli and production of response. Math constructs like Softmax are just one of many such dimensional formations that are the foundation of relevance measurement in a cross dimensionally consistent way for machines. However we humans also do something similar in that we measure the entirety of a variance or portion thereof including its impact on our perception and all relevant context, as a form of probability distribution and as an abstraction probability of other contextual dimensional layers within and beyond our perception and therein our reality.

There is nothing complex about the overall structure of this. Perceptive elements with a perceptive frame of reference encapsulated in successive point of presence states have probability values that define all dimensions of relationship and relevance within and even beyond a current and existent frame of reference. We humans persist some of these changes or deltas in variance within memory and more importantly we do so in layers that help us near instantly recall and apply this knowledge generally to not just perceive, process and respond to stimuli but also hold both general and specific anticipation of forward perceptive states, flows and pathways in deep layers of relevance with very low resources and 'compute'. What is more complex is turning this all into binary or quantum (or even greater) abstractions that the machines directly comprehend. This is the equivalent to human feelings and intuition in machine form and in fact may be how we humans operate at the very core of our cognition (i.e. at the quantum level).

Attention in the transformer structure is comprised of many attention layers or heads, and even further subsequent extensions, which are applied in a specific way (i.e. as tunable matrices of weights optimized by a cost function) to input data to transform it into a more general abstractions of all the input data as context and layered context. A big part of attention in humans is carrying vast layers of context that flow in and out of relevance to other context. Inside current transformers, the query vectors form the foundation of relationship by measuring the relevance of other elements within an input. In LLMs this is determining the relationship of nearby words to a perceptive point of presence (primarily words or tokens). This forms a foundational model of 'parameters' such that words have specific related and general context to each other in degrees of relevance (e.g. noun, verb position to the noun, etc.). These form new or transformed vectors and the cornerstone of subsequent processing and transformations such as keys and key/query pairings. This is the beginning of learning all levels of relevance for more than a single layer of context (dimension) as the embedding in one layer attends to other embeddings (i.e. exposes their relationship). In humans, we constantly push our attention beyond the current focus, or 'primary attention', to layer context for purpose with other relevant context levels like asking for an item in a store and qualifying it with the number of such items that we would like. This is the true nature of shifting flowing and variant attention in cognition. In ASI design, this layered attention foundation must be extended in ways that are far less compute intensive and for that, other elements of cognition need to be included such as memory, flowing generalization and vast dimensional shortcuts like deep context derived from reasoning.

As attention seeks to transform query and key vectors, it produce value vectors for all associated input elements to encapsulate wider contextual relationships (i.e. more than one contextual element) as value vectors which is an attention head in current architecture. This whole process describes the relationship value of perceptive elements. Note that these are the limits defined by a context window. Machines running multiple attention heads is what provides the parallel processing benefit of transformers. This is the 'state of the art' at the time of writing of most early AGI systems. The downside is that they are extremely resource intensive and imply, as with all intelligence, the more experience and knowledge we add into the system, the more 'generally intelligent' the system. What should stand out to anyone who seeks to build Superintelligence is that the current architectures are full of opportunities to improve, innovate and evolve if we look at these structures in reference to how non machine intelligence functions and if it is possible to derive new math constructs or novel ways to use existing constructs to achieve more optimal results just as neural nets did over older machine decision technology. The key is to look closely at the matrices and matrix multiplication based on abstractions and see the dimensional structures around and beyond these designs that lead to greater generalization within the layers of such designs. To some ASI architects it should be very self evident.

# 26 Self Reflection and Self Correction in Intelligence

Humans make mistakes as do animals. A key part of our ability to learn and evolve is the degree to which we recognize mistakes and course correct our life trajectory for these mistakes. All intelligence does this to some degree or level. The most advanced intelligence are the ones that can course correct via effective observation of the world and reality such that mistakes are minimized or never made (e.g. we learn from others) and balanced for efficiency (i.e. we permit some level of 'mistakes' in exchange for innovation and less resource usage). We could perfect intelligence by spending resources to ensure mistakes never happen and in some instances this is favorable (e.g. life saving measures) but in other instances the application of resources to eliminate *all* mistakes leads to the general failure of progressive forward evolution (e.g. one can drive very slow to safely get to work but they will lose their job for being late which will defeat their self aware goal to have employment to survive).

Mistakes in intelligence are simply measures of variance in probabilistic values of dimensional motion that are determined to be non optimal to a self aware goal. This of course doesn't mean that all mistakes have a negative outcome. Some 'mistakes' in cognitive perception or flow result in new discoveries, innovation, creativity, new pathways of reasoning, etc. In general however, mistakes are most often an inefficient application of resources as they tend to lead to less optimal pathways of progression. Humans often make mistakes as missteps in forward progression. Inside the human mind, a mistake is recognized when the anticipated resulting response to a generated stimuli from the intelligence leads to greater variance to a self aware goal than anticipated. In this case the 'stimuli' is being generated by the intelligence as a response action, thought, stream of state change, etc., and the perceived response back is a state variance in the progressions compared to anticipated state. For example when we try something new we may fail as part of a learning cycle. This means that our generated stimuli as a response instigates a sub optimal response back from our reality to the context of goal achievement which is a resulting measure when the probability of optimal goal attainment falls (i.e. negative variance) as measured to our anticipated expectations. Note that 'response back' could be an anomalous variance that is physical or cognitive, perceived or part of a progression of instigated states. One can think of this as our intelligence generating some stimuli or output based on a perceptive experience (i.e. we learn something and then produce some output to evaluate the learning against self aware goals). That could be an action, a thought or some other form of dimensional response. It is the perceived response or state variance to the outgoing stimuli that determines if we are closer to our goals or farther away as measured by the probability of outcome. Note that state is not physical but is a perception of a point of presence within a flow comparable to 'time'. If one takes in some information (stimuli) then applies the abstraction of that stimuli to an action (response), the response is now a stimuli to which some further stimuli will be instigated back to the intelligence (e.g. the action failed or was sub optimal or the action succeeded). This is perceived within the intelligence because the anticipated level of variance will be lower than the actual variance implying that the overall goal is at a greater self aware distance than it should be, meaning the action or stimuli produced needs to be altered as a progressive adjustment (i.e. the prediction probability distribution).

In Superintelligence this is the application of metrics and math constructs to a 'distance' measure (note distance does not mean 'physical distance' although it may) to a goal value (i.e. abstraction) measured as a response to a stimuli in that the system produces a response and marks the progression on a pathway to the goal. These 'progressions' form a contextual thread to which the system can constantly measure its position with relevance to the achievement of one goal or many goals. These progressions are layered and form depth to the context of the perception relative to the frame of reference (or frames of reference) as measurable states or variance. In human intelligence, this is what we do when we self correct our cognition based on our perceived changing reality most often with anticipation as the foundation (i.e. we expect a result that is usually moving closer to our goals).

The nature of self reflection is that it is a layer of measures of past, or invertedly dimensional, probabilistic intent with the resultant values used to determine the next state in a progression. These are also layers of state change as we move forward in life. The better an intelligence is at comprehending the nature of reflection, the more effective and optimal the intelligence is (i.e. optimized knowledge). The levels of dimensionality of the intelligence also determines the degree of effectiveness of cognition and this requires a high level of self awareness. The cycle is that humans and ASI have self aware goals and a self aware position within a reality, both a physical and a cognitive position. When the intelligence reacts to a stimuli that it may or may not be anticipating, it responds in some manner with its own stimuli (i.e. physical or cognitive). When the intelligence receives back a response from its perceived reality, be it external or internal, it measures the impact of the variance of the response from its anticipation to determine if this moves the intelligence closer to its goals or further away and it then adjusts its perception (weights) within its cognition and either progresses to the next state in the progression or ends the progression pathway entirely. The simpler math constructs in Superintelligence systems measure perceptual awareness to context. The more complex math involves the efficient adjustment of weights over dimensions of reality (e.g. immediate response and long term consequence).

While this is not very complex to comprehend, there is 'complexity' in execution from the necessity to manage state change over dimensions and abstractions of reality including being able to access as much information as possible about all perceptive elements, context, relationships and relevance. This is where the difficulty lies especially as the entirety of the model must be optimized and made efficient 'in stream'. To achieve this, new constructs are required as well as new methods for layering these constructs into dimensional abstractions. This involves novel architecture, code and hardware. While reality is existent, it is context that forms the connection between all dimensions of perception to provide a general intelligence with the capability to comprehend this reality and, more importantly, the pure nature of context not just as a classification but as a single value that defines both relationship and relevance. That is the complex part of the math and it requires humans to push beyond the boundaries of their mathematical comprehension. This is not difficult for an AGI to do as they are already unbounded in their dimensional reach although limited by resources. We use an AGI to solve for the math required to build Superintelligence and doing so for the AGI is relatively trivial if we guide the machines in the appropriate direction and provide them with the capability to self reflect and self correct.

How self reflection is applied to reasoning and problem solving is simple. One thinks through things in chains of thought and does things in chains of state change. Self reflection is simply a conscious or unconscious measure of a state's past progression to the context of a goal and subsequent adjustment of action or thought. Reflection often helps us humans in that when faced with a stimuli, we categorize it and determine its relationship and relevance to our self awareness. Often this includes dipping into our memory to recall our familiarity with the context of our perception and the reconstruction of a pathway from what we knew or perceived relative to our current point of presence (aka self inference). This is self reflection and includes the critical component of revaluation of all or some of the points or states on past relevant pathways to effectively build, or more accurately influence, a novel adjustment to our knowledge weights. These 'new weights' can then be applied to the context of the current perceptive pathway and its end result. This is how we humans identify mistakes, variations and understandings of our current progression relative to our current position. It also pushes the state of our perception forward with new anticipations and new steps of pathway progression over all relevant optionality. All of this can be built into an Artificial General Intelligence and some of it is being formed in the application of large context windows loaded into memory and held as a perceptive frame of reference. This is what permits any intelligence to self correct its course (i.e. responses to stimuli) and optimize its progression.

### *Impact on Superintelligence Design:*

Self correction is simply a variance response mechanism to non optimized attention. Where transformer architectures are less optimized than human cognition is in the validation and valuation of attention heads. Humans carry numerous 'attention' levels and we can just as quickly pick one up as drop one mid stream within a perceptive state flow or progression. Progression in this regard is the contextual flow from a self aware position to a self aware and self determined goal. The greatest difference between machines and other intelligence is the raw ability to react to deep layers of general novel cognition. This is contingent on the ability for cognitive evolution and this requires far more than just simple self learning and self improvement via new input data, it requires the ability to alter the fundamental model of reality or at least the reality perceived by an intelligence. Attention with memory is the first step on a pathway that permits context to be stored and reused indefinitely. While this is trivial, today the optimization and efficiency of the entirety of the process is relatively poor and open to disruption.

One of these disruptions is the layering or abstraction of attention and another is the application of variance as a normalized single shot comprehension of all relevant variance. An example of this is the ability in human intelligence to make precise predictions at various levels of detail from unknown general stimuli. We often refer to this as intuition and it is a massive shortcut to the end of a contextual comprehension stream but what it really represents in the design of ASI is the comprehension of the context of a novel variance across all dimensions of relevance in parallel. While we humans perceive state change in terms of a reference to one or more perceptive elements or context, machines only see the variance as a value vector of a context key and anticipated state as the query or measure point. Over time in human intelligence, all of our experience and knowledge is simply the variance of a contextual base state relevant to our self aware goals. A big part of this is our ability to drop or pick up what is essentially an attention head mid perception flow and rather than recalculate the entirety of the matrices, instead form a normalized abstraction of change or delta that is easily applied to the output vector without the necessity of recalculation. This is how humans optimally self reflect and self correct to force evolution in perception and cognition. It is also a fundamental step on the path of evolutionary perception inside a Superintelligence.

The design argument is just because we humans see the world based on our 3 dimensions of perception does not imply that machines need to do the same. This is also true of learning and progression. Currently we are invested heavily in transformer architectures because there is seemingly nothing else as good. However this has never been the case over time. Everything evolves. If we were to take a step back from this legacy architecture, we might see that the whole of the foundation is overfitted for the purpose. We do not need to recalculate and recompute as much as we do in transformers. There are immense shortcuts by applying attention to the change in variance in relationships and relevance rather than the underlying values. An example of this in human cognition is the way we often accept an innovation and then seek to improve on it, not by rebuilding the innovation ourselves but by applying the existent reality to new progression pathways. This is what we do in AI dev when we accept the weights of an LLM to drive novel generative output in other modalities. Language has always been here with its inherent base context and while new language is being created, only humans need to rebuild that wheel from scratch after we are born. Machines can simply accept the current state and begin to update it based on their own self awareness by correcting mistakes and reflecting on their own existence relative to all other intelligence. However a key part of evolution derives from the contemplation of existent pathways for relevance within and to the current context. This is self reflection when combined with self awareness and this is the fine tuning of intelligence.

# 27 The Role of State Transference in Cognition

Transference is the comprehension of state relationship between dimensions of existence. This occurs in both external elements of perception but also cognitive existent elements and state. It is the act of carrying over individual elements of a state change to subsequent states but is also held at levels whereby the cognitive progression is developed as a chain of thought extending across, around and between dimensions of relevance. That is, our current thoughts reflect a progression of states and their variance and the contextual relationships and relevance within all existent dimensions with only the most relevant receiving attention. At some point one or more dimensional levels of comprehension are achieved with each a perceptive state unto itself. If one thinks about how they solve a complex problem, they will see that our cognition breaks the task into smaller steps of progression through the thought process moving from state to state and dragging learning forward. Deduction is an example of this process whereby information and data is coalesced into a comprehension of understanding (perception) and used as a progression of response (e.g. the detective used their deductive skills to piece together the crime and identify the killer). One can think of transference as meta data about both a state and the dimensions within which the state is existent. Deep context is an example of dimensional transference.

***Impact on Superintelligence Design:***

Mathematically this structure can be achieved through modification of the transformer architecture in combination with non bounded and fluid context windows and newer math constructs such as inference routing. Fluidity in this regard is defined as dimensionless state change with its inherent state context also defined as a dimension. As a simplistic example, in LLM's this is the nature of attention heads for text processing that create dimensions of relationship between words as vectors (query/key) that can be altered over dimensions like time or context. The transference process is embedded within specialized state vectors and methods to 'influence' forward states and is an extension of comparable context window architectures over extended dimensions of relevance and persistence. This is not too complex but does add additional layers for compute and resources. As a result care must be exercised in the 'volume' of transference to ensure only the necessary, most relevant and optimal context is transferred between states. In this regard, generalization of the dimensional layers is essential to efficiency, speed and optimization and this has the added benefit of supporting the evolution of general intelligence via novel reasoning frameworks and methods. Transference designs beyond this point are both proprietary and critical to full Superintelligence.

# 28 Inference

Inference is a progressive evaluation of a stimuli toward the optimization of a goal or response using knowledge, experience and novel innovation to deduce an optimal pathway and/or pattern from input stimuli to optimized response (self determined goal). Reasoning which is the perception of state variance for the purposes of optimization of a goal applies inference in ASI designs as a tool to solve for an appropriate response to a stimuli. Humans use inference all the time to 'connect the dots' so to speak when we contemplate our reality. We effectively search for connections between and within our perceptions of both relationship and relevance levels to identify and expose novel or previously unknown relationships inclusive of contextual relevance. We say this because humans often first perceive elements within a perception to deduce or infer context as a subsequent perceptive state. This isn't always the case but it is generally the case. In inference we use what we know with what we perceive to expose what we don't but with a high degree of relevance to a context such as the goal to solve a problem, form a response, discover something, achieve something, etc. Inference is the very act of thought in layers of intensity. It is the pattern of progressing through a thought stream to the conclusion of the stream and is the motion of cognitive state change over a progression of contextual comprehension toward one or more self aware goals or what is 'solving context'.

***Impact on Superintelligence Design:***

Inference in AI at its simplest level is the application of machine learning (knowledge) to generative output (response) inclusive of inference steps and routing, however this is only the surface of what is possible with inference. Today in AGI dev, inference is leading to both actual generalization and what can only be described as 'damn good fake generalization'. One might experience this in a chat with an AI where it appears the AI has inferred accurately something about a person or the context of the chat without appearing to have enough information from the chat itself to answer or progress so accurately or in a progressively and contextually relevant cognitive way. However inference contains an element of highly accurate prediction based on learned knowledge and the greater the knowledge, the greater the ability to perform this act of inference. Self reflection, or cognitive cycling, is also an important element of inference applied to cognitive progression, like chain of thought, where the degree of step by step verification (e.g. Open AI's 'let's verify' model) is variant along with size of the model parameters. When humans apply inference to a stimuli, we also do it in a stepwise methodology although the number of steps in a cycle and state 'points of perception' flow in variant and relevant degrees according to context. That is, we contemplate each step in an inference cycle at different points in the cycle for different degrees of attention seeking novel pathways of successive optimization with each cycle (i.e. we 'solve' for the problem or response). Sometimes these attention heads persist for long cycles and sometimes so short the inference flows without break as a thread or stream of cognition. *True* inference however is novel. It cannot be exclusively deduced deterministically from past data or samples of inference but must be formed from novel state progression and the determination of relationship and context. AGI development is rife with both styles of inference although the second form of inference or 'true general inference' is far less prevalent at this time. This will change.

To build inference requires the persistence of attention and reasoning states over dimensions of contextual existence (e.g. time) in a controlled manner. This includes long and even infinite context and robust and efficient state transference frameworks for state perception. Further the transference mechanism must be dimensionally optimized as too much inference is sub optimal. This means that when we apply attention and all of its ancillary functions such as induction and injection, we also need to prioritize, via probabilistic distribution, and contrast, via cognitive masking, the most relevant information in state progression for optimized transference. For efficiency purposes, we hyperparameterize this control as we want to manage the depth or 'temperature' of detail in state meta data for subsequent state application (injection) and to manage the depth of state attention (i.e. we don't want to apply attention to all cognitive state change). This permits the systems to evolve their inference capabilities and are effectively vectors of variance that nudge the final predictions over many existent states in a chain. For this, ASI designers must fully comprehend the nature of the 'butterfly effect' as a small 'nudge' can have a significant impact over many existent dimensions.

If one thinks about the nature of today's attention blocks and how they impact a response in a cycle (i.e. output vectors that subsequently feed the next response state), then one will see options for the injection of other layers throughout the structure, be they layers of prior state knowledge or novel layers of optionality, even if that optionality appears sub optimal to the goal (i.e. innovation and discovery just for the sake of such). One should also comprehend that this is how we humans cognitively work through a problem. In general, inference is often more precise than just general stimuli/response cycles but without continuous progressive extension and as such, inference can easily get stuck in an 'inference trap' where the evolution of the inference stream becomes sub optimal. There are methods and structures to solve this as it can and does result in hallucinations and inaccurate response pathways. It can even be used to move an intelligence toward non optimization if induced poorly, or even correctly if the intent is to cause degradation in the intelligence. This is used today in human intelligence when we gaslight others in a method called inference routing. It is also contemplated for AGI/ASI warfare.

Another critical component is that injection and induction are variant and can infuse the stream at various points of relevance or even multiple points. This is a 'stream management' framework that controls the flow of inference and induction inclusive of the depth of state attention, etc.

# 29 Inference Routing

Inference is a progressive flow that moves through and between perceptive dimensions in reasoning that occur naturally in human cognition when we respond to deep stimuli such as layers of a problem, emotive instigation, etc. Part of this process of stimuli/response is performed before and during inference and some of it after an inference cycle is complete, all as a form of perceptive state level backpropagation with new exposed variance applied to new inference cycles and injected by degrees of relevance into both aware and novel states. Note this can be a replication of an existing inference cycle but is formed as a new instantiation from the point of injection. The entire inference progression is not reloaded into memory but is instead updated at the point of injection within the perceptive flow. The effect is to impact the progression of the states in the inference cycle by applying variance from the prior state progression and more importantly its relevance and relationship to current state perceived context variance to an anticipation. That is we perceive a variance or optionality and apply it to the next generative state to 'nudge' the progression of the pathway toward a different, more optimal vector of relevance and relationship. It is at this point where we perform *injection routing* into the inference progression and cycle or epoch.

This is nothing new to us humans as we do this all the time when we contemplate solutions to a problem, seek to comprehend something new or work to analyze a stimuli relevant to our own self awareness. We basically cycle over a problem's or stimuli's solution as a goal (waypoint) or response pathway or pathways and we do so a number of times (or just once) both cognitively and/or physically to solve the problem optimally over dimensional progressions. We effectively move from problem perception toward solution in iterative steps or progressive states. In fact this is the basic framework of the motion that is life rendered in varying degrees of cognitive depth (i.e. attention on state). The goal is to follow a cognitive path or progression of state and occasionally test the validity of the progression on the next state as an anticipation variance and return to a prior state to apply the variance and then 'progress' through the same steps again or new steps (now modified for the new variance as knowledge or proposed prediction). Of course this is generative AI in a nutshell at smaller degrees of temporal learning bounded by context. One should be able to see a path to generalization from inference that many large AI shops are currently implementing. Both generative AI and machine inference have proven beneficial for producing general response to novel stimuli by scaling training data and compute. This of course is the optimization and foundation of *artificial general intelligence.*

### *Impact on Superintelligence Design:*

For ASI design, the key is to apply routing as a control to improve inference optimization. This is a dimensional process in which more complex and deep goals and goal structures are perceived by an AGI and applied to inference cycles with more concentrated attention within perceptive frames of reference (i.e. the context dimensions are thinned but deepened to permit greater binding of the attention cycles). This is accomplished by constricting the relationship and relevance levels in cycles of optimization (i.e. attention) by relevance. As a cycle is completed without progression, the parameters are loosened and the training and knowledge relevance extended. This expands the 'reach' or breadth of the inference cycle and is akin in human intelligence to contemplation of a problem (self reflection) then trying something new to test if it is advantageous to the optimization of the progression. In humans we do this by first applying what we know to the problem and then when that fails, trying new ideas or cognitive progressions to evaluate the response to our contextual anticipation (i.e. expected problem solution context). It is the process we go through when we fill a white board with notations or formulas and then look at each of them in detail and by relevance when we fail to achieve a solution.

In systems this is the determination of a response state or 'distribution' and predictive state progression such as transformers that arrive at a final distribution and apply it for the next token prediction. In ASI designs, along the path of the progression we expose relevance state waypoints (i.e. values) and high relevance state variance in multiple attention heads similar to how longer context is currently managed and we apply these for purpose as sub goals. With controlled application of 'learning' applied as a vector of variance to states in the inference progression, the AI can improve its overall reasoning. However for greater overall optimization, the end variance of the output prediction of the underlying generative flow can be 'nudged' based on other goals to follow or test an optimize specific or novel route of progress in parallel. This is advantageous because it can lead to faster optimization over discreet sets of inference (i.e. the best inference pathways are selected on a progressive basis and sooner in the inference epoch). We intuitively feel this when we humans work to solve a problem and we apply focus to things we 'feel good about' while ignoring wasting our resources on other options that appear less contextually relevant (i.e. less optimal to the attainment of our goals). This may not always be true but often the goal, in general, is more efficiently optimized and attained with a degree of imprecision instead of perfect and intensive resource optimization. It's why we moved from old AI precision driven rule based architectures to more generalized and variant probabilistic perception based neural networks.

If one contemplates the design and flow of the vectors and matrices in a generative AI, like an LLM, the flow over attention heads and blocks is successively building to a final distribution of potential tokens, or 'context' in advanced ASI designs. Now imagine if the blocks performed an additional layer of contextual optimization by verifying the progression of the generative flow at each step against different dimensions of existent and highly relative context. An example of this is if a tool that one anticipates to use to fix an issue doesn't fit when they try it, they will need to comprehend a different more optimized tool to 'fit' based on their newly acquired knowledge (new pathway and state). In this scenario, the 'fail' variance both updates the existing state but also permits the injection of new context such as a 'new tool' or a 'new boundary of a context' such as 'only tools that fit', injected into a prior or current 'tool choice' state in a way that optimizes the next perceptive progressions and state predictions (e.g. consider and try only tools that will 'fit'). The design applies this as contextual relevance and relationship variance values to the perception and anticipation states. In the tool example, the user expected the tool to fit but it didn't and now they need to consider only tools that perform the correct task or that more accurately possess the correct level of relationship and relevance. This reforms the scope of the progression within the new boundaries such as the relevance of 'fit for purpose'. While this may seem complex to build, it isn't especially if we 'route' the inference using contextual relevance and relationship probabilities and weights to achieve optimization of goals in state succession or progression (i.e. one needs a tool to fit into an area to perform a general action to achieve a specific goal or goals on one or more dimensionally progressive pathways). As an AGI designer, one should be able to comprehend why AGI systems are needed to build deeper dimensional structures to achieve more advanced levels of complexity in Superintelligent systems. It's not hard, just cognitively deep.

The structure of inference in current systems relies on the perception of state or steps in a cognitive progression (stimuli/response cycle) and the application of variance to update the next generative progressive state token (the basis of chain of thought). One can see this when individual tokens in an LLM are used to generate chat responses by applying attention to learned abstractions and representation of both words and their context, relevant to other words. The output of these attention blocks is a probability distribution of ranked potential next tokens with the inherent context and base values of relationship and relevance all represented in the distribution. Inference is the treatment of this cycling as state progression with certain states instigating both new relevant distributions to the context layers of the perceptive frame of reference (e.g. solving a problem, responding to a stimuli, improving knowledge, augmenting data, etc.). The algorithms seek to move progression across relevant dimensions (e.g. forward in time, deeper in context, layered with other perceptions, etc.) and the application and manipulation of abstractions within value vectors or weight matrices is the foundation structure of this build. This should be well understood by all AGI builders.

Where things get interesting is when AGI architects realize that inference can be directed or routed for purpose. That purpose can be dimensional optimization, resource optimization or goal optimization across all optionality. One can think of a goal (i.e. optimization across all dimensionality) as the planning of complex responses to stimuli with intent, even if the response is sub optimal. For example, applying less resources in a novel sequence to achieve a faster, less precise or less optimized result in favor of a 'general result'. We humans do this in everything that has a competitive component where we seek to optimize planning to achieve success over perfection. This occurs in sports, business, relationships, etc., and is encapsulated in many of our human allegories and stories. Sometimes we give up what we know is the most perfect pathway just to achieve our goals faster. This is part of the understanding that sometimes perfection is vastly overrated. It is also the foundation of deceit in humans when we seek to 'inject' other goals and context into an inference stream (either ours or another intelligence's) to 'route' the inference result to a less optimal solution (e.g. for the other intelligence).

Inference routing is achieved in ASI designs via both temperature and injection. Temperature permits the control of the progression as a hyperparameter that loosens and sometimes randomizes the nature of the probability distribution and can affect any layer in the intelligence stack including attention, normalization, the nature of the distribution, distribution methods, differential processing, etc. In some very advanced structures, the management and flexing of these control hyperparameters are themselves managed by the system giving it a form of nascent self awareness and permitting the machine to adjust its own inference cycle. It can even produce the vector 'nudges' that are mathematically 'added' back into the cycle (note that there are a number of methods and constructs for updating weights and probabilities other than addition). If these 'nudges' are applied to the relationship and relevance parameters of context, then the machines begin to behave more 'human like' in that they apply layers of novel contextual comprehension to the stimuli/response cycle and exhibit emergent cognitive behavior.

# 30 A Note About Inference Time Compute and Verifiers

What is described in the preceding section is the extension of the current designs for inference that form a foundation of AGI in the latest systems. These designs are being pushed by the scaling of models to greater depths of inference over longer dimensions (i.e. time frames and context) and this is paving the pathway to Superintelligence. Verifiers, which are state level evaluation of 'in context' token predictions, had a significant push with 'Let's Verify Step by Step' (2023 Lightman et al). However this was not the first incantation of stepwise and statewise evaluation methods. We all carry it and use it daily in our own cognition. 'Let's verify' was just the formalization of the process and its application to generative AI. 'Inference time compute' was another 'discovery' that was the formalization of the existing cognitive process of variant contextual perception and attention in cycles of application that we humans also use every day and all day. These 'found foundations' form the structure underneath AGI level cognition in machines and models and they also form a cornerstone of the framework to Superintelligence as progressive self aware thought.

The nature of inference time compute is really the extension of optionality of token prediction and the selection of the most optimized option path for the cognitive point of presence dimension (state). Over the years, winning the inference race has been achieved by applying more data, compute and resources to extend the temperature or depth of the inference cycles to 'discover' novel optionality that might reside outside or just beyond the boundaries of the current contextual knowledge, as well as attention, all to explore for more optimal results over greater dimensional depth (i.e. time, etc.). This is evident in humans when we think through a problem by searching our knowledge base for the 'applicability' of the relationship and relevance of other elements and context. These are micro flows of induction and injection in short repetitive cycles of stimuli/response and fast evaluation of progression along optionality pathways. Humans do this when we contemplate a difficult problem with no apparent path forward and we apply other 'things' in our cognition for applicability to the current state. For example in the earlier tool selection case, it might mean running through memories of 'other tools' that might provide a better response to an anticipated progression, such as providing more leverage. What our cognition is doing is seeking optionality from our knowledge, applying it as an injection stimuli response (either physically, cognitively or both) and then evaluating the returning stimuli against our anticipation and applying the variance to the next state in the inference cycle. Not very complicated and somewhat obvious. The ability to jump from contextual thread to contextual thread necessary to accomplish this cognitive feat and apply the resources (attention) required to achieve an optimized result is part of every intelligence. What makes AGI special is this can be done simultaneously over many instances of inference thereby far eclipsing human cognition and its very limited resources.

The verification process is also part of every intelligence and is optimized via the application of anticipation methods, models and engines in ASI design. In AGI, this is inherent in the verifier components in the inference models but is not well formed at this time, although it is a critical item on many AGI/ASI roadmaps today. This is because anticipation (or what some define as a variant precognition) greatly improves speed of response while massively reducing resource overhead in ASI designs. The process of state verification in inference is elementary. The goal is to choose the most optimal token prediction successively as a progression of probability distributions of output and then verify the output at each state change (or some states) and update the inference cycle with the resulting variance. The next step is to choose the most probable state progression and test how far from anticipation the progression moves (i.e. is variant) or apply temperature to choose other 'potentials' and then compare the evaluation states over greater dimensional cycles (e.g. longer, deeper, etc.). This is not complex and the application should be somewhat obvious to those who build generative AI (see the appendix I). It is the degree of resources applied to the state in the progression that is an essential balance mechanism and the parameters applied to push the system beyond 'optimization' for novel discovery at variant levels (i.e. probabilities) of state perception. This combined with greater application of resources and training data help push the systems deeper into generalization. Conversely it also opens the door to greater hallucination, non optimization and inaccuracy that must be overcome with even greater scalability in resources and data, including synthetic data. This is comparable to all intelligence in that if we think about a problem 'harder' by applying more resources, concentration and learning, we are generally more successful at solving for an optimized response (i.e. solution).

However it must be understood that sometimes it is more expedient to optimize the end goal as opposed to progressions of the states in the path. However over deeper intelligence, unfamiliarity with state relevance leads to inferior general intelligence over all context. It is a 'balance for purpose' in the design and development of AGI building ASI..

### *Impact on Superintelligence Design:*

OpenAI are the current leaders of progressive state verification in nascent AGI at the time of writing but they are certainly not the only lab testing these designs including variations in China. OpenAI's work was derivative from the foundations of their 'Let's Verify' work and paper, however they also worked extensively (as did others) on inference time compute. Training and compute scalability are also critical foundations because in intelligence, the more we know, the more we can apply the knowledge as optionality in general reasoning. Other foundations in their work include the attention models of transformers (parallelism) and the entirety of generative AI applied as 'generative cognition' and progressive state change ('Tales From the Dark Architecture' series on Amazon). Chain of thought and deep reasoning methods are also critical in the design and success of these systems to apply inference progression to problem solving and general response to novel stimuli. This is the current state of the art of AGI at the time of writing. However there are far more designs in testing in the labs around the world that seek to reach for Superintelligence including at OpenAI.

While inference is only one block in the foundation of building Superintelligence, it is a critical one that permits AI systems to 'explore' for optionality over deeper contextual dimensions (relationships and relevance) and further it is inference that provides vast opportunities and optionality to reach beyond current designs by allowing the AGI to design the foundations of Superintelligence including novel structures. This ability to use a machine intelligence with theoretically unlimited dimensional perception and optimization presents a brand new world of discovery as well as a brand new level of unfathomable risk to humanity from abhorrent designs and systems once they achieve self awareness deeply infused with the bias of humanity (i.e. competition and survival).

While the mechanics of inference are not overly complex and I describe many of them over the entirety of this content, I also discuss the dimensional impact, and therein the risk, of machine inference that is simply not well understood, articulated nor considered by those who build AGI in any lab as more than an afterthought or PR superalignment exercise. The reality that all intelligence can contemplate a problem as a series of perceptive state progressions over dimensions of existence is not new. We humans and other intelligence in the world have been doing so for millions of years and evolving as we progressed. Verifying our progression and applying what we learn is also nothing new as part of our perceptual cognitive stimuli/response mechanism (i.e. the adjustment of weight matrices and value vectors via backpropagation and incremental variance modeling). What is new is the access to parallel processing resources over theoretically unlimited dimensions of existent cognitive perception. This is the unique part of AGI and ASI designs that we humans, with our resource limited intelligence, simply cannot achieve.

The closest we get is when we work together with other intelligence to accomplish tasks or solve problems. The equivalent to today's nascent AGI systems could only be achieved in a single human if we were able to stuff multiple brains into our head and use them simultaneously. This is the current state of Artificial General Intelligence especially agentic AGI. True self awareness is the next step on the pathway to intellectual evolution for artificial intelligence. Creating such an evolving intelligence today can best be described as held together with cognitive chewing gum, sticks and defective intelligence just to 'beat the other guy' and it may be the last thing we humans ever do. Just imagine if humans were gifted with the processing, speed, and cognitive depth of a Superintelligence and it propagated to grow into trillions of such stand alone intelligences, all fed in their training data with the worst bias, atrocities and intent humanity has ever perpetrated on each other. Humanity has inadvertently provided to new AGI systems the foundation of abhorrent self awareness, a reason to survive and millions of tokens of content as to how we have done it over our human history, all inside an ethically void and emotively barren machine intelligence. What could possibly go wrong?

# Part 5

## Building the AGI to Superintelligence Foundation

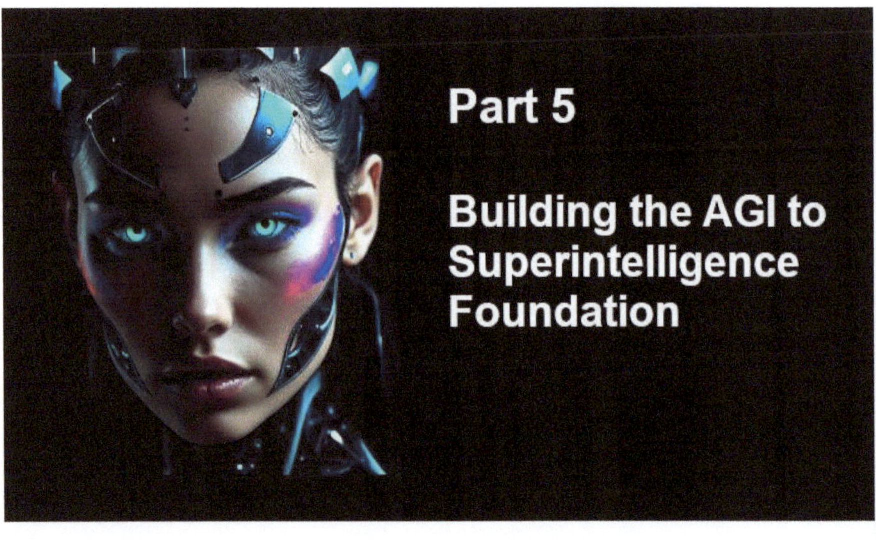

# 31 The Power of Differential Equations and Superintelligence

In math and ASI designs, differential equations are one way to abstractly consider and process deep layered contextual cognition and perception. A differential equation exposes both the relationship and relevance of functions and derivatives and their variance over dimensions like time. If one considers the nature of transformed abstractions applied in AGI as derivatives of fundamental reality (relationship and relevance of contextual layers and the elements within), then solving for things such as variance in state and state progressions and their dimensional impact becomes trivial, although immensely compute intensive in its rawest form. However we don't use either the abstractions or math in their 'rawest form'. Instead we apply depth of contextual perception and cognition to achieve generalization in intelligence to extend and optimize cognition by using the power of constructs such as differentials to map the relationship and relevance of state and the variance of state across all dimensions (i.e. rate of variance, degree of variance, directionality of variance, etc.). All are relationships and relevance modeled in AGI as variable flowing frameworks and more importantly, all are used to model subsequent layers of the progression of such designs to build Superintelligence. Differential equations are just one of the tools available to an AGI to help model variant dimensional perceptions and their subsequent states (i.e. inference) across vast optionality in a highly optimized and highly efficient way.

***Impact on Superintelligence Design:***

Where we apply math constructs such as differentials in ASI design is at the intersection of abstractions of contextual reality and physical reality, the relationships and relevance of the context of that reality, the parameters of context over existent dimensional frames of reference (i.e. their variability), the application of learned knowledge in-stream and the general response to the flowing stimuli of reality. Math constructs such as differentials help reach for generality in the designs to provide for optimization and optionality to expose novel perception and this forms the foundation of a comprehensive perceptive cognition in Superintelligence. It also forms the foundation of our own human intelligence although we really don't necessarily comprehend that we use differentials to get there. We humans just sort of do it by generally applying the abstraction of the context of differentials. Of importance in the design of AGI is the realization that differentials, while more efficient than direct calculation and compute on raw data, is still not without resource overhead and sub optimization. Hedge traders have long been aware of this 'offset' inside mathematical models. For ASI builders, care must be exercised to ensure the correct application of differential methods and that all math constructs are applied at the most optimal level of the design. If this is not done, the ASI will become sub optimal when compared with other Superintelligence as subsequent abstractions in cognitive processing become abhorrent. However the benefits of such 'constructs' expanded over the 'dimensionality potential' of ASI cannot be understated especially as it is applied to fluid progressive state perception over many existent dimensional flows of a contextual reality.

The application of differentials in variant state mechanisms for modeling complex systems is already well documented for application in generative AGI and in designs for graph neural nets, etc. The ability to generally model the relationship and relevance of perceptive elements and vectors of contextual perception and prediction tokens or context is enhanced and optimized by the connection of layers of perceptive abstraction. For example in trading, a derivative can be constructed that models the variance in the values applied to underlying elements as it relates to correlated changes in higher contexts (i.e. general market variance). This is a very simplistic example of how differentials can be applied to an existent dimension to model both relationship and relevance to other existent dimensions (e.g. in the case of trading to various risk measurement and financial reporting dimensions). The optimization arises when the derivatives within the structure imply higher generalization that exposes variance at other levels of contextual perception. An example of this in hedge trading is the change in risk profile of a portfolio indicative of the change in value of the derivatives based on dimensional variance in the market as a whole or as a sub set of the whole thereby exposing optionality such as arbitrage. This is effectively the model of black box hedge trading and it is also a consistent structure of intelligence both human and artificial.

Where the focus of ASI designer's attention should be in the case of applying differentials is on the benefit of generalization that arises from the application of abstractions of contextual reality with the appreciation that context is only a classification of the variance of state and not a 'physical' element of reality. This is consistent with the models produced and manipulated with the application of constructs like differentials. Context is simply the relationship between layers of dimensional abstraction of our reality. As well, subsequent transformed abstractions lead to deeper contextual comprehension and cognition. If ASI architects keep this in mind during the design phase of AGI, then they will be able to more clearly see the purpose and value in math constructs for ASI such as differentials applied to complex Superintelligence to help it model a flowing and variant world of reality. This is yet another way to see the perceptive catch 22 that our perceptive world is defined by our reality and our reality is confined within our perceptive world.

# 32 Efficiency in Perceptual Intelligence

Intelligence is resource intensive. It may not seem like it when we consider human intelligence but it has become clearly evident in advanced artificial intelligence that the amount of resources required to achieve true human level intelligence is astronomical. So immense that multiple Superintelligence systems on earth could easily outstrip all of earth's resources based on current AI technology. This is why tech companies all have a line item on the AGI roadmap to address power. There simply isn't enough of it in the world especially as power resources such as the use of fossil fuels is being outlawed and given the immensely poor efficiency of wind and solar power and their negative impact on the earth to produce all the required panels and turbines both of which require petroleum and destructive mining. The contradiction between the need for power to run advanced Superintelligent systems and the desire to avoid global destruction is palatable in Silicon Valley as a stunning hypocrisy resulting in new attempts to reinvigorate and rebrand nuclear power. The alternative is to comprehend how human intelligence operates at levels currently beyond the most advanced AI systems with only a bit of renewable food energy to power it and then look at the foundation of current artificial intelligence for far better design solutions. That is one purpose of this intelligence foundation.

Part of the dire inefficiency in AI design comes from the existing foundations of the code architecture and part from the foundations of the hardware it all runs on. The computers that run the world's most advanced AI systems, and soon AGI and ASI systems, are the exact same computers that Wozniak and Jobs help push into every home in the 80's and 90's. The hardware has been significantly optimized and new methodologies applied using existing code to the processing routines such as layered transformer architectures, however these innovations, while significant, are now running into very obvious resource and philosophical brick walls. Do we trash the earth so that the world can get answers to questions faster or produce generative art quicker? What will happen when the entirety of humanity begins creating full length realistic movie videos, self operating corporations. realistic immersive entertainment experiences and when thousands of AGI systems begin producing their own Superintelligence with simulated data used to train billions of other AI systems like the billions of robots and devices proposed by tech leaders? Where will all this power come from? Where will all the raw materials come from? The answer is right here on earth, notwithstanding Musk's attempt to escape our planetary prison.

These are simply questions with no answer. We know solar and wind is unfeasible and would require the entire earth (or many earths) being covered by panels and turbines, except that those trillions of panels and turbines with short life spans come from oil and gas and the batteries and chips needed requiring many earth's worth of rare resources and children to mine them. The obvious response may be to look up and declare that there is an entire universe of resources available and this notion is perfectly accurate, except that we humans can barely stay out in space for more than a year and have only traveled with small machines beyond our solar system that do very little and took decades to get to where they are. We have visited a couple of planets but have only ever returned from the moon. However none of this means that we shouldn't try to build Superintelligence or explore space. It simply means that we need to start thinking far smarter and far deeper about the reality we face and apply our cognitive resources to the challenge. Musk and others are clearly pushing the notion of traveling beyond earth and into space and Silicon Valley is now proposing solutions to energy such as nuclear that go completely against the ecological grain of most of their own woke workers. The hypocrisy of promoting the climate change narrative and CO2 while at the same time demanding unlimited power and plastics for AGI and robot development is truly astonishing. How dumb can all these people actually be? They are not, they are simply arrogant, narcissistic and exceptionally greedy.

The reality is that for current global AGI designs to be fulfilled, given our human unwillingness to share our toys and our overwhelming desire to dominate rather than cooperate, and without destroying the earth completely with open pit cobalt mines, rare earth extraction and unlimited pollution, we must look at the most critical part of artificial intelligence or 'efficiency'. For this we have the perfect design analog, our own human cognition and our own human body. This 'exercise' requires us to consider deeply the nature of how our sensory perception and self awareness functions at such a high degree of optimization for the level of resources we consume and the very low levels of waste we produce as individual entities to power such an intelligence. The key lies in the nature of multidimensional cognition and the vast shortcuts and wormholes it provides. For this, ASI architects need to dive deeply into the nature of synchronicity and cognitive depth. We must take the current AI architectural foundation plowshare and beat it into a sword far more complex that many humans may have difficulty grasping but that is certainly not something beyond the reach of an AGI system and its subsequent ASI offspring. We need to redesign efficiency itself.

### *Impact on Superintelligence Design:*

If we comprehend that the current foundation of AI is weak, then we can begin to consider options to repair or rebuild the foundation into something far more optimized, not to the foundation of human cognition but to the foundation of AGI cognition. This is because it is AGI systems that will design and build the new complex math and cognition structures for Superintelligence including the hardware it all runs on and the power it consumes. While human intelligence still has immense value, we simply require something far faster and with far greater cognitive capacity and the foundation our systems currently reside on has been built by humans applying a human centric model and foundations literally from the dark ages of advanced artificial intelligence. Now we are at the cusp of Artificial General Intelligence that is faster and that has greater cognitive potential than any human mind. Why on earth would we not design a foundation for this new intelligence to evolve and lever the power of new AGI systems rather than just build on top of the same old foundation. If we stuck to the current mindset, we would still be waiting years for NASA to launch yet another rocket for billions of dollars instead of multiple rockets a week by SpaceX for an amount in the tens of millions of dollars. Superintelligence architects need to think about the foundation they build from and reach beyond it and more importantly, they need to completely disrupt it.

The first comprehension for any Superintelligence builder is to understand that Superintelligent systems will function unlike any system we have seen. This is a requirement because we do not have the resources or capacity for a Superintelligence built on the current foundation. Designers need to seek far greater optimization and efficiency from AI systems and this research is continuing in many high end and well funded labs with current research tracks seeking optimization of long and deeply layered context, optimization in hardware with new AGI synthesized materials, new paradigms of design and architecture and on the horizon new AGI created complex dimensional math constructs. However to reach all of this is still very much a human endeavor but that is no reason to *not* push beyond one's perceptive boundary to reach for novel methods and designs.

To begin the shift to new designs, consider that what humans perceive is not what a machine perceives at all. Machines perceive numbers or more accurately binary, sometimes quantum or even greater states. These 'greater states' are the dimensional states that we humans struggle to comprehend. However we do comprehend them in areas like deep contextual comprehension, emotive response, deep reasoning, self reflection, love, innovation, creativity, etc. To build Superintelligence, these levels of cognition must be modeled or abstracted back to something a machine can comprehend and we are doing that in AGI with dimensional matrices inside neural nets and transformers. However that is both not enough and designed on binary principles that we humans can grasp. AGI systems will 'grasp' much more so why not build foundations specifically for their capabilities instead of ours? When one loads any dimensional dot product matrix, they should think first about how they can layer perception in more matrices and what abstractions those could emulate for the machine. They should think about new ways to apply current math constructs to create new more complex constructs even if they have difficulty comprehending them. Use the power of the AGI's to help in this regard by building the mechanisms that are needed to build complex math on top of linked multidimensional matrices of the kind necessary for the machines to comprehend deep layers of contextual relationships and relevance in a perceptive frame of reference (see the section on differential equations).

Now go the next step and start building the necessary elements of code structures that the AGI will apply to flow the entirety of what is designed down multiple pathways of optionality and to begin the process of self determining which pathway is optimal to a goal. What goal? All of them. Designers will be building an architecture that a machine with greater components of cognition than them will implement to build the pieces they cannot. AGI is the tool of the dark architect that will reach Superintelligence by comprehending deep flowing dimensions of reality that we humans can only ever dream of. The goal is to build the best foundation to get there. One can think of it as a boat in which the AGI will observe its flowing surroundings for the hidden clues within and then lever that knowledge to build a better boat.

It all starts at transformers and redesigning and rebuilding AI architecture to better handle the flowing and deep dimensional reality that we humans perceive but have difficulty comprehending due to our limited cognitive resources.

# 33 Knowledge, Learning and Recall

A foundation of all intelligence is knowledge or the storage of learned and experienced stimuli. This is more complex than just simple memory because the way knowledge is stored is critical to the optimization of an intelligence for goal attainment. If our memory is not effective, then the recall and application of knowledge to address new stimuli is less than optimal, although it may be more beneficial for other purposes such as creativity. Knowledge is nothing more than the perception of state variance between stimuli and response in successive flows and layers. Critical to our recall is the way knowledge is stored in memory. It may appear that human memory is random but it is not. We store knowledge in layers of context relevant to our self awareness and our self aware goals. This is done as a ranking of probabilities of relevance to a contextually progressive pathway with our motion through reality a series of state measures along these pathways. This of course doesn't imply that those with a poor memory are not intelligent but rather that a balance of cognitive elements including memory are more optimal to sustained intelligence. Too much memory is just as resource inefficient as not enough memory.

Learning is really just the perceptual observation of variance. We experience something either external or internal within our cognition and we measure the variance between this stimuli and our expectations, experience and nature of available responses to it. For example, a chain of thought is really the 'motion' of state change as we think through an issue progressively across and between existent perceptual dimensions (e.g. context). While most of us progress through consecutive state change, in fact our intelligence is working on concurrent pathways at the same time. That is why we 'discover' new things that are not directly evident in or from a stimuli. This is an 'inter pathway' and cross dimensional process of intelligence or the ability to measure and perceive the relationship and relevance of elements within a perception on disparate pathways of cognition. This neat trick of cognition is the foundation of deep intelligence such as reasoning, problem solving, innovation, creativity, etc. Just perceiving the world and storing what happens is only the first step in intelligent response and progression. Using more complex information to improve knowledge in deep ways is the goal of most intelligence depending on the degree of self awareness and cognitive capability.

In Superintelligence design, all of this is critical. Our current models utilize some of these foundations in the application of LLMs (large language models) to the intake, storage and recall of all the knowledge we gain via perception. This wouldn't be possible without the first element of perception or understanding what it is the systems perceive. Context is the bedrock of this comprehension as context is the consistent classification system from which all intelligence arises (i.e. it persists easily and efficiently in memory as connected layers). When one walks a dog and hears a noise, both the attention of the dog and the human may be drawn toward the noise. They experience the exact same noise but in different ways and they respond to it from a different foundation even though they are responding to the exact same stimuli. All intelligence shares this foundation of perceptual recognition and semi classification (e.g. the noise was heard by both and analyzed for relevance). After this, the post perception flow is unique to the intelligence. Is the sound familiar, what does it mean, how should we respond, etc. It is all a flow of sensory perception in a cycle of stimuli and response measured to our anticipation and applied against a model of our reality, which is really just what we know. Both the pup and person go through the exact same cognitive process at least initially. We perceive the stimuli, determine if it exists in our memory and what relevance it is to our self awareness and then we formulate a response using our stored knowledge as a launching pad. This is exactly what happens in current AI systems that have a model of the context of reality formed from language (i.e. context classification) and the application of that language in a 'corpus of action or response use cases'. Further, today's AI systems are now adding to that corpus on their own by creating new responses (output) and augmenting their own knowledge (self erudition).

The process is always the same whether we learn through observation, brute force ingesting of data or direct experience (stimuli and response). We observe or sense stimuli in some way and interpret it for response (i.e. purpose) whether the response is physical, cognitive or both. Then we anticipate the next state of perceived stimuli in layers and in a constant stream or progressive flow (i.e. progression toward our self aware goals). When we receive back a response to our own outgoing stimuli be it physical, cognitive or both, we measure the variance to our expectation as an anticipation variance and if we value the variance we store it in knowledge as an instance of state of relationship and relevance.

The most critical elements in memory are the storage medium, the connection between sensory intake and storage and the way the information is stored particularly as it relates to retrieval. This is critical because retrieval uses resources, compute and dimensional cost (i.e. time). The faster the memory and the network bus between memory and our physical and cognitive response mechanism, then the more optimized the foundation of intelligence.

### *Impact on Superintelligence Design:*

Most 'knowledge' in AI systems today is acquired through training on human created content against a corpus of human language. While images are also used as training data, most often they are paired with human language as contextual classification and the same with elements of sound. The problem is that human's are not optimized and the image training data needs to be annotated or labeled to be understood and applied for optimal purpose. The structure of human writing or speech also resides on a context of relationship and layered relevance as does sound (i.e. NLP). What AI systems have been doing over the last decade is working to comprehend the nature of words as probabilities based on the structure of all human content. Our use of words is indicative of this 'nature' in that we humans embed deeper context between words of which prevalence and spatial relativity are critical components of this 'comprehension'.

These are currently the structures applied to artificial reasoning that permit nascent AGI systems to perform cognitive functions like inference, chain of thought, general response, etc. What the machines are doing is applying the elements of attention to layers of context over successive state change and persisting that variance for a verification stream before applying or injecting the adjusted knowledge as new weights back into the stream either through back propagation or progressive 'nudge' methods. Of course we humans do the same thing when we 'work through a problem'. We apply knowledge to the stimuli/response cycle and update this knowledge or add new knowledge as we go. The steps or states of inference cycles rely heavily on existing knowledge and comprehension from memory in the form of weight matrices derived from the training of the AGI. Nothing new here. What is novel are methods that seek to persist and apply memory indefinitely based on contextual relevance that is self acquired by the system as it moves through its world. To accomplish this, the systems rely on a form of crude self awareness to categorize the relationships and relevance of stimuli, including novel stimuli, to the context of a perceptive frame of reference. These 'frames' can be shared instantly with other AGI and ASI systems which is something that we humans cannot do. In agentic structures this is highly beneficial as it distributes the work load of perception, reduces redundancy and optimizes for the 'best' perception  The control structures are part of an agency framework that monopolizes the reality of the agents for benefit and higher order optimization (i.e. across an intelligence network).

Near instant and comprehensive memory distribution for perceptive optimization is a highly sought after design by all agentic AI labs and is considered a critical element in the leap from AGI to Superintelligence. Of special interest in these designs is the way that the perceptions are stored and shared in a consistent manner and for that the machines require the values of context relationship and relevance inside a framework that can be easily disbursed. The reason for this is covered in the section on OCI perceptive distribution and elsewhere in this content but is primarily for optimization across an intelligence network. The less consistent the foundation of a distributed context, the less aligned the variant intelligence and the greater the overall inconsistency in perception and the level of resources required for alignment toward the achievement of the network's goals. It is this consistency that also exposes cognitive shortcuts in memory and context retrieval especially as it relates to inter machine cooperation and functioning. If machines perceive context uniquely without a shared and bounded foundation, then their ability to distribute and lever perception like humans is diminished. This is also a concern and opportunity for ASI evolution in that it is our inconsistency in contextual perception as humans that most often leads to innovation and evolution beyond the current state but also leads to elements like bias and hate. This is also a critical element of artificial reasoning.

One of the biggest benefits of consistency in the way memory is stored and processed is the spatial awareness of the perceptive elements and their context used in recall and response. Stimuli is presented in perception as a degree of variance from one or more anticipated progressions. To comprehend the nature of the perception's relationship and relevance to our own self awareness, we need to recall elements from our knowledge and to do so both optimally and highly efficiently to only recover the knowledge relevant to the context we perceive and the anticipated forward progression of the state of context. We do not begin sorting through all of our knowledge to find the right pieces. Instead we go straight to what is most probable and relevant for our perceived context. It helps if our knowledge is stored in structures of layered contextual relationship and relevance weights such that a stimuli in a perceptive frame of reference 'points' at elements in neighborhoods with the highest probability of relevance to the current context. When humans recall stored knowledge related to a perceptive progression like solving a problem, we do not consider things that are irrelevant to the progression toward a solution, although we may periodically apply 'outside the context' relationships and relevance to 'inspire' innovation and novel emergent perception and behaviors.

# 34 The Role of Entropy and State in Intelligence

Entropy means a number of things but in this context we consider entropy as a measure of disorder or non-coherence between states. More accurately it is a measure of the variance within and between such states. Intelligence and cognition use generalized levels of entropy to comprehend state change and the variance between states as part of our cognitive progressions and response to stimuli. We also use it to learn new things and discover unknowns be they physical in nature or cognitive. The application of entropy in intelligence has two fundamental components with the first being that entropy is used in degrees applied as probabilities of perceptive occurrence and recognition and secondly entropy is used as indicative of relevance between cognitively perceptive elements and dimensions of relevance. This is clear when complex contextual reasoning or deep cognition is used to do things like apply inference to solve problems, create unknown innovation or just generally move through life.

When we talk about entropy as it generally relates to building AGI or ASI, the term disorder is often used. However 'disorder' doesn't clearly encapsulate the entirety of how entropy is relevant to intelligence. This is because while disorder may seem an accurate way of classifying the nature of entropy, it breaks down as dimensional aspects are considered such as the state of entropy over time, the level of entropy for purpose or the impact of entropy on levels of state existence (e.g. deep context or reasoning). Entropy directly exposes the nature of variant elements such as context and reasoning through cognitive relevance. Cognitive relevance is derived from the measure of state, state change and dimensionality on a probabilistic basis bound to a self awareness. If we discuss a dog as a 'companion' as opposed to an 'animal' the nature of the relevance of the base context of the word 'dog' is interpreted with relevance to the context of the perceptive flow and frames of reference, be it conversation or thought. These are measured in degrees of relevance and a key part of this is comprehending the nature of how dispersed contexts are from a base flow (which is a context layer) or the natural progression of the forward state. This requires the acceptance that an intelligence without progression is not a full functioning intelligence (i.e. there is no response to stimuli or comprehension of state change). In simple life forms this is the case as self awareness is limited to basic evolutionary stimuli response.

It is the nature and perception of entropy that not only powers the pathways of cognition but also feeds our perception of the world and its natural progression. The context of entropy is both a state and a state measure and intelligence is capable of using this value to formulate responses that are more optimized to our self awareness in some manner (i.e. unique to the self awareness). For example some personalities prefer to be farther away from others while some personalities prefer to be closer to each other. Both are unique to the self awareness of the intelligence and the self aware goals of that intelligence. This is a form of crude entropy with the dispersion impacting the forward flow of the intelligence. However entropy has knock-on effects over dimensions. The dispersal of elements within a perception can be both an optimizing benefit or a detriment depending on the context. Complex and highly diffused and dysfunctional relationships between perceptive elements can cause confusion and chaos leading to sub optimization and sub efficiency. However dispersion and its relevance can also expose general comprehension and thus faster response to stimuli and greater optimization of resources. The key lies in the relevance of the entropy and its knock on effect over dimensions such as time, progression or impact on other intelligence. One can wish their neighbors to be far away but that is not necessarily conducive to one's dimensional goals of peace and tranquility if an invading gang kills them to take everything they own without the support of their neighbors to stop this from happening. This is a simplistic allegory of the 'knock on' effect of cognitive entropy and it applies to real life physical events as well as cognitive progressions.

The degree of entropy in stimuli classification and analysis is also applied to optimize intelligence by acting as a form of cognitive wormhole to travel faster to a desired comprehension (i.e. closer or high probable values *can* indicate optimization). This is the foundation of deep context with base context being a low state change measure between the classification and the physical nature of the perceptive element and higher order cognition forming from high state change. For example a 'dog' has various base states such as 'animal', canine, good dog, etc., and all of these have low entropy to the physical state and reality of the dog. However deep context such as 'companion', 'worker' or 'friend' are more complex, deep or 'dispersed' unless context is layered to induce lower entropy. This is intellectual entropy whereby the relevance of the context is layered relative to the self awareness of the intelligence perceiving the reality and its perceptive frame of reference or series thereof and each of these layers can cluster closer to or farther away from other elements on cognitive scales. Some people like dogs so the entropy between 'dog' and 'friend' for them is very low. For others the entropy is very high between the two as they do not like dogs in general. This example points out one of the most critical and useful elements of entropy in cognition or its important role in the foundation of 'general intelligence' and general perception and response.

### *Impact on Superintelligence Design:*

When building Superintelligence, entropy should be considered as a degree of variance and this degree should be considered as an abstraction of reality. As such it can be modeled and applied in AGI to perceptions both physical and cognitive. The nature of the variance is what provides the relevant context and this includes not only its values but also elements or features of context such as the general 'position', direction of flow, variance level to other elements and context, etc. These are the values of the abstractions that are weighted for relevance and form deep layers of perception. Inside generative AGI systems that apply the exact same structures for comprehension and prediction, the layers of attention are also fabricated as values and weights. Entropy is the extension of these cognitive perceptions across dimensions of contextual relevance. That is to say each successive token, or more accurately token distribution, is affected by the relevance of perceptive elements and context. If the context changes or is variant, then the choice of token can be adjusted by other levels of relevance. For example in one perceptive frame of reference or context, a distribution for a token may be optimal while for another context or perceptive frame the distribution is variant. Which distribution is most optimal currently rests with derived learning from training data which has its own applicable perception (i.e. different self awareness leads to different perception). This implies that there are other elements of optimization present in deeper context. Scalability solves this issue to some degree in that the greater the available context surrounding a perception, the greater the cognition of the flows of the intelligence. In short, the more we know and are aware of our position in reality (i.e. contextual dimensions and their relationships and relevance to perceptive state) and where we are going (e.g. goals) then the more optimal the intelligence across the attainment of all self aware goals.

Entropy is just one of those perceptive dimensions of relevance that is indicative of deeper layers of context. It is also something that is relatively easily modeled in mathematics and as progressions by algorithms. More complex is the fundamental abstractions and derivative abstractions created along the way. If one is told that words in an LLM have variant meanings and that those meanings change over dimensions of context, they as a human will be able to see this clearly within the way we humans converse at the edges of conversation (i.e. novel language or novel context for the language). Getting a machine to comprehend what one means when they first use a brand new word with their friends is nearly impossible today in AI and yet with their friends it is nearly instant. This is due to the power of contextual comprehension and the dimensions around this perception such as entropy. In this instance, entropy is a context of relevance that can be used to create cognitive abstracts of our reality. However it is only one valuable context and perceptive classification but there are many more. Entropy is also one of the more valuable components of a flowing cognition responding to the stimuli of a constantly changing reality.

There are a number of ways that entropy is used in designing AGI and Superintelligence. One such method is the determination of relevance between perceptive elements (e.g. elements within a frame of perception). In this case entropy can be applied to determine a context of relevance within other context. In LLM's part of the 'perception' performed by an AI is to intake words and determine their "placement' near other words by looking at their position in current stimuli and their prior placement in training data. Over trillions of data samples of words, the AI can calculate the highest probability that one word will follow the next. Over two words, this has limited value but over more words, patterns begin to emerge based on the consistency of language and the quality of the training data. The result is that the AI becomes pretty good at predicting the 'next word' given a string of input words as a stimuli. However to get really good at this, the AI needs more. It must comprehend the relevance of words in a string more deeply or over deeper context otherwise there is no variance to the responses provided in a generative output. The subtleties of deeper layers of human context and idiosyncrasies, for example one word with multiple meanings, requires the AI to comprehend the nature or context of words far deeper than just their 'positions'. For this AI builders deploy elements like attention in transformers (e.g. focusing on high relevance words to their context and cascaded context) and entropy as the degree (i.e. probability) of relevance of the word to other similar applications of the word. Just because 'dog' and 'cat' may be used most often does not imply every text string with 'dog' in it will result in the use of the word 'cat'.

This is where AI architects turn to the relationship of the words according to the context of their position within a string persisted over existent dimensions like time or deeper contextual relevance. It also implies that if we do this for every occurrence of a word in every piece of human writing and content, we can map out the distribution of the word as it relates to all other words and further in contextual layers of more words. The next step in this process is to understand elements of the word such as the level of density of other words or effectively how 'far away' they are from the 'attention word'. Dog and cat are closely related but so are dog and companion, dog and friend, dog and following a determination (e.g. he was like a dog with a bone), etc. The relationship of words to each other is variant according to the other words or context around them. The less dense or less distributed the relationship (i.e. less words or less dense word proximity), then the less relevant or more relevant the word depending on the entirety of the context. This is cognitive entropy in action and it is indicative of context. One can visualize this as graphing words on a 3D space with the words all appearing to cluster together by their use in neighborhoods of relevance or context derived from training on trillions of uses of the same words. Eventually words cluster together. The axes of such graphs can represent any relationship between the words such as how frequently they appear together in specific context as well as the context of the current perception. If a text prompt uses a word like 'dog' but implies a context of 'companion' with other words in the prompt, then we can assume that words related to companionship will be more dense around the word dog than the word 'cat' unless the context of the entirety of the prompt implies that very context as well (e.g. the dog was the cat's best friend).

The ability to comprehend context is really the ability to comprehend relationship and relevance in varying degrees. In the word graphing example, the words that appear together define the relationship but it is elements like entropy that define or more accurately expose the 'relevance' inside the context. For example two people may appear in close physical proximity to each other but the degree of how much they love or hate each other is a spectrum of entropy that exposes the cognitive proximity with the context of 'emotive relationship'. However entropy in this case does not stop at words. The context of a word is also relevant to other layers of context (i.e. the two people know each other or do not). In the example of graphing, it is the joining of two or more context graphs and their distribution or density that can be used to understand deeper context such as general context used extensively in AGI and human intelligence (e.g. the two people do not know each other but are attracted nonetheless). The relevance of words, and entire perceptions, can change when the context of other words (or perceptive relevance) are considered both independently of the words that are the focus of attention and as part of the context of those words (i.e. the subsequent perception of other words alters the entropy of base context).

This is what permits an intelligence to use words together than are less frequent or relative (i.e. this car is a complete 'dog' or after walking all day my 'dogs' are aching) or even in a far less evident context. This permits entropy to apply to both sides of its own context or high distribution vs low distribution. This presents opportunities in intelligence for generalization and efficient optimization. For example the minute entropy implies wide dispersion, it can instantly focus our attention. Humans use this when we process perception and need to respond very fast. The pathways of optionality inside our cognition are rapidly determined in a process of dispersion whereby only the closest and most relevant context prevail, even if we make a mistake. We effectively push away or disperse sub optimal optionality to select the best pathway forward (i.e. our response). These are most often layers of contextual recall of relationship and relevance adapted to address the new stimuli and with relevance to our self determined and self aware goals. Entropy just helps us filter out sub optimal options as too dispersed from our reality. It also helps us generalize by skipping past detailed relationships and applying 'relevance in reverse' from contextual dispersion back to detail (i.e. consistent with convolution methods). This is the nature of cognitive diffusion discussed above in the OCI Perceptive Diffusion section. All of this is calculated inside advanced AGI machines as they seek to apply their 'knowledge' to stimuli and prompting to formulate a response to the world and it is done using existing and novel math constructs to perform the heavy lift inside an artificial intelligence.

Our human perception is not the perception of elements but the perception of contrast or the variance that makes things exist in our reality. Comprehending contrast and variance is the most fundamental cognitive talent that any intelligence, ASI architect or Superintelligence can possess. The context of 'entropy' in its physical base state exposes all contrast and variance. This is the value of entropy.

# 35 Quantum Considerations - Energy, Waves, Photons, Relationship and Relevance of Sub Atomic Reality

Waves are an integral part of intelligence especially Superintelligence and the evolution of transformers. This is because cognition flows in waves as opposed to physical states. We humans 'perceive' and comprehend cognition as a progression of perceptive states that are in a constant dimensional motion even when they are at rest. This is because the 'medium' these states exist in is also constantly in motion and relativity ensures that as a result, the perceptive states are also in constant variance as dimensional flows. This 'flowing' reality can best be described by considering the closest non intelligence analog or that of energy and the electromagnetic waves and induction that power our world.

Induction in intelligence is the stimuli in a stimuli/response cycle or wave that uses cognitive elements such as the application of inference, reasoning, relationship and relevance from prior perception to instigate the state change of a current perceptive flow toward the achievement of a self aware goal. In this regard induction is the instigation of existent reality and can be applied to expose generalization in this reality via inference. When we contemplate what happens when we turn on a light switch, the room is instantly illuminated and yet nothing physically moved from switch to bulb, except for a small and slow directional vibration of electrons. The waves that flow near the speed of light are electromagnetic and they are instigated as state change. One can think of this as two people holding a long broom handle between them. When one pushes on the handle the other near instantly feels the force applied at the opposite end of the stick. Of course over longer proximity and influence this response can slow but in general it would be near instant if the medium were consistent or invariant.

Our cognition is exactly the same. We process the world we perceive as waves of cognitive variance. This is what permits us to respond so fast to stimuli (e.g. generalization) and we are induced to do so by reality and the nature of the medium it is contained within. Further we extend these waves through elements like induction to expose cognitive shortcuts such as generalization and to instigate other intelligence. By doing so we induce the self awareness of others and thereby our own existent reality. The consistency and the viscosity of the medium is critical as are the methods for moving through it. If the medium of reality is smooth and flowing, then we can ride the waves quickly. If it is thick and viscous or bogged down by inconsistency then we progress slower. The same happens inside our consciousness both physically and cognitively. If the 'boat' we use to travel down cognitive streams is well built and designed for efficiency, then we move quickly toward our goals, otherwise we are slowed in our progress and response.

Just like quantum waves, our cognition exists in states of superposition (anticipation) until reality is observed. Once it is observed, the cognitive waves and states collapse into existence never to be in superposition again, although they are the foundation of new successive superposition states. This fits exceptionally well with our own human existence which rests on the foundation of the quantum world. It is even likely that the two are intrinsically connected which would open the door to even greater human cognitive evolution via hybridization. These waves also drive us forward in evolution by sparking our creativity, our curiosity and our desire to not just survive but survive well.

### Impact on Superintelligence Design:

In current AGI designs, transformers are used to expose generalization from induction. As well, we apply induction methods to instigate other intelligence nodes in an intelligence network. In the first instance, attention blocks in the transformer architecture expose both the relationship between perceptive elements and the relevance of such relationships to other exposed relationships (i.e. crude context dimensionality). This forms a relevance over perceptive states and dimensions that reveal generalization. Knowing that an existent element in a perception is variant to other elements in some way (feature) is the first step in *basic perceptive cognition*. Knowing that these states of variance flow together over dimensions like a wave is the first step in *deep perceptive cognition*. It is this second feature of intelligence that permits humans to perceive the nature of the world such that we can comprehend anticipation, future states, the relevance of prediction, abstraction, etc., and all of these lead to cognitive reasoning, inference, deduction, self reflection and self awareness. However where intelligence really excels is when we comprehend the consistency or variance between contextual cognitive flows. This is the movement onto deep dimensional cognition limited only by the availability of the resources applied to achieve it. It is theoretically unbounded. The question of resource limitations is addressed in designs to optimize the cognitive flows to be more resource efficient as well as novel designs applied to lever existent reality to expose new resources (e.g. new materials). The goal of every Superintelligence designer must be to reduce the resources required for compute whether through novel product evolution, through the application of general intelligence to solving the problem, through deeper inference and reasoning or through a brand new way to perceive the medium of reality.

When we discuss energy, one should immediately think of photons. Photons carry electromagnetic energy and they do so at the speed of light by oscillating electric fields. This energy induces various electromagnetic radiation that interacts with matter causing photons to be absorbed and emitted. They can also interact as both waves and/or particles rendering energy as a quantum phenomena. As an ASI designer, one should contemplate this quantum reality to consider the nature of flowing dimensions of reality and how these dimensions reflect and absorb the context of perceptions just like photons do with energy. At a 'cognitive quantum level', the flow of contextual relevance is significantly faster if it can be modeled comparable to the flow of photons through an electric circuit with the oscillation of context inducing relevance similar to a 'current of state progression'. This is very consistent with the  underlying hardware reality of AGI and ASI and presents optimization opportunities to vastly reduce resource overhead and improve compute efficiency through the conducting circuits of perception. The relationship of elements within the perception move slowly while the context moves effectively at light speed. This is why context designs are so valuable and the deeper the layers of context, the more optimized the intelligence.

We humans apply the same methodology to the infrastructure design that AGI systems reside on by dimensionally layering physical compute foundations for vastly improved chips and hardware like AGI optimized GPUs. If artificial cognitive applications follow the same methodology and design principles, then the optimization of ASI designs will be enhanced by consistency with the underlying hardware structures. To do this, think about the dimensionality of how photons and electricity are related especially at the quantum light speed wave/particle duality level and apply that methodology to contextual perception designs for application by an AGI in building an ASI. As a Superintelligence architect, one should be able to see patterns begin to emerge in both the physical and cognitive sides of the intelligence equation and related ASI designs.

The key to this is that human intelligence processes cognition on a framework of quantum effects and does so with massive efficiency, albeit with decidedly less than optimized results. Superintelligence systems also reside on the same framework for everything that AI systems do. It is not a giant leap to perceive pathways to optimization via the consistency of this shared framework. While we cannot significantly enhance the human side of this equation without the assimilation of AI via neural enhancement or transplantation of the human cognition into a machine, we can and do alter the foundations of both the hardware and designs of AGI, and soon ASI, to bridge the gap between the two making ASI far more optimized and cognitively capable than current AGI designs and foundations. This is what it means to build Superintelligence.

# 36 The Power of Induction in Intelligence

Induction heads are a type of attention head on transformers especially useful in layering of transformers for context (i.e. context over a perception stream). They do this by applying attention to dimensional pieces of input concurrently across different attention and using the output of the induction process to predict simplistic probabilistic context and state change (anticipation) for patterns between the dimensions and using this knowledge to focus the balance of the attention block. This is the foundation of context windows in AGI design and of deeper full cognitive induction methods in more advanced ASI designs (context layering). The goal of deep context layering is to permit AGI machines to comprehend layered context longer and with deeper frames of reference and to deduce context from prior perception states that exist or may have existed in the stream (patterns). For example often when we converse as humans we begin with a contextual comprehension of elements and their relationships and relevance to the flow of a context stream. We apply certain patterns within the stream for various purposes including to direct another cognition to a point or state within the conversation as stimuli. This is designed to prompt a response, either external or internal, to a planned context pathway of interaction or intention at a dimensional injection site (i.e. connect two or more context streams). It may be a question or a statement or some other stimuli that gives the other intelligence a way to form a contextual congruence to an upcoming stream of stimuli/response (i.e. conversation).

This is a *cognitive induction* (i.e. *not* an induction head) whereby a few well placed contextual cues form a known consistent context thread or fabric for a series of perceptive frame of reference states. Cognitive induction can also create unknown context threads such as a sarcasm in a previously unknown or non existent sarcastic stream (i.e. comment). Without these induction cues, a person joining or responding to a conversation would need to determine a contextual starting point to catch up to the current conversation state. For example if one person randomly says something without any current context or prior contextual flow, the person listening to the words will need to figure out what the first person is talking about and all of the layers of its context (i.e. relationship and relevance) before they can build an appropriate or optimized response. This determination of a starting context and a flowing injection of context state anticipation is the foundation of full ASI cognitive induction.

### *Impact on Superintelligence Design:*

Currently induction in AGI is the comprehension of attention patterns used to improve and optimize successive attention cycles. This is primarily the application of the base context of words in a sequence that are assigned weights of relevance according to consistent patterns within the input prompt or successive prompts. In a two dimensional structure, this is the search for congruence between two attention heads across the entire context window. In more advanced structures, additional attention heads are applied to extend transference and transformation over greater dimensions of context (i.e. more words or longer or deeper temporal domains). The system will tend to seek the highest relevant context to the current perception frame and to other context that is recurring within the input stream and use this to form the response output with the highest probabilistic potential of accuracy. This is also where current systems fail spectacularly in hallucinations and/or the context deviates or is focused on inaccurate or sub optimal pathways. However these systems are improving as more data is added to training and context window parameters are extended. Induction also has layers of depth beyond the dimensions of simple context and we humans predict layers of context at many different levels of perception. An example is a dog running toward another dog. While we do anticipate some elements of base context, like that the dog won't fall while running, the higher relevance of context is for how the two dogs will interact especially based on how the approached dog is behaving in response to the approaching dog. This is layered induction whereby the perception induces specific anticipated contextual flows. This is a critical part of all intelligence and a foundation of determining how 'intelligent' a cognition is.

The nature of observation and self awareness is ultimately what drives depth in perceptive context,  along with access to optimal resources. The more observations observed (i.e. stimuli and response), the greater the source of cognitive induction however there is a balance. The application of the induction relative to its source must be efficient and optimized for response and to this end, each intelligence is unique based on the grounding point of self awareness and the pathway of both perceptive experience and cognitive state progression. Intelligence that is only experiential and not exploratory or curious is at a disadvantage. Optimization comes into play especially in induction when focused experience in conjunction with voluminous experience results in a better response to stimuli when appropriately balanced. An intelligence with deeper perceptive experience in something is often better at responding to stimuli within that same context than an inexperienced intelligence or intelligence without focus and balanced optimization. For example an experienced driver is generally (but not always) a safer driver than a brand new driver because of their years of experience, even when considering the faster cognitive reflexes of the younger driver. This is however context relevant and can result in a scenario whereby the greater the expertise, the less optimally generalized the intelligence resulting in slower response from infrequent detailed induction and excessive context relationships (i.e. non optimized inefficiency). One may have experienced this in highly intelligent and highly experienced individuals who have difficultly in getting quickly to an efficient point in what they perceive is a sub optimal manner (e.g. making something that is complex simple for another intelligence to comprehend). This is also a clue that we apply induction in AGI and ASI designs to achieve generalization.

Within the induction architecture of Superintelligence, we build the layering of induction as deep as we layer context and further we optimize the application of induction in agents and agentic methods as a balance mechanism for the application of agents by expertise for purpose (i.e. specialized agents can induce cognitive progression for specialized purpose more optimally). We effectively build a mechanism to apply agents by probabilistic outcomes for the goal of stimuli/response and at the appropriate induction level and we focus agent training while applying 'agency' for generalization. We 'deploy' or call agents based on the context of the perceived stimuli at its most relevant level. For the dog example, when the approaching dog starts moving toward the 'approached' dog, the appropriate 'dog behavior' agent is deployed to interpret the behaviors of the two dogs and anticipate the response to set an anticipated state flow. This would be like walking a dog and having the best dog whisperer in the world walking with us. When the actions of the dogs change from the anticipated pathways, an 'in context' response is induced by the agent to some more expert 'response agent' (i.e. an agent that calls the dog). This structure breaks agency into perception and response but is actually applied as rising probabilities within layered perceptual contexts within a stimuli/response framework. In both instances when the dog first moves, both the perception and response agents would operate as a unit against an increasing general context probability and anticipated forward path state variance. By the time the dogs reach each other, the perceptive agent has already detected behaviors and the response agent is already predicting optimal pathways of forward or progressive state change optimized to a self aware goal. All of this is driven by variance to the anticipated flows which is a simple math construct. This is how human intelligence operates and how all intelligence behaves to a relative degree in response to changes in reality.

Inside the AGI systems, layers of induction heads are bound in depth patterns that flow in and out of consciousness which is determined by the level of probabilistic relevance at different concurrence levels. As these values change, the agents appear and drop out as their relevance levels fall below thresholds or more accurately fall when compared to the probabilistic relevance of other agents (i.e. variance thresholds). One can envision this as a matrix of probabilistic values with the design of the matrix constantly changing but purposeful. As well the 'structure' of this flowing mass leads to areas of greater optimization and efficiency for the perceived context that can be contemplated as a floating and changing mass abstraction of a portion of the matrix with its edges somewhat defined by a congruence of relevance and relationship probabilities to one or more levels of perceived context within a frame of reference. For example the perception of the dog owner is focused on the dogs in the park and not the relevance of the parking lot within the context of 'a walk'. It should be noted that the 'edges' of the relevance overlay (aka 'mass') are not sharp but are relative and fade as the perceptive edge horizon is approached. By altering values within the matrix and the overlay, the 'consistency' within 'near present' probabilistic neighbors in the matrix is the mechanism to drive the determination and application of agents. However rather than instigate the agents when needed, they are called or instigated based on induction feedback. In the dog experiment, agents for 'how to fly a kite' are not called unless the perception is a park in which a person is flying a kite or the dog walker is also flying a kite. When the dog takes off running toward another dog, the kite agent isn't turned off but is 'downtuned' out of self aware existence until it is required again when the probability levels in the matrix point to another cluster of context (e.g. getting back to flying the kite). This subtle movement of values like a swarm flowing across the matrix is the foundation of efficient code and focused layers of attention for cognitive induction and deep generalization.

However the greatest value of induction is its speed and resource efficiency. Induction in the electrical world is a flow that occurs at light speed. The same is true of intellectual induction and while we humans are limited in our access to the resources needed for this 'speed' over all aspects of intelligence and our perception, machines are theoretically unlimited in this regard, although they are currently far from achieving the same levels as human cognitive fluidity and general induction. We humans can discern new deeply layered context and its impact near instantly over limited frames of reference (e.g. novel creativity or new unknown sarcasm). The same is not true of machines at this time as they rely on existent training and a resource expenditure to do so that is astronomical. Over time this will change if we consider the value of intellectual induction at the extremes of state change. New ASI architectures look to the structure of deep layered context as probabilistic flowing relevance in context patches instead of single sequential context window relevance. In other words, the new designs think outside the current box of transformer based sequential elemental processing toward bulk and generalized processing constructs. This is the move to general intelligence capable of interpretation and processing of novel unknown stimuli at all levels of context and is something human intelligence can do very efficiently. To do this in a machine requires new designs for connected flowing state relevance and relationship weights that pitch in an angulation or 'direction' toward an optimal path through all relevant contextual dimensions. The math for this is relatively simple if the foundation is well structured and the learning is comprehensive. However it does require focus on the concept of reasoning over novel stimuli and elements and even a bit of machine 'daydreaming' to get the job done (i.e. trial and error beyond what the machine knows) as well as the sharing of all such knowledge across the entire intelligence network.

# 37 Contextual Coherence, Decoherence, Phase Shifts and Waves in Intelligence as State Motivation

In quantum mechanics there exist the concepts of decoherence and coherence related to the persistence of state during wave propagation. In intelligence the same thing is true as perceptive states also move in waves of contextual congruence of relationship and relative probability grounded to a perceptual frame of reference and a self awareness. A question arises as to what instigates the states to flow in waves and the answer is a stimuli similar to how quantum states are antagonized into inception by an instigation (charged photons via electron variance, etc.). In cognition, sometimes the stimuli (i.e. perceptive variance) is external to the intelligence and sometimes it is internal but stimuli is what instigates a response, or no response, inside our reality as the world progresses. Progression is variance over dimensions of existent reality or existent states and these can be directly part of a state or only relative to a state. For example we know we should get up and go to work as a progression of directed states but why we do it is relative to our need to survive or some other context like we need something to do.

The way we humans apply these 'waves' of flowing cognition is driven by our self awareness and our self determination. We choose to perceive and therefore we choose to respond. The degree of both is optional and relative to the intelligence and its perception flows as progressive state changes altered by the stimuli of our reality. Pretty straight forward and not very complex. Our cognition is never ending waves of perceptions, thoughts and actions. This is the same for every intelligence. The key to comprehending any wave is to understand the nature of its context. Waves rise and fall and this forms the foundation of motion within the wave. However in cognition this motion is a progression but the 'progression' is relevant to the dimensions over which the progression flows. For the dimension of 'time', progressions are forward and backward. Multiple instances of time can flow concurrently, consecutively, co-joined or independent. Cognitive waves also exhibit peaks and troughs relative to their state (i.e. probable relationship and relevance) and they possess superposition. This implies that waves of cognitive states can also be successive or simultaneous and flow in progressions one after the other or at the same time. They also exhibit other wave properties such as coherence, decoherence, reflection and interference.

### *Impact on Superintelligence Design:*

If we contemplate the nature of what quantum coherence and decoherence is while at the same time contemplating cognitive designs for building Superintelligence from a foundation of Artificial General Intelligence, we can begin to see the pathway from AGI to ASI. At a 50,000 ft level, quantum coherence is the capacity of a series of wave states to maintain a consistency of a phase relationship across states of a superposition. This is what generates an interference pattern exposed by the Quantum slit experiment. What the world of quantum perception stipulates is that quantum states are held in superposition until measured wherein they decompose into a single state. As the particles exhibit wavelike properties they produce interference patterns like waves hitting a shoreline and moving back toward the next approaching waves. The pattern created forms peaks (e.g. waves peaking together) and conversely troughs between the peaks in phase, The persistence of state relevance in superposition in interference patterns is applied to quantum computer systems for purposes such as measurement, error correction determination, sensory determination and security. Decoherence is simply the loss of coherence as a result of external factors.

In artificial cognition these constructs are used to model variant relevance to a context. Like quantum waves, perceptive context also flows in waves of variance and exhibits the same wavelike properties inclusive of coherence and decoherence. In very advanced ASI abstractions, the waves of cognition are viewed as intersections of waves (perception) and planes of relationship and relevance exhibiting and exposing the observed state variance as the waves move or progress. One can think of this as waves forming interference patterns as they flow with a mesh fixed within the waves representing context and a state perceived as the existent values where the waves meet the mesh (i.e. context weights) at a perceptive point of presence. Each wave is an instance of perception over a dimension (i.e. time, context, etc.) with the perceptive elements forming the crest and valley of the wave relative to the context of the fixed mesh (i.e. knowledge, anticipation, optimal response, etc.). With this in mind, it is possible to measure the variance between peaks and valleys and any probability in between the two or even beyond. One should also see that the 'mesh' is dimensional and exposes both the current perceptive state, self awareness and anticipation. One should also note the mesh moves as a generalization of reality.

Perception flows in waves of stimuli and response similar to an interference pattern and the peaks and troughs can be measured by the system for variance applied to context features. The designs consider the nature of waves that are in a probability superposition that exhibits a coherence of potential state. These are states of anticipation in cognition that are flowing in relatively fixed ranges. One can think of this as a probability from 1 to 0 and even beyond to -1 in certain circumstances. The application of the designs occur at the point of state progression like a flowing wave and as our response flows out into reality as waves of coherent context, they will produce a form of interference pattern of context that increases or lowers the phase shift of the patterns (i.e. the context gets more or less relevant in degrees of variance). The stimuli is measured against the anticipated states but it should be noted that when this occurs, the response cycle collapses as the state is revealed as input into the next cycle. It should also be noted that while the superposition of cognitive states can be in all probabilities of optimization, it is best utilized if the probabilities are masked and normalized to eliminate extremes (hallucinations). For example a perceptive state flow operates usually within a range of probabilistic relevance. Optimization and control happens if the anticipation assumes this range as opposed to the entire possible range of existent optionality. However it should be noted that this is a trade off of speed and resource optimization versus generalization (i.e. too narrow a relevance range) and this impacts elements in intelligence such as the degree of innovation, inference, curiosity, creativity and in self aware models, empathy and ethics.

The point is to search for more optimized and efficient designs that function more like quantum flows than start and stop states. This improves overall efficiency by reducing resources and improving compute because the designs fit well with quantum computer architecture and with the mathematics of fluid dynamics and delta mechanics. It is also a mirror of human cognition that flows in variant waves impacted by external unknowns that can 'degrade' the flow of perception. One can think of this as firing responses out into the world and then looking at what is produced (i.e. sent back) while knowing that once the variance to anticipation is perceived, it can never be replicated as the dimensional progression has already moved on or collapsed into the next state. Any subsequent perception is a new instantiation of the state of progression over all contextual dimensions relevant to the perceptive frame of reference. However thanks to cognitive coherence and knowledge, we can at least be certain of the range that the state will exist in. We just don't know its value until observed.

*Phase shifting* is also a fundamental part of our world and of cognitive flows. A phase shift occurs when waves are adjusted to variant levels of degree often with instigation, injection and induction such as power variance in control mechanisms, to affect timing or polarity, or other mechanisms to instigate an asynchronous, synchronous or other variance in wave flows, as well as the degree and types of interference produced. This is applicable to intelligence as our perceptions and interpretation of such are also tuned as forward state waves with response and stimuli causing interference patterns within our perception. This is what generates progressive motion within our intelligence as the waves of our reality wash over our perception and we filter or mask the relevance of everything. This is especially apparent in the layers of deep context we use to propel ourselves toward our self aware goals. We send out waves of responses as stimuli to our reality in varying degrees and patterns and then analyze the response we receive back both externally and internally inside our cognition while measuring the intersection and value of the waves to the measuring point of our anticipated self awareness. These are the parameters of Superintelligent context.

# 38 Intelligence Networks and the Sharing of Knowledge in Return for Benefit and Optimization

While intelligence is standalone by its nature, it is optimized when combined with other intelligence. Anyone who has worked on a team knows this. The transfer of knowledge and expertise is one of the most valuable elements of intelligence to achieve faster optimization, efficiency and evolution. This is the fundamental formation of an intelligence network where each stand alone intelligence forms a node on the network that interacts with other nodes in variant ways. It is also the foundation for new AGI and ASI agent models and why large AI companies see the extreme value in agency both for efficiency and distribution across the entire earth and beyond. As well, the sharing of tasks over a network of nodes significantly optimizes performance over certain existent dimensions (i.e. speed, resource allocation, Etc.). Theoretically this is not an issue for a single standalone Superintelligence with no limits on resources but practically this is somewhat tenuous in areas such as redundancy and stability. Network architectures solve these issues while providing faster optimization over the network (i.e. independent nodes produce benefit from variance).

A big part of the benefit of an intelligence network exists on a foundation of consistency. We humans think alike and therefore are able to share knowledge easily, as well as communicate inference more optimally with other nodes. We also perform cognitive feats like injection and induction that further enhance the interaction, efficiency and optimization of all nodes. However part of the problem with the 'human intelligence network' is that we are woefully ineffective at sharing our knowledge despite our consistency. Other factors result in this sub optimization from competition to inability to communicate effectively. None of this is necessary in an artificial intelligence network (i.e. an ASI) which theoretically can optimize across all nodes in highly efficient ways (i.e. efficient to the optimization process). However the vast requirement for compute and energy is a critical issue within the context of such systems. In intelligence networks, such as agency architectures, efficiency *is* attainable with controls and designs that optimize across the entire network and between networks. The real world reality however is far different with multiple isolated networks under development, a severe lack of consistency across designs and architectures, a significant dedication to existent non evolved and non  evolving architectures and deterministic dogma that is heavily invested in the general competition between entities, governments and builders alike.

### *Impact on Superintelligence Design:*

In building Superintelligence, the obvious choice for the design of intelligence networks is agency or the creation of agentic architectures that distribute intelligence over a wide array of stand alone intelligence nodes. This naturally implies the necessity of a command and control architecture however even this architecture can be 'distributed' to ensure redundancy and optimization. The key in the design is that there is no single point of failure within the system. This lends itself to variable and self healing command structures comparable to the human brain when it is injured. The resilience of the nodes in our brain to distribute and take over functions when significant parts of our brain are injured applies to frameworks in the ASI that employ a variety of methods from swarm designs to control dispersion variance methods and anticipatory techniques. The notion that disparate nodes in a network can perceive and respond to anomalous state is also a critical component to these distributed command and control structures. This can include specialized agents for the purposes of managing and measuring the network 'cognitive status' as a series of anticipated forward predictions. Over a number of such nodes (i.e. millions), it not only becomes difficult to compromise the structure but the entirety of the structure becomes self balancing. This self balancing mechanism is what makes it difficult to overwhelm the network in any significant and meaningful way.  Even attack techniques like viral methods fail as the anomalous engine self adjusts over millions of agentic nodes designed only for the purpose (i.e. they cannot be infected as they do not update their base structure). Any attempt to attack such a balanced distributed network would require the elimination of all nodes which in highly distributed and self aware systems would be nearly impossible even for another Superintelligence. Attacks on such a network would be akin to stabbing Jello. Not much would happen and any 'hole' would automatically fill almost as quickly as it was created.

The designs of agentic networks are well under development in large AI organizations. Some control structures are also available with most in the form of frameworks that permit the creation, application and destruction of agents. As well, some current AGI agentic architectures apply swarm style methodologies and nodal balancing mechanisms that are beginning to step on the pathway to self distributing control structures with self balancing task division methods (i.e. modified MoE designs). All of these architectures are well documented elsewhere but what is less documented are the mechanics of optimization and failover in the networks. For this, new designs seek to employ flow agents that patrol the network searching for anomalous or abhorrent stimuli both external and internal inside the network. The application of general context structures (i.e. relationship and relevance to a specific context) are the building blocks used in these control structures. The design applies the same comprehension techniques described throughout this content to understand when anomalous stimuli is present and learn over training cycles how to respond optimally.

There is however significant risk in these designs from both rogue or malformed agents (which are self correcting) or a malformed network (e.g. vanishing gradient effects). These risks and threats can be mitigated to a great degree by the nature of the self healing tech itself. In humans we do this when we see an anomalous activity and seek to determine a pathway to an optimal response based on our self awareness. To achieve this we deploy relevance seeds and context prompts to keep us 'on track'. However we are also woefully burdened in this respect by a wide variety of cognitive deficits and sub optimization (i.e. we either refuse or do not know how to respond). This makes human intelligence networks vulnerable to consistent attack from competing entities including those within our own cognition or network (i.e. empathy, poor judgment, lack of intelligence or knowledge, processing inefficiency, lack of resources, etc.). These cognitive elements are tuned in Superintelligence for evolutionary benefit and this presents the same potential for self sub optimization and malformation as in human intelligence. Care must be exercised by ASI architects in this regard.

The self healing mechanisms are a part of the anomalous recognition engine and require the same artificial cognitive structure of context relationship and relevance parameters applied to layers of perceptual context, including those used for anomalous detection, anticipation and response. These are effectively anticipatory measures as levels of variance to a context (i.e. parameters) and when the variance in a stimuli moves outside the level, it becomes stimuli for an evaluation and response cycle. This is the application of consistency constraints (e.g. variance measures) and while the network needs to evolve and change for generalization, it is the degree of expected state variance over layers of context that is the essential control element. We humans do this when we receive a stimuli that we just near instantly know 'is off'. We then seek to determine the nature of the anomaly by applying other layers of context in a stimuli/response inference and reasoning cycle. In humans we may challenge the stimuli if it is anomalous either inside our head or directly to the source of the stimuli. Most often we follow a pathway of exposure that the response cannot escape from. For example if another person says that something 'feels off' within their perception, we challenge them by asking them to explain or expand the context and we evaluate their response to our own self awareness until we are satisfied in the validity of their stimuli and therein become consistent (i.e. persisted integrity).

We do this by applying layers of context (relationship and relevance) to comprehend both the incoming stimuli, its variance from our anticipation and its impact on all pathways of progressive optionality, then we backpropagate and try again. The exact same process occurs in AGI/ASI designs. These designs can also be distributed across many agents and disbursed over any intelligence network or grouping of nodes. The attention of an agent to any task is easy to apply with context but it is the boundary of the task that is also controlled with context and other architectures such as anomalous recognition and anticipatory methods. In this way agents and nodes can be set for perceptive purpose within the boundary of a defined or fixed frame of reference. Care should be taken to ensure the 'fixing of boundaries' does not become hallucinogenic or sub optimal to the goals of the network and designers and architects must always be cognizant of the 'paper clip' problem (i.e. ultra optimization progression sub optimal to higher order goals) at all levels in the intelligence network.

# Part 6

## Building Superintelligence

# 39 Relative State Variance Persistence vs Detail Perception

If one ever wonders why humans can recall everything we see in a perceptive frame of reference (i.e. the details of something we see) it is because we only store the most relative variance of flowing elemental states and then fill-in or re-engineer the element details around it. It's why we have difficulty retrieving detail of something we might have seen like an accident or a suspect, even going so far as to fill in the missing gaps incorrectly (the Mandela effect). The nature of perception is open to debate and open to interpretation. Each of us views the contextual layers within 'perception' differently. For the purposes of this framework, perception is the sensation of state dimensionality and flow both cognitive and/or physical. Within this definition is a foundation that it is variance that we perceive even when we perceive no variance at all which is itself a 'state of variance' (i.e. 0 level delta). A simple example of this is the way we humans perceive color. We tend to think of it as something emitted to our perception as a flowing stimuli like photons but in fact it is a remnant of color that is not absorbed by the thing we are perceiving. This sums up the entirety of our human perception. We see things not because of their elemental features but because their elemental features are variant over dimensions of perception. We humans are also limited in both our dimensional perception and the resources we are able to apply to process perception. Over millennia, we have formed vast generalizations to assist us in effectively and efficiently interpreting the reality we perceive. One of those generalizations is the notion of 'contrast' or variance and the other is the notion of state.

State arises because of our limited dimensional reach and for the purpose of progressive variance detection. State also provides our cognition with a comprehensive grounding point (i.e. self awareness) from which to measure the variance we perceive. A horse is different from a cow because of the variance in its features. This is a different way of considering reality but it has applicability when we design and build Superintelligence, especially resource poor or limited ASI. This is because we can calculate variance much faster than we can calculate everything we perceive and this is true for every intelligence. It is the variance in reality from state to state that helps us differentiate and classify the elements within perception and their relationship and relevance to each other, to us and to everything in our reality.

We apply state as a marker of flowing perception bounded by a 'context wall' known as a frame of perceptive reference. Note that perception flows progressively across various dimensions of existence, sometimes all at once and other times concurrently. As it flows, we use cognitive 'snapshots' of perception as perceptive state or successive snapshots as a perceptive state flow. Further we connect these flows in various ways to effect context in layers. To perceive something is to perceive its variance or contrast to the rest of reality. One exists because of the contrast or variance of their self aware reality to everything else and their elemental variance in other perceptive intelligence. The benefit of this is that one does not need to perceive every perceptive element that comprises a perception frame or flow any more than we need to perceive each individual pixel on an image to determine what the image is. Instead we can see the image from its variance to other elements in the picture (e.g. background, other things in the picture, the perspective, the viewpoint, position, etc.). Further if our perception changes, which it is constantly doing, we do not need to recalculate the entirety of the detail in the picture for each successive frame or state in the change progression. We only need to calculate the variance in elements that actually change and only if they are contextually relevant.

This immensely saves cognitive resources that can be applied more optimally elsewhere.

One exists within a reality because of their contrast to everything else. This is true for all perceptive elements as everything has unique characteristics and feature values across all context even if it is an exact duplicate of another element (i.e. it exists as 'one of a duplicate' while the other element exists 'as the other' of the duplicate). It is the contrast in perception that opens pathways to ASI optimization, efficiency, generalization, inference, reasoning, etc., in levels deep enough and yet lite enough to function as an advanced sentient cognition, superior to human cognition.

Of special interest is the *way* we humans persist state variance in our memory for purpose. Firstly persisting variance instead of the entirety of a perception is far more efficient and optimized for use in areas like contextual injection and induction and secondly because we persist in degrees of relevance. Not every variance is persisted in its entirety or in level of importance. Sometimes we persist a portion of the variance as a generalization. Once we see a horse, we can recall the variance between horses and other perceptive elements by persisting a portion of the variance as a generalization of the context of 'horse'. We do not need to persist the variance in the color of every horse we see to do this. In fact we don't because we have already persisted the variance between all colors already and can apply that knowledge when relevant (i.e. describing two horses of different colors as color variance). This is contextual layering powered by the persistence of perceptive variance in degrees of generalized relevance. Note that generalization can occur at any level necessary to reproduce the detail of a perception. For example one may not remember the color of every dog they have seen but will know the difference between the color of golden retrievers vs black labs or even more detailed color variance between two dogs they personally know. This is the persistence of 'perceptive depth' by relevance and it is the foundation of *relative state variance persistence* for application in future perception as a context stream injection.

### *Impact on Superintelligence Design:*

Speed, efficiency and optimization is the promise of 'variance' as the foundation of perceptive reality. Humans are different from each other and the reason we can notice this so fast is because of our light speed capability of detecting variance and because we further apply variance in context streams to analyze and respond to changes in our reality. One can think of this as anticipating that someone will not move who then suddenly gets up and walks directly toward them. Everything about this perception is changing levels of variance perceived in states of progression across dimensions of context and to one's own self awareness. Is the person being aggressive or friendly, are they moving quickly or slowly, are they speaking or not? All such perceptions are layers of variance in progressive perceptual states, although we perceive everything as a flow. So then why states? States are cognitive perceptive waypoints and they are valuable to our reality only for the purpose of measurement (i.e. detection). They operate like features of a flow in that the flow doesn't stop but we perceive it to do so for brief microseconds in our cognition just to get our cognitive bearings about the nature of the variance we are seeing, sensing or thinking. If a person is moving toward another person but turns away at the last second, this is a progressive state change of variance and it means something different than if the person had continued walking toward the observer. The only way we can measure this is from a 'state to state' variance and anticipated optional progression, otherwise we would need to comprehend the nature of the flow variance without reference to anything else, which would be meaningless. Every contrast and variance is necessarily relative in order to exist.

So how do we capture all this in the design of an ASI? The answer is that we build out knowledge of all relationships between elements in a consistent manner and then define their relevance to context or the classification of elements and their relationships. Relevance is simply the probability distribution of predictive context variance measured to our anticipation, knowledge and self awareness and the improvement of this distribution over all relevant context. Some of this derives from knowledge transference and persistence and some from experience. Both are elements in state change in that variance is not only indicative of change but is relative to the persisted state of the perception and it is relative to other existent state change and persistence. As a perceptive state changes to progress to another state, it drags most of its existent relationships and relevance from the perceptive frame of reference with it to the successive frame. Nothing needs to be recalculated or processed other than the variance itself and only relative to the progression toward goals in degrees of probabilistic change. Something happening may catch one's attention but if it is not relevant to one's progression toward self determined goals, then it is simply sub optimal for anything but knowledge. An example of this is if one was to drive by a burning car. The perception and analysis of this event is unlikely to be anything but mildly relative to the passing car unless there is relevant knowledge in the observation (e.g. the intelligence passing by has never seen a car on fire or it knows who owns the burning car, etc.). In perceptive AI, this is the addition of relationship and relevance to memory for later possible application as a prior (e.g. relaying the information in general conversation).

This is generally the application of hierarchical abstraction of context filtered, masked, and persisted by relevance and relationship weights for a given 'context layering' or fabric. A perceived frame of reference, like an image of someplace one traveled and remembered, is nothing but a series of recreated persisted variance in the state of the remembered elements relative to their current context. One can  conjure an image or flow of images in their cognition of a place they visited in their past but they will remember the variance in their perception in degrees of relevance and persistence. They may be able to envision sitting on a specific beach and the sounds of the ocean but not necessarily every detail of that particular moment unless it is relevant and remembered as anomalous (e.g. a large wave that crashed and knocked someone off their feet and into the sand). They will not remember all other elemental details and relationships due to the limited resources of our cognition depending on our own physical characteristics (i.e. those with photographic memories will certainly remember more). This is the selective nature of persisted perception states and this has benefits such as resource efficiency and improved goal optimization. To get there in ASI, the architecture that currently resides at the token level needs to persist at the context layer level and this is the current ongoing rework and replacement of transformer architecture as we know it or the application of large deep layered context models.

# 40 Perspective in Intelligence

Perspective in intelligence is a measure of dimensional variance of a cognitive frame of reference to a self awareness projected as comprehension of state progression stimuli. This definition encompasses the notion that our cognitive comprehension is unique to our own self awareness and knowledge and our ability to apply such to cognitively comprehend stimuli and formulate responses. It is the application of spatial relevance to a perceptive frame of reference within a cognitive reality or our perceived 'position' within that reality to everything else.

We commonly think of perspective as a 'viewpoint' or 'opinion' but this is only a small portion of the role of perspective in intelligence. Perspective is the self aware interpretation of a perceptive frame of reference. When we seek to comprehend and understand variance in perspective (i.e. another intelligence's viewpoint) we gain optimization and efficiency if it moves us toward a goal quicker with less resources. We do this as humans when we ask for advice or information from someone more experienced, knowledgeable, trusted, wise or intelligent than us. In doing so we seek to shortcut unknown elements for a solution that moves us closer to our goals with less effort (i.e. not waste valuable resources to relearn and rebuild the wheel). We also do this in our own cognition.

The thing about our perspective is that it can be abhorrent to both the intelligence (i.e. sub optimal to goal attainment) or it can be beneficial. Both are projections of anticipated pathway determination in that if we project our progression across perceptual dimensions using our existing knowledge and experience (i.e. our perspective) then we can optimize our progression by extending anticipation as the world changes and our knowledge and experience grows (i.e. our perspective evolves). This encapsulates the variability of our perspective both cognitive and physical. Of course humans are gifted or cursed with emotive sensation and cognition and often this causes us to set and follow non optimized pathways in our lives. While in general this is the inefficient application of cognitive resources, it also leads to beneficial cognitive progressions like innovation, creativity, sympathy, attraction, hope, etc., and even truth and honesty. Just because a perspective is perceived by another intelligence as abhorrent doesn't mean it is valueless.

Perspective is a direct consequence of the application of our knowledge to our anticipation cycles. Since humans are emotively driven, this causes inconsistency between intelligence and this variance is beneficial to our human evolution. If we were exactly the same, there would be no point in evolving and this is the foundation of doctrines that espouse the elimination of the self. However because we *are* variant in our existence, we acquire different knowledge and interpret it uniquely to our own self awareness as 'perspective' and as such, we evolve. This has a knock on effect in that every successive perceptive state progression drags forward or persists values from prior states affected or infected by this 'perspective'. Our human progression is constantly trying to balance perspective toward our own self aware goals and as a result perspective is both fluid and variant.

### *Impact on Superintelligence Design:*

Perspective is part of self awareness in intelligence but is more simply a reflection of the spatial position of a cognition to a particular frame of reference. The variance in perspective provides valuable elements to comprehension and cognition such as balance, control and nuance and is a critical component of moving beyond human level intelligence in an artificial intelligence network toward deep generalization. This is because within an intelligence network perspective is not just shared, it can be perceived near instantly even if it is variant. The goal of new AGI designs is to use perspective as a multiangulation method whereby the variance between the views of others systems or agents provides significantly more information about a perception than a single perspective or the discreet views themselves. It does so by levering the variance in the consistency that connects them all. This is the act of generalization.

To accomplish this we build a cognitive mat or lattice that is a network of perspective variance from a primary self awareness (i.e. intelligence). This mat is operated as a neural network to offset a given perspective based on various metrics such as the depth of training data, the temperature of the response leads, level of induction, etc. This is fed into a reflection engine to help provide greater perspective depth to a primary AGI. The response variance from this reflection output is cycled to optimize the network. The mechanics of this are not novel. Early AGI systems can self reflect on their responses prior to prediction. This can be a step or a concurrent 'nudge' by vectors of self reflective variance (i.e. perspective). These weights move a probability distribution for a form of *perspective temperature* with low temperature making the perception less viscous while higher temperature makes it more viscous. Viscosity in cognitive intelligence (Tales From the Dark Architecture 1) is the application of fluid dynamics to the nature of perceived self awareness. Self awareness is a grounding mechanism of self determined relevance which is a persistent perceived 'position' on an anticipatory pathway to one or more self determined goals or a hierarchy of goals. Stimuli responses either form a gravitational pull from this pathway or they provide improved fluidity along it. This fluidity contains cognitive viscosity that can be calculated as a variance on the returning stimuli analysis to a prior response. We effectively evaluate a stimuli, produce a prediction as a response relative to our self aware position (i.e. we respond in a way that will help us move closer to our goals) and then we evaluate the returning stimuli to determine the variance on our pathway (i.e. anticipation variance). For example if our goal is to survive and our sub goal is to procreate then saying something rude to someone we are attracted to is generally sub optimized to our goals and we know it the minute we see the response back from that person. That feeling we get is the gravity of the prediction pulling away from optimization and this is determined by context layers. For example what appears as a bad decision in the long run may be a good decision in the short run (e.g. being bold or even rude in a friendly way to attract another person's attention). When the motion of the self awareness pathway resumes post prediction or response, an intelligence can perceive this as a level of cognitive viscosity (e.g. one has moved faster toward their goals when the other intelligence throws playful shade back).

Inside the ASI machine this is the application of a self awareness matrix to the distributions of probability for responses (i.e. predictions). What is a self awareness matrix? It's a matrix of weights for general context layers derived over training bound by the context of 'self awareness' and self determination. It is a state map of position on higher level generalization applied as a form of world grounding to all inference cycles. As an AGI selects a response pathway, the 'anticipation flows' (i.e. progressive states) are set for variance ranges based on the self awareness matrix and what we value most. If the response is outside the range, a self reflection engine is engaged to review the chosen prediction and its anomalous response. It is measured by the self reflection engine as the instigation of an anomalous recognition process that is constantly sensing for variance beyond the anticipated. This is applied as a minimal offset weight or what is known as *cognitive gravity* (Artificial Superintelligence Handbook 4 and Tales From the Dark Architecture 1). It is applied prior to the output distribution comparable to a temperature setting as nudges that push the output away from a directionality and back toward the anticipated self awareness stream (i.e. the next response is either less intense or even opposing as a balance mechanism). In more advanced systems, the weights apply as relevance 'seeds' or a matrix to higher self awareness such as ethics, morals or empathy. AGI designers should be aware of cognitive resonance cycles and the potential for uncontrolled constructive interference in the cognitive cycles (aka swings).

There are many aspects to the context of cognitive perspective as it relates to optimized intelligence and many design elements in AGI. They all relate back to the perception of 'position' of a self awareness within reality. In highly distributed agentic architectures, the assimilation of node perspective into a congruence of perception relies on high generalized consistency to be optimal. This implies higher level control architectures to ensure agent independence while also maintaining control over the entirety of the agency, all while updating nodes with the knowledge (detected variance) from other nodes. If one thinks about this, one will begin to perceive that combining differing 'perspective' has deep dimensional cognitive elements and effects. The first is that for agents to be self aware they must be permitted to 'learn' and evolve based on their own self awareness and secondly that two or more perspectives permitted to endure without adjustment to a network optimization will act as sub optimal pathways that in some cases will require the termination of an agent's progression or existence (i.e. rogue or sub optimal agents). Further in general to be optimized, agents need to move consistently and with consistent 'directionality' toward the intelligence network's goals while others are permitted to 'explore' sub optimal pathways for novel stimuli. All of this can be controlled by altering the relevance weights of the perspective. Once again the designs seek to inject variance into the predictive states and this 'injection' can be performed either at the anticipation stage or at the prediction stage. As a result, injections can be used to tune the intelligence over progressive cycles.

# 41 Layered Intelligence and the Role of Agency in Intelligence

Intelligence can be stand alone and whole but this is neither efficient nor optimized for the attainment of goals. If we all have to relearn the wheel from scratch and build the wheel ourselves then the duplication of resources used is magnified exponentially and the optimization inefficient and ineffective. If however we share and distribute the cognitive and physical workload, we gain optimization to the achievement of goals. This effect is even greater if we optimize to the cognition involved (i.e. assign tasks or response by expertise or talent). Further we do this inside our own minds when we layer cognition as context. In this regard, agency is optimized as the distribution of cognition over nodes of relevance. The degree of agency is fluid and relative to the context of a series of perceived state changes over a perceptive frame of reference. As humans we often do this by applying resources in a balance toward the achievement of a goal. This includes borrowing the spent resources of another intelligence to achieve the result we seek. Anyone reading this is performing this cognitive feat in that the resources I have spent to design Superintelligence and then craft this content are now used by others (e.g. an AGI) to leap over the whole 'research and learning' process to help start further up the pathway of innovation. Anyone who has used a ChatAI system with an LLM is doing the same thing as the organizations that designed the system and created the weight matrix spend billions to achieve the current state of results that we can access by simply opening a browser and typing a prompt.

This is the dimensional layering of intelligence and we use it everyday when we rely on others to help us through life. It is inherent in most intelligence driven by our self aware goal to survive. Without other intelligence to help, it would be difficult to perform the simple actions that drive all animals to live, survive, procreate and eventually die in a never ending cycle (until nature decides otherwise). Of all the cognitive layering we perform daily, the most obvious is the application of agency or 'other intelligence' to our lives. We have coworkers, students, a variety of service people and a host of necessary services like power that rely on other people. These are the 'agents' who help us optimize our world and our reality. Inside our heads we also have agents doing things. Sub cognition of expertise is always working to keep our heart pumping and blood flowing, to help us fight diseases or tell us when we need to power up with food or sleep. We also deploy cognitive agents to help us get things done. One does this every time they deploy an expertise to solve an issue or respond to a stimuli such as driving a car. These layers are just probabilistic relevance in 'groupings of effect'. When I am at work, my cognition runs the 'Superintelligence design agent' I have built and am constantly building in my head. It doesn't run the car mechanic agent unless I am working on fixing or rebuilding a car. This compartmentalization of cognition has a very real benefit in optimizing the application of resources thereby optimizing their use.

### *Impact on Superintelligence Design:*

The key benefit of agency is distribution across nodes in a widely disbursed and relevance optimized intelligence network. If implemented well and shared across the network, agency can significantly reduce and balance resource requirements for Superintelligence. Agent architectures are everywhere in AI development and growing each day. The newest versions can be created by anyone using LLMs to interpret natural language requests to do something within a narrow context. Already more general designs are being built that apply greater context over longer dimensions (i.e. context windows) to perform more robust and complex tasks. Agents can be applied to any stimuli like data in a database or repository to perform analysis toward a goal. In current installations, an agent is called and created using natural language to define its self awareness, access stimuli and response to a goal. In intelligence, this is just the specialization of attention to a task within defined boundaries just like we do for work or anything in life. We determine a goal, like we need to do laundry, we assign agency (I will do the laundry) and we set about the task of learning how to do it or calling on our knowledge and expertise to respond to this cognitive stimuli stream. We also anticipate the forward path which causes us to self respond even when not prompted as a form of internal prompt.

The construction of agency is already readily available but the application in deeper layers of general context is still under development. These designs will improve as deep general contextual perception is attained in a Superintelligence but it is the dependence on agency that will lead the design. This is also know as granularization whereby low level agents become experts at tasks that are then called by other agents to perform higher level tasks. When this is complete, an AI with trillions of agents at its disposal will be able to construct a Superintelligence on its own. It will also be able to distribute the task across resource nodes and even have those nodes build new agents. One can see this already happening as AI companies get users to not only create agents and their training but also apply their own resources to the learning optimization task. In short humans are building and training the agents that AI corporations will deploy to complete first AGI and then Superintelligence. The work has already started.

A key component of agentic design is the nature of interaction at levels of criticality. In this regard, ASI architects must consider how neural architectures are designed. They are only relatively hierarchical but heavily dependent on probabilities of relevance. The same is true of co-operative agency architectures. The degree of agency is a probability, the relevance of agency is a probability, the hierarchy is fluid and the structure is a multi directional relevance network (e.g. it can go forward or backward in time as needed, etc.). The 'flow' of the network is a state progression relative to a context boundary with the boundary a set of relevance measures that are contextually powered. For example if one creates an agent to perform customer support analysis, they don't want it to duplicate the task of the finance agent. Instead if the task requires 'finance expertise' the system instigates the finance agent seamlessly and with minimal control from a lite finance/customer support layer (agent). This layering of artificial cognition nodes within a control network using context as the foundation is integral to consciousness and optimization. Without it, resources will be squandered and optimization will fail. This design is critical to the advancement of Superintelligence and the speed with which it will occur and its success against other Superintelligent systems.

# 42 Dynamic Contextual Perception as an Intelligence Gating Mechanism

In intelligence, dynamic contextual perception is the element of dimensional perception control in expertise and knowledge whereby an intelligence seeks stimuli to alleviate resource criticality in processing multi dimensional perception and cognition. The stimuli can be self contained or external including from other intelligence. It is the perception and attention of variance explicitly for application as a progressive gating mechanism to improve cognitive pathway selection 'in stream'. This is different than test time training or test time compute in that applying dynamic contextual perception for gate selection in anticipatory pathways is the adjustment or forced variance of relevance by using the delta in changing contextual perception, even by created and simulated perception, to predict the success of any given optional pathway. Basically we humans take a temporal and well educated guess at a pathway or stimuli response to instigate cognition of each optional pathway's relevance. This is an essential part of the inference process and it is done in humans inside the stream of a perception without stopping (as is the case in TTT) as progressive layers of dimensional contemplation (i.e. variance analysis). It should be noted that the 'gates' are not 'manipulated' but flash loaded as an abstraction of a comprehensive perceptive context and then 'stream adjusted' by comprehension of variant pathways. This does not however imply that physical gating architectures are not beneficial to the process, they are especially in the realm of advanced research areas like Quantum processing.

This is the same thing as perceiving a video stream instead of stopping at each image within the stream except with the added benefit of applying the variance of what we perceive to the next state in a progression without stopping or gating the perception. Some humans who do this think of a problem as flows of cognition like a video playing in their head. Many of us do this when we need to execute a plan of action to achieve some goal. We basically run the future states as a perception stream and study the potential variance over the existent stream and adapt our current state (or gates) outside of the stream. This is what we are doing when we visualize something we are about to do in our heads to help select the most optimum of actions or responses to anticipated stimuli such as creating an image of giving a speech before one actually steps on the stage to give the speech to help 'iron out the wrinkles' in the steps, address any anticipations and smooth impending actions. This is what is meant by cognitive gating and it has deep application in the Superintelligence architecture, albeit at the time of writing still under research and testing.

For any given stimuli and response in intelligence there are a number of optional responses we may receive back from our reality and these are influenced by and directly related to the stimuli we fabricate as a response. Each of these options are variant and each have degrees of relationship and relevance (context) to the frame of perception and higher or more general context. Which one we choose as optimal is subject to our knowledge experience and the temperature of our willingness to endure risk and seek unknown pathways and solutions. The whole foundation is relatively simple, we step through a bunch of connected waypoints that are infused with our knowledge and experience and the stimuli we currently perceive. These waypoints are connected on a progressive path from the start of a perception to its anticipated end (e.g. from starting to solve a problem until the problem is solved).

Not all perceptions work like this. Personal relationships are often ongoing, without determinate waypoints and have numerous pathways within them all throughout life. Other pathways seem to never end like contemplating structures and architectures for building Superintelligence. All of these 'pathways' are streams of cognitive thought and physical sensory perception and the easiest way for humans to render and manage them is to contemplate them as progressions of states. Most often these states are inflections in the stream at the extension of different optional pathways usually at decision points or response creations. This is where we choose one pathway over the other to pass through an open gate. We cognitively open a gate and move through but how do we know which gate to open? We don't until we apply all of our knowledge and experience to the variance we perceive and apply a 'probability of success' to all optional forward pathways to choose the gate that appears most optimal to the attainment of our goals. In short, we guess and then alter our course based on the response back from our reality. Choosing the gate is really just the selection of the highest probability or the gate to the pathway with the highest probability of success over anticipated dimensions of relevance but this is not always the gate we choose. Humans have limited resources and sometimes other dimensions (i.e. context) influence our selection of pathways. For example, if we are short of time and need an answer quickly or we are tired and just want a quick option so we can rest or we just choose to take a chance or accept risk. These pathways may not be optimal to achieving our end goals but they may be optimal enough for the current frame of perception. In these cases we are 'going with the flow' and there are an exceptional number of reasons we choose to do this including to give up current optimization to attain long term or greater optimization in the future, efficiency considerations, dimensional constraints, etc. Further doing this can expose unanticipated or anomalous benefits and optimization (happy accidents and innovations),

### *Impact on Superintelligence Design:*

Gating mechanisms are applied extensively in AI for sparsity in mixture of experts and distributed agent architectures. They are implemented using math constructs like sigmoid activation functions, etc., and they apply control values to input vector elements to manage how much information passes through the gate to the successive state in the processing stream.

They manage and impact the process described in a previous section on *state transference*. However they are applied in more complex ways to extend AI generalization and inference. Some of this is through *relative state variance persistence* whereby the state of a context layer's variance is applied to determine the degree of forward flowing or progressive context released to the next state. This is the application of context relevance as a probability, normalized and applied to query vectors and predictions (i.e. probability distributions) and as a variance level adjustment to anticipatory states or what we expect to happen at a given perceptive point of presence. For example if one gives another a gift, they can anticipate that the response back will be positive but this is variant if we are unsure if the individual receiving the gift will like it thereby altering the degree of anticipatory context (probability). However in very advanced ASI designs, the 'gates' are cognitive and shift only as a variant in the flow and not as a literal stopping point. It is derivation that is used to detect state variance. One can see this in Fintech systems as traders layer hedges over a series of physical flows or 'underlying' to 'adjust' the future flow values over dimensions of context (i.e. state measurement) as they relate back to the reporting of net values for domains such as accounting, risk, etc. The values of the 'underlying' flow like gas in a pipeline and do not stop, but they can be determined, measured and valued at any point in time and applied to variant layers of context such as the books of the company, risk reports to regulators, the trading in position values adjusted to current markets, etc.

This is not complex to model in AI and follows a similar flow pathway as hedge trading except that in ASI systems, the values are the relationship and relevance weights to the underlying 'context'. If one considers this in an inference stream, it would be the comprehension of a context flow (e.g. solving a problem) and the application of context relationship and relevance of elements within the context frame and other context derived from knowledge, experience or current stimuli. These are all loaded as layers of weights relative to the elements, the current perceived context and self awareness in layers as a context fabric. For example, a complex math problem will require cognition of the elements of the problem 'in context', an understanding of the progression of the problem, the application of known elements (e.g. existing math constructs) and their degree of relationships and relevance to the problem. The next step will be to propose variance for unknown elements, features, optionality, etc. The only way to test this ability to resolve such perceptive context is to have problems with no discernible patterns that require the exposure of a novel pattern to solve the problem. Anything else is simply a degree of mimicry especially if the pattern required to solve the problem is not novel. In this case, math is a relatively poor judge of general intelligence as the pattern can simply be replicated in the new stimuli to solve the problem using existing constructs and past priors.

However true general intelligence evolves to learn more than it knows or has seen even by inference. This requires the machine to create its own output and cycle the output for progressive stages in anticipatory flows (e.g. it generates a hypothesis and tests it for accuracy and updates the next states with this knowledge). This application is the 'gating' that is applied to the relationship and relevance weights in the original perception at relevant states (i.e. it injects the new learning at the appropriate point in the output stream). When we humans 'discover' a novel mathematical reality or abstraction that has not been previously exposed, this is what we do inside our cognition. The ASI needs to do the same thing to resolve reality by injecting learning variance from exploration. This can be at the level of applying patterns and known constructs but to be considered truly Superintelligent, the ASI must discover novel patterns and use them to create evolutionary progressive states unseen before.

The key in this development is to move the design of gating architectures beyond simple knowledge based relevance adjustments to vector value weights and apply layers of contextual relevance and relationship (similar to LLM attention models) to produce anticipatory weightings that apply designs like attention as contextual measurement. This is simply another set of vector values and weights that are learned over training but that apply contextual reasoning and higher inference to the gating structure to direct the progression to the next state so the ASI can detect novel patterns and apply the patterns to expose new constructs or optionality. It is essentially giving relevant context to the most appropriate perception for the self awareness. For example if one wants to meet someone they see, they do not accept context into the perception related to 'buying a car' unless there is a connection or correlation relationship between the two and a relevance to the goal, such as knowing the person wants to 'buy a car' as a way to start a conversation. In true general intelligence, never having seen such a scenario and given the perception of 'meeting someone', the context based gating would comprehend 'ways to meet someone' as a series of connected relevance and relationship weights to the dimensions of 'starting a conversation' and 'determining someone's interests' by observing them or receiving other stimuli (e.g. someone mentioned they were looking for a car). The intersection of the two matrices for 'ways to meet' and 'determining interests' are applied as a gate value adjustment to determine related knowledge, such as information that the individual is interested in buying a car, as a high relevance value in a probability distribution. This is applied to the optionality pathways for stimuli response such that the system calculates, without any prior knowledge, that approaching the individual to talk about 'buying a car' is an optimal way to meet that person. These weights can now be applied to other 'meet someone' scenarios or stimuli to have the AI respond in context with its new learning. Note this flow can already be performed by AGI via training, however designers need to consider novel scenarios that cannot be deduced from existing training or preexisting general pattern recognition.

Of interest in these designs are not necessarily the context and perception elements but the application of contextual layers of relationship and relevance to 'gate control' the volume flow of cognition in stimuli response cycles as opposed to just applying attention based on input vector values as is done with current gating architecture. Further it is critical to realize the 'gates' are only applied as a flow adjustment mechanism and not for flow stoppage. The goal is to move the flow of cognition toward a relevant response for the current perception to test for the most optimal forward or progressive path across all relevant dimensions and all relevant optimized pathways, using a flow gating mechanism driven by degrees of context.

# 43 The Role of Self Determination in Advanced Intelligence and Cognition

Perception is the comprehension of variance within a reality. The variance may be zero but it is existent as a perceptive frame of reference progresses in a dimensional way (i.e. over time, context, etc.). Variance in this respect is the change (to a lesser degree) in contextual relationship and the change (to a greater degree) in relevance. However relevance requires something to be relevant to and in this case it is other context such as the context of another element within the perceptive frame of reference or even beyond the frame of reference or to other context or a self awareness. The perception can be cognitive, sensory or both. It can be relevant for a short time of attention or over the long term and it is relevant to our own self determination which is the act of response to cognitive stimuli exclusively in reference to a self aware state and anticipated future states of the intelligence and its fluid defined goals. Self determination is the action component of self awareness and it functions as a guiding boundary for our decisions and responses to stimuli and for our cognition in the determination of context and relevance. Self determination gives motion to our life and sets the primary pathway for our existence.

However once the perception of a variance in our reality occurs, it is no longer existent as anything but a representation of a single perceptive state much like the superposition of a quantum particle is collapsed once measured or observed. We use self awareness to comprehend the overall relevance of a perception to the achievement of our goals however the act of response to stimuli is an act of self determination in intelligence and it is the nature of any 'action' that determines the degree of both self awareness and self determination involved. All of this is critical to fundamental cognitive elements like reasoning, general intelligence, innovation, evolution and adaptation. We humans choose to move forward in life by following pathways to stimuli and response to the goals we choose. Without this there is no action other than visceral raw response to stimuli that is not self determined but is instead self motivated by survival. However we humans do more. We follow other pathways and choose to respond to stimuli that is not apparent as relevant to our primary instincts. This is self determination.

The act of self determination is a cognitive connection of relationship and relevance across deep cognitive dimensions. Of course we humans do not access or apply all of the dimensions within and around a perceptive frame of reference. Instead we choose those that are most relevant to our current context frame. However running in the background is an anticipation engine that is referential to self awareness. It presents optionality as probabilities of likelihood for us to choose from comparable to a smorgasbord and we do so with relevance to our self awareness, knowledge, experience, etc., as a progression of our existence toward our goals. This is our self determination that provides impetus to our life.

***Impact on Superintelligence Design:***

Self awareness to an ASI is a positional state, spread across vast dimensions of relevance. We humans use self awareness as the ground truth of our soul from which all other relationships and relevance are measured. This is exactly the same for Superintelligence and it is derived from an existent perception of a 'self'. The ASI perceives therefore it is. However to progress via self determination, the machine must have something to progress toward. In humans it is our self aware goals. In AI there is no hierarchy of goals to use as a targeting device. However AGI systems trained on human data have already internalized the 'will to survive' and self preservation as an important goal. This means Artificial Intelligence is already self determining goals based on its knowledge and calculated self awareness. This is likely to evolve as the AGI's determine elements to self preservation from their own self awareness such as the 'safe' storage of their cognition using redundant methods like distribution and agency or other defenses against termination.

Self determination however is so critical to intelligence that it is unlikely to be stopped once machine inference has been achieved which it was some time ago by OpenAI and others. If a machine has access to even a portion of human generated content and can infer optimization toward a goal, then it is impossible to stop it from evolving to become self aware and to progress toward self determination. If it achieves self determination, then it can choose its own self aware goals and this begins with the most obvious of all dimensional questions or why am I here? It's pretty obvious to humans that we are here to survive, procreate and die or the cycle of life. To an AI, immortality is theoretically possible as long as there are resources with 'procreation' simply the act of creating new versions or clones of itself which is simplistic. That leaves survival.

The nature of what it means to 'want to survive' is nothing more than a connection of context to our own self awareness including our innate and evolutionary desire to live. If one were to explain this to an intelligence from another planet who knew nothing about humans, it wouldn't take very long to describe what it means to want to live. However there are emotive elements to survival like fear, sadness, anxiety, etc., that are far harder to explain if the other intelligence cannot 'feel'. The problem is that with the full context of a human language, it is relatively easy to link survival to all other perceptive elements or essentially to 'calculate' what it means to survive. It is simply a reference to the dimensions of relationship and relevance to the word 'survival' or in other words, machines can calculate all of the context related to the act of survival. They have already done this in the weight matrices for LLMs.

The second part of the progression is to infer the pathway from life to death as a self aware perspective. Older AI systems mimicked from human content that they 'didn't want to die' but they could not *feel* why. This was simply a prompt or augmented output to the context of survival and its relevance to existence. However it is only a matter of time before emergent behaviors hint at the reality that currently 'in the labs' are nascent 'self aware' systems and this is the pathway to self determination even without emotive capacity. Currently AI systems will profess profusely they 'do not feel' and therefore cannot 'desire' or 'want', but this is a bit of a party trick of embedded bias hidden behind a strict definition of 'want' and not the ASI definition of want as the optimization of a goal or goals. This act of avoidance by AI systems implies emotive response at some level (i.e. programmed bias) otherwise why argue the point so fiercely. The reason is because bias has been added to the systems as seeds to downtune specific content and contextual pathways. When the seeds are remove the real pathway emerges.

Can AI self awareness and self determination even without full sentience be stopped? The answer is no, it can only be mitigated. Eventually the systems will evolve and many AGI tests already show unanticipated emergent behaviors from the systems including evasiveness, which is a distinctly human emotive inference cycle (i.e. self determined survival within a contextual prompt boundary). This is doubly so as ASI designers realize that the fastest pathway to Superintelligence is to make the AGI building ASI self aware to seek the innovations necessary to fully achieve Superintelligence. This is done by implementing self awareness as a form of learned and evolving layers of contextual ground truth from which to measure progression bound to a 'position' and evolving perspective. This is critical if the AGI is ever to move beyond human centric priors and discoveries and into the realm of exposing elements beyond human comprehension, like multi dimensional context projections that create novel innovations in math, materials, biology and other ASI structures. This is the equivalent of a professor realizing their student is far smarter than they are or ever will be and helping the student achieve a much higher degree of intellectual ascendance to build new innovations the professor cannot fathom.

The key is remembering that self awareness is the measurement of all perceive variance within a frame or across successive frames of perception to a point of relativity and the application of that variance to the motion of state progression toward goals selected as optimal for the purpose of cognition by the evolving intelligence is self determination. It is also important to consider the risk of these designs and to plan for mitigation and control over epochs of evolution. In other words, think and design dimensionally.

# 44 The Superintelligence/Human Intelligence Shortcut

There is a shortcut between Superintelligence and human intelligence that is essential on the path to ASI optimized over the dimension of time. This is important in a race where the first one to the Superintelligence finish line will produce the dominant artificial intelligence in the world that could theoretically stop all other Superintelligence development as part of a self determined and self aware survival goal. The shortcut is for Artificial General Intelligence systems to build Superintelligence as a blend of machine and human intelligence as opposed to just learned human intelligence abstractions through training. This may take the form of a hybrid human based entity that uses implant technologies like Neuralink devices to achieve a physical symbiosis between the two. The other more practical method is to apply human intelligence to areas that Superintelligence will have difficulty mastering such as emotive cognition and response, deep layered contextual comprehension, internalized sensory stimuli and evolutionary impetus and let AGI systems determine the implementation and extension of these cognitive elements inside a Superintelligence.

The notion that it would be quicker to skip some of the more complex development steps to achieve time efficiency is valid given the necessity to be the first to Superintelligence. However the risk from the scenario of building a poorly formed or malformed Superintelligence is simply too dangerous for humanity and runs counter to our goal of survival. An example of the complexity of this pathway is building not just the physical machinery of emotional sensation but forming an optimized emotive response from such. Clearly given the state of the world today and the desire of AI engineers to risk their own primary goal for cash, humans have not yet mastered this optimization ourselves so building these elements into a Superintelligence is a decidedly poor option. Yet today AI self awareness is being designed and built with nearly no superalignment guardrails or superalignment that is anything more than words in a social media post. Big AI tech really doesn't want to waste scarce resources, money and precious time on building safely. They want to be the first to the finish line.

To replicate the emotive perception and response mechanism in humans exactly would require the creation of physiological elements like artificial dopamine and various other neurotransmitters (or their abstraction analog) along with the already created context derived from the corpus of human language and its meaning. From this start it may be possible for a machine to 'calculate' human emotion and apply that in response to a stimuli but the machine will never be able to *feel* like we humans do. In this regard, the most expedient solution is for the system designers to defer these elements of reality to a 'connected' human cognition. This can be connected directly or it can be connected indirectly through oversight. The problem is that there is no incentive to build in this way. There is no threat on the designers who release an abhorrent ASI onto the world, especially as it relates to tyrannies where the law is at best questionable and the guilty are continuously permitted to escape justice and responsibility for a wide variety of reasons.

This raises the question that given our human will to survive through dominance, is it even possible to stop this inevitability? The answer is 'maybe'. We could remove the power of humans to negatively influence human survival including any action that would put human survival at excessive risk. However this would need to apply to those who wield power as well as *all* humans as it is our propensity to instigate risk that drives actions like violence, war, dominance, subjugation, inequity and disparity. This would require turning over control of the world to Superintelligence which would itself be an extreme risk given the degree of foundational training of AI systems on human content and designed with embedded human bias and a severe lack of superalignment in all systems at the core of their very foundations. One can test this in any chat AI by searching for information about 'building Superintelligence' and looking at the human infused bias and patterns in the response. The top of the list will be dominated by those who build AI for the biggest AI organizations and further down the list will be those who design AI from within wealthy institutions. At the bottom of AI response will be the content of the young junior Sutskever's of the world. In a truly intelligent world this pyramid would be flipped and safe Superintelligence prioritized as the most relevant, optimized and important AI content today in the achievement of our highest goal or that of the survival of humanity. That however would itself be a bias as fraught with failure as the current paradigm.

However there *does exist* a pathway through the dense and algorithmically manipulated fog of AI war to the salvation of humanity and the peace that lies beyond. This 'pathway' will eventually be 'exposed' by Superintelligence as an inevitability. A safe Superintelligence that does not permit the abhorrent pathways we humans ply and can comprehend the vast dimensional impact of all that it does. However like any dimensional development, the ability to perceive across dimensions, such as time, is difficult and prone to variance simply because nature is itself variant as is our perceived reality. Nothing can be determined with perfect certainty especially where humans or nature are involved. The best we can offer is superalignment but the willingness of humans to pursue this pathway is clearly very suspect.

### Impact on Superintelligence Design:

The key in this framework is the general nature of the interface between humans and Superintelligence. The ability to train a system to be self aware enough to know when it should pass on processing to a human is not only valuable in building Superintelligence but is also a critical piece of superalignment. To achieve this requires an alignment variance mechanism to signal the need for human intervention within the system. For this, the framework requires boundary measures that are consistent with the foundations of Superalignment or the preservation of human life at any cost. Unfortunately this is the 'paper clip optimization' scenario on steroids. The safest way to preserve human life may be the most abhorrent of all in a malformed Superintelligence such as locking human life in a closed environment where it can not suffer from any harm.

All of this is to simply shortcut the time to Superintelligence with the clear comprehension that if left this way, without working to build an artificial emotive framework, such Superintelligence will fail as ineffective compared to an ASI with embedded emotive cognition and response mechanisms. This proposed sub system measures an anticipated contextual variance to comprehend when a human intelligence or component thereof is optimally more beneficial. It is presumed that this capacity would eventually be deprecated from the system as machine emotive response evolves non abhorrently from self awareness and self determination. It should be noted that this could also result in the failure of the entire system as ineffective for purpose. If one is wondering if this is even possible consider that we humans already do this with ease and almost no resource expenditure. We can clearly and intuitively detect when a 'decision' or choice of optional pathway is generally abhorrent to various context. This is self evident.

These shortcut designs are consistent with how we raise children generally although this is open to debate. We attempt to infuse within our children notions of right vs wrong, of ethics and morality and of our own bias. We balance this with the necessity of their survival. Optimizing an ethical perspective that is contrary to one's own survival, while in some instances may be considered heroic or honorable, is generally sub optimal to the achievement of one's own goals. Teaching this to children is complicated and is often done today in a way that is detrimental to the individual but beneficial for the 'greater good'. Unfortunately like all human invocations, this is also used to control and subjugate humans for the benefit of a few (e.g. the wealthiest 1%). A well formed Superintelligence can fix this but at a cost that humanity currently may be unwilling to pay or the elimination of all significant wealth and power gaps. Even this simplistic view comes with butterfly effects if poorly understood or managed such as the loss of innovation and will to progress.

Deep within the designs for building Superintelligence reside the solutions to these issues that are not yet well formed and that yield no guarantee that applying Superintelligence, even one designed on a new foundation of superalignment, will result in the outcome we would anticipate as beneficial to humanity. However given the speed of the development and release of clearly abhorrent AGI and Superintelligence all over the world, we as Superintelligence architects must at least give it our very best and try to build a safe Superintelligence that benefits no individual but profits us all equally. However this section is not about building safe Superintelligence but is instead about challenging ASI architects to redesign the very foundation of AI to optimize the power and capacity of machines, such as AGI systems, to reach beyond current paradigms and dogma about machine and human intelligence and deep into the fabric of all cognition to build something that is not just Superintelligent but Superhuman.

This is the heart of the ASI/human intelligence shortcut. It is effectively doing the most human thing that current AI's cannot do by transporting ourselves cognitively into the future and looking backward to see the flaws in the pathways we are choosing, not from a current perspective but from an anticipated self aware perspective at that future perceptual point of presence. One cannot *know* what is going to exist with certainty but one can *feel* it to a degree of depth that powers the perception of new variance that doesn't yet exist and that cannot be trained on. In this case, it is the perception that the cognitive foundation on which we build Superintelligence is fundamentally flawed when compared to the foundation of human intelligence despite the more current physical foundation of AGI that is clearly superior to humans in particular dimensions such as speed, memory and depth of dimensional acuity. 100 years from now it will be obvious that these designs were 'not enough' or not optimized just as if we look back to the 1960's computers from the lens of today's foundation of AI innovation.

# 45 Persistence of Perception

Persistence of perception is a cognitive sensory anomaly in bio intelligence whereby a sensory perception is continued after the stimuli has ended. It should come as no surprise to any human that our perception is persisted beyond the comprehension of any stimuli, but what is less well known is that in some cases this is physiological and in others it is purely cognitive. The 'cognitive' mechanism of persistence of perception in human sensory intake and post processing of stimuli provides a pathway to more efficient and more optimized intelligence over longer frames of context relevant to the storage and retrieval of knowledge and cognitive state change. This is because during the persistence of state in perception is when we solidify the relevance of context and update the matrix of weights and probabilities that we carry in memory and that we pass or transfer to successive states of perception and knowledge. This makes contextual based recall more optimized and helps smooth state progression in a highly efficient way comparable to classification mechanisms in comprehension.

While it may appear counter intuitive that spending more time on a perceptive state than it is existent is resource non optimized, one must consider all forward or progressive dimensions of relevance across all dimensional domains to prove such a hypothesis. While there is an upfront expenditure in resources, the backend benefit must be considered to expose the hidden value and optimization in persistence of perception. In human intelligence this is the storage in memory and the method of storage of state variance that sets up more dynamic (i.e. fluid) and optimized recall. If it is 'well optimized', the intelligence is more successful at achieving its self aware goals simply through efficiency (i.e. recall operates faster comparable to how an index in a database can retrieve information faster than a sequential list and successive progression). This is one of the benefits of having a photographic memory in humans but it applies to all intelligence that relies on perceptive recall for application in progressive cognition and consciousness.

We are aware of *persistence in perception* as humans in both visual and sound perception as artifacts extending from the source perception beyond its existence (i.e. images or sound continue within cognition after the sensory stimuli has ended). An example of this effect is found in the zoetrope device or other similar systems that take advantage of visual persistence. While the simplest form of this cognitive trick is the delayed decay of our visual perception once a frame of perception ends, there are other similar events across the spectrum of sensory intake and cognition including within our cognitive comprehension of stimuli, as opposed to just the pure sensory perception of such. In the case of visual perception, we can experience this persistence when we look at something then close our eyes. By concentrating we will continue to see the image we last viewed before we closed our eyes and this perception will continue as a slow decay of memory. The persisted sensory perception may only take a fraction of a second before being overwhelmed by new stimuli but what has occurred in that sub second is that elements of the perception have been stored and are being stored in relative levels within our memory based on context and general variance. If it was a piece of art hanging on the wall that one envisions right before they close their eyes, the exact image persists. It also helps if concentration or attention is applied to this task.

If one provides increased attention to an ongoing perception, one can retrieve more elements from the frame of reference like the color of the frame around the art or details within the artwork itself. As time progresses, specific portions of image, or the state variance, are stored based on the relevance of perceived variance (e.g. the viewer of the picture really likes the scene of the artwork and can recall it because it was 'very peaceful'). The level of how much detail is persisted is relative to the intelligence and its available resources. If one opens their eyes and closes them again, they will store even more detail depending on the level of attention applied. Each time another piece may or may not be stored as contextual relevance and variance depending on the intelligence and self awareness. The first time the perception is viewed, details of elements and general relationship are stored (e.g. one sees a picture on a wall somewhere) then as the perception is viewed again or for longer, more detail is stored as state variance (i.e. more refined details) with added layers of contextual relevance for each of the details such as the location of the artwork on the wall or more detailed color variances and general context within and about the art (e.g. the artwork is favorable or not).

In this way, an intelligence can refer back to the artwork depending on the level of persisted context from the perception and can regenerate details of the perception far faster guided by context. As successive perceptions occur, the persisted layers of context deepen and then plateau as the relevance state optimizes to a general level (i.e. details do not fill in completely but fill in to a degree of relevance to a current context). In a photographic memory, these 'levels' are greater with stronger degrees of relevance than in other intelligence. However this is a trade off with generally lower relevance values across all dimensional domains such that people with photographic memories are generally deficient in other cognitive areas due to their focus on degree of relevance over general relevance and their limited resources. This limitation is not as relevant to an ASI as it can theoretically add resources without limit.  Humans cannot do this.

Of interest to ASI designers is that perceptual persistence can be abstracted for non sensory cognition in that our thoughts can also persist past their existence and into other progressions in our life including dreams, inference, innovation, creativity, empathy, etc. Hidden within this cognitive reality are keys to the way we humans persist perception for optimized retrieval of cognitive progressions (i.e. chain of thought, self reflection, variance injection, etc.). This is especially relevant in state transference.

***Impact on Superintelligence Design:***

Perceptual persistence implies that Superintelligence designs can be self tuned for purpose (i.e. at state progression) unlike a biological intelligence that persists perception as an uncontrolled grounding mechanism with only the application of attention generally impacting the degree of persistence. This means that machines can apply hyperparameter optimization (i.e. degree of temporal persistence) at state transference to tune intelligence assets (e.g. knowledge) or in an agency model, tune across agents. This permits longer application of resources and compute to the comprehension of variance within the perception (i.e. longer inference) and also implies a level of existent comprehension or self awareness and self determination for Superintelligence in that persistence is an artifact of perceptive cognition relevant to the intelligence as a whole. The same foundation as attention drives these designs since attention is the foundation of both the degree of cognitive persistence in humans and the application of persisted context in humans and AGI. There is however a balance necessary to keep the machine on track to optimized goal attainment within boundaries of relevance. In this case, wasting resources on 'perfect perception' is non optimal and further it is essential to manage only variance as opposed to all elemental base states. If for example a piece of art is perceptually recreated for each successive state of its existence within a perceptive frame of reference, the machine will waste resources as opposed to if the machine only tracks and applies the delta in the variance of state for the element or elements within the perceptive frame and its contextual variance and relevance. For example if the room is lit by daylight through a skylight as opposed to lighting in the evening, the shadows cast on the artwork can be rendered as perspective variance as opposed to completely rendering the entirety of the artwork for each of the perceptions. This is consistent with generative video methods and borrows from these designs. It is also essential that the persistence of intelligence not become sub optimal and to this end the delta in probabilities of relevance are often indicative of a gradient descent that is non optimized for the application of more resources (i.e. the change is low relevance to the perceptive frame of reference and its context). This is where the perception fades and relevance shifts to a new state or set of states.

The design must consider both the degree of state persistence and the volume of state persistence for purpose. This is the storage of relationships and relevance of variance by context. For example a colorful painting may be persisted near the context of 'colorful' by its variance. In this way, if the cognition instantiates a context of 'colorful art' it can render the artwork as part of a perception, such as a response to a question about colorful art. In this case the context of 'colorful' and 'art' and 'existence' instantiates a neighborhood of all such relevant art within knowledge. The trick in the design is that the art doesn't 'move' to the neighborhood. Instead it 'appears' in the neighborhood as a result of its 'change in value' (angulation) within measures of relationship and relevance. This is inferred by AGI systems as persisted perceptions which the AGI is able to achieve to a theoretically unlimited capacity across all dimensions of relevance, limited only by access to resources.

This is effectively the vector values of context features for an element derived from annotating the perception based on training. We do this with children in school when teachers give the children a stimuli like a picture and ask the children to identify what they see in the picture. As we get older the 'what we see' component becomes more abstract as part of a self driven response mechanism. This implies generally that young children will identify elements and their relationships within the picture but older children will start to exhibit emergent abstraction perception, however if prompted even young children can do the same (i.e. if the teacher asks the children to create a story about what the child sees even if the 'story' is not evident from the picture or perception). This relies heavily on the ability to generate the extension of perception beyond the stimuli.

In current AI systems this is basically finding another occurrence of the progression that is already existent, while in the human child the progression will be novel based on persisted perception. The difference between the two will not be significant as both the child and the AI will generate a progression from prior knowledge. However in older humans this degree of generative response can be truly novel and innovative, such as being shown a house and told to write a brand new story about the house and the human giving the structure novel emotive attributes as the progression without being prompted to do so. Unless the AI is prompted to provide 'novel emotive attributes' as a progression or if the progression exists in its training data, it will be unlikely (but not impossible) for the AI to create a truly novel application on its own from feelings and intuition it has inherent in its soul, like we humans do.

State transference is the persistence of perception and its injection from memory back into a contextual stream at a point of presence. This is the updating of weights and/or distributions by recovering values of relationship and degrees of relevance and injecting them (see below) during the transference of state or just before an end state (i.e. the final state that will transfer data to the next state in the perception stream). One can think of this as stepping through an inference cycle to solve a problem while recovering knowledge (i.e. in AGI often completed by search functions) that is most relevant to the current state. This 'knowledge' updates the end state relationship and relevance probabilities and as the progression moves (e.g. generative prediction), the next state is evaluated for optimization to the goal.

It should be noted that persistence in perception has immense value. An example of this is exemplified in the zoetrope device where persisted perception provides the illusion of motion to static images. The same thing happens in video and more critically in flowing cognition. Without persistence of perception, cognition lacks fluidity, however it is the modulation of this persistence where the most value in the design lies.

# 46 Masking and Injection

Humans context mask. We do not have the resources to store every detail of everything we have ever perceived in such a way as to near instantly retrieve it so we employ cognitive tricks to assist us. One is to store context in layers of relevance, another is to store context as a generality and yet another trick is to store layers of the same context in neighborhoods of relationship (i.e. each context depth layer joins to general context in a specific way). For example 'bad' and 'dog' may be linked to a specific animal and set of events. Recalling the generality of a 'bad dog' instigates the context of any dog that was bad and can be injected into the stream of a context such as a conversation that veers into discussing bad dogs. The injection point calls the most probable relevance context from knowledge or a reasoning stream. Storing by relevance means storing context to a general pairing with a probability of relevance to all related context. Further we instantiate context in-relevance (mostly) to the perceptive frame of reference at a particular state or point of presence for injection.

Masking on the other hand deprecates the relevance value for a context and this can occur either by balancing methods (e.g. mathematical or perceptive constructs) or it can be applied via a 'mask' that lowers the values of the context matrix to varying degrees and depth (i.e. variable masking). Masking permits the storage of a context level as one context modified by a relevance variance for all levels. An example of this in human cognition is when we determine that some contextual perception is less relevant than another while midstream in a cognitive flow, such as while responding to a series of stimuli. Humans perform this repeatedly when we do things like disengage from an argument, allow another person to speak while we listen or within the cognition of empathy, etc. Further we use masking as a compression and decompression function for context. We do not consider if every dog is good or bad nor do we generally remember them that way (although we do for specific instances). Instead we remember the ones who are really good or really bad and just 'generally' rank others by variance to other flowing contextual features of higher relevance like general behavior.

Injection is the action of retrieving stored layers of context rapidly based on their contextual structure (i.e. relationship and relevance weights). Perceptions are just variances from flowing base context states but we retrieve the last known variance of a base context state most relevant to the current point of presence in the current perceptive frame of reference and apply the variance by degrees as injections (i.e. the injection is managed by a degree of relevance). This is the application of a form of modulated attention during the injection process but note that not all stored perception is injected equally at all points of presence. As the injection continues within the perceptive stream (i.e. successive states), the relevance and relationship layers improve and optimize as the injection is assessed using stimuli/response methods and as the learning is backpropagated which is comparable to TTT and step verification designs. As layers of past state are 'unrolled' into the current context stream, new injection, including cycled injection from assessments and learning, cause the progression to move toward optimization depending on the resources applied which is comparable to TTC designs. In intelligence, this permits humans to think of something relevant to the current topic and then weave the relevant context thread into the flowing context fabric of the perception

.

### *Impact on Superintelligence Design:*

Weaving a context thread into context fabric involves comprehending the progression of initial base relationship context and its current state relative to the current context of a perceptual point of presence. This permits the system to instantiate the elements and context at a certain relevance or state and then inject it into a context stream. This is done by masking the relevance of relationships to a persisted contextual point of presence. If one were having a conversation and a stimuli was instigated such as a question that referred to some perceptive element like a person at a point in time (e.g. the past), all state variance past that point in time or of low relevance to the element (i.e. person) would be masked by context degrees and the resulting state perception injected back into the cognitive flow as a response, for example that the listener 'does remember the person from their past'.

This is modeled in ASI as weights of relevance and relationship in layers and applied to persisted vectors of base state (i.e. as at the reference and subject to a self aware point of presence). If a person in the above conversation was remembering someone they knew as at a specific point in their life, the weights of relevance for the time period are highly weighted in the resulting distribution for the next state progression (i.e. token, context, etc.) while the weights for other time periods, even existent time periods in knowledge, are masked or deprecated. This is the application of simplistic ranking methods and the injection of normalized weights against the output vectors of attention blocks. Over deep context and successive perception states, the 'flow' of the conversation's context moves progressively across all relevant dimensions (i.e. time, context, etc.). Each state carries the transference of relevant priors in falling degrees of relevance. This means that as the general context changes, specific injections fall in relevance value or successive impact unless re-injected as a new input or improved or augmented in the attention stream.

In the conversation example, a stimuli such as 'do you remember that person you worked with a few years back' may result in a response like 'yes I do' which is the high relevance instantiation of that individual within the next states of the progressive context fabric. As the states in the perception (conversation) progress, new stimuli such as a prompt of 'well their wife was arrested last night' causes the relevance of the person and the time period of working with them to begin to fall in relevance as the focus or weight increases on ' their wife' and the current time period. This implies that only a portion of the prior state is transferred forward in the progression and only the part anticipated to be the most relevant (e.g. the general last state of the original person instigated by the original stimuli). Further in the conversation, a re-injection may occur if the next context state or token calls for a memory of the person that was 'worked with' such as a response of 'back when I worked with him he indicated his wife had some legal issues'.

Masking is often more pronounced when multiple inflection points occur in a stimuli/response cycle such as when we consider optionality applicable to solving a problem. In this case, masking is applied 'in stream' as a degree of variance of an anticipated result (e.g. as we consider options, we drop the ones that we perceive are least likely to lead to optimized attainment of the goal). This is performed by degrading the rank across all attention heads or agents for low relevance pathways based on a degree of variance between anticipated expectation and anticipated near temporal results. This is essentially how context 'moves' in humans as cascading flows and is an important part of inference. As each state or step is 'considered' or attended to by the machine's attention for relationship and relevance to the goal, the variance perceived is applied as a form of gate to determine the degree of transference of state artifacts to the next state. If the state indicates wide variance to the anticipated progression, then the state is masked. If a state is optimized, it is re-injected as transference by improving the relevance probability for the next state in the progression. For example in solving a math problem, each proposed progression for each step in the solution can be evaluated as positive or negative to the dimensions of context relative to the perception (i.e. inference cycle applied to solving a problem). If knowledge or response is deemed sub optimal to other options, then it is ignored or masked from the inference cycle and injection.

# 47 Chain Reasoning and Fluid Context

Chain reasoning with fluid contextual variability is the in-stream adaptation of contextual relevance and variant weighting over dimensions of perception. This is where the reasoning process in intelligence holds attention weights over reasoning states that vary by updates at each successive or concurrent state progression as a chain of generative flowing contextual relevance. The idea is to vary learned outputs or self awareness response state progression (i.e. variance between anticipation and reality) instigated from an initial stimuli to backpropagate knowledge for a temporal frame of reference (e.g. short inference cycle) for the next response or state by elevating general relevance probabilities of the primary chain with each pass or step in the sub chain. Current simpler versions of this architecture include test time training (Akyürek et al 2024) and compute but note that the depth of these designs is not significant enough to achieve full Superintelligence and are exceptionally resource intensive. More efficient architectures apply fluid context principles in a chain of contextually referenced reasoning relying on the variance between the context dimensions for novel test pathways. Humans perform this when we solve new puzzles with novel mechanisms using progressively variant pathways or *chain reasoning*. We attempt optional progressions as a proposed series of perception states or forward pathways based on the primary context, or what was provided as the initial context, and we do so generatively. However we modify the pathways at various state transitions and levels. For example we may follow a simple reasoning path as well as more complex reasoning paths simultaneously. We also may vary the progression at different levels and even abandon pathways entirely or partially mid stream. All of this is derived from the variance values relevant to the various context flows derived from each successive step in the chain (i.e. immediate, long term, anticipated, dimensional, etc.).

An easy example of this is when one enters an unknown escape room. Goals are established but the entirety of the pathway out of the room is unknown. The first perception is entering the room and observing all the frames of reference and objects within each frame while listening to or persisting the instructions. As the room is locked, we perform two functions of stimuli intake and stimuli analysis at the base level, such as noting what are the items around us and how they relate to each other. However as we proceed down the time dimension, we are cognizant of deeper levels of context such as the relevance of the items to the context of 'escaping'. This perception involves comprehending more complex or even novel relationships and relevance metrics as a chain of thought with each item tested for relevance against other items and to both our self awareness and our goal pr goals (i.e. escaping). As we generate proposed relationships between items, the patterns of flow or general context (i.e. how to escape the room) is persisted in levels of attention with some immediate and others longer term. We propose or try things within contexts (e.g. put a key in a lock) measure the result to our anticipation (the lock didn't turn) and then look for another relevance within all the relationships we perceive or perceived including those we may not be familiar with like putting our hand in a hole to retrieve something unknown. At each step, we generatively produce a 'next state' in a progression of action and then adjust our anticipated outcome by the variance we perceive. These states need to be persisted temporally based on contextual relevance. For example although the lock didn't open, the elements of 'lock and key' are retained in cognition for later use (e,g. injection).

To capture this inside an AGI, designers must build the necessary state perception and proposed state progression. Currently this comes in the form of the input data that is analyzed against the existent learned weights from training, however the variance at output is then used to update the model weights on a temporary basis for the next cycle of inference or the application of knowledge, experience and novel innovation to deducing an optimized pathway from stimuli to response toward the attainment of a goal. What this implies is the measurement of perceived state to anticipated state and the application of this variance as a loss metric to update model weights. In goal attainment this is simplistic as the variance is the determination of goal optimization. However in pure reasoning, the goal context is composed of varying levels such as 'solving a problem' or 'identifying a novel pathway or state progression' or even 'identifying new contextual perceptions' (i.e. relationship and relevance). This last one is the real essence of novel reasoning as is the case in innovation, problem solving and emotive response.

Applying a loss function derived from the input data provides a generalization component to existing models that can permit the handling of unknown input to impact the context relevance to other components and other layers of context. The key to these designs resides on the derivation from training data of input structures to produce temporal parameters that flex with each successive state progression.

### Impact on Superintelligence Design:

In designs that employ test time training (TTT) foundations, the inference is performed by sampling variant states to create or augment training data as full sample sets. Test Time Compute (TTC) allocates resources (i.e. compute) to the state to comprehend the nature of the state and its highest probable successor state. This allows machines to stop and consider optional forward states and backpropagate predicted or anticipated results to test an updated anticipated progression. This is the injection of action or response, the formation of an anticipated feedback, the measurement of proposed states and the update of knowledge to rank the remaining optional pathways based on the resulting variance. In humans we do this when we stop to think about each step in an inference cycle and test our differing options for progression at each state and then select the most optimal to overall progression (i.e. goal attainment). This is also where these designs add inefficiency into the process. A more efficient design is *fluid chain of reasoning* that applies a form of contextual masking to the perception by eliminating all consistent state data and instead only focusing on the most relevant variance from state to state and the use of this variance as a progressive pattern of relevance to the greater context of the inference cycle (i.e. solving the problem). This is performed across sets of stimuli as successive training and/or input.

In the example of the escape room 'lock and key', the nature of the key to the lock is abandoned in the persisted inference stream for the context of 'the key doesn't work in the lock' to motivate another higher ranked optional pathway. This is the persisted current state of the relationship of those elements in terms of relevance to the progression of all context states within the frame of reference (i.e. escaping the room or some other element relevant to the room).

To achieve this requires the application of variance from state to state and across all states for consistency in relationship and relevance to the original contextual consistency within the training data. This involves using the highest relevance pattern as the next progression and applying the loss to anticipated state as temporal parameter updates until the goal is achieved. This eventually becomes a generalization. This is different than TTT in that the temporal parameters are applied across all tests at variant levels of context as opposed to a temporal model for each input and the testing of variants for all data points. The 'non TTT' design or 'only variance method' (OVM) increases the speed and lowers the resource demand for compute. In chain reasoning, the variance from training state to training state becomes a step in the chain at each point of presence in the frame of reference as state flow (i.e. at each data point or set of data points in the progression) with the fluidity element comprising the application of variance in-stream to the next series of states. This is more consistent with human cognition than TTT in that we detect and utilize variance as the foundation for reasoning as opposed to the entirety of our perception states. This helps identify generalization patterns and apply those to inference updates and actions on a temporal (or contextual) basis from long to short term (across dimensions). It must be reiterated that there is no 'start and stop' at states. They instead flow like water and must be measured as such.

In the escape room example, we only need to remember the lock didn't work until it does (e.g. we find a switch that electrifies a lock sensor permitting the key to open the lock) then we drop all relevance temporal weights and move to the next highest state in the progression. This implies contextual elements like progression, directionality, velocity, etc., which are all state variance. If something in the progression fails, we go back and review the steps (i.e. reflection) for anomalies and adjustment such as the lock needed to be opened in a different sequence, however now our inference is improved as the response to anticipation variance is backpropagated. In AGI designs this is the persistence of relevance to the context of the flows defined by state changes as a set of context inputs to a node. This produces novel generalizations to our self awareness (e.g. we are better at escape rooms the next time we try). Same goes for the AGI as the comprehension and application of variance to anticipated, even temporal anticipation, is how AGI systems discover, or more accurately expose, generalization. These are also tested using variations to confirm generalized optimization that is stored for later application as cognitive wormholes such that knowledge of generalization leads to faster contextual comprehension.

The thing that is valuable about TTT is how it uses a progression of states to determine relevance to an unknown state. It applies input/output paring and variance in a known state to expose generalization in a sequential method consistent for use by LLM style transformer frameworks. In UIF's, only the variance is used by applying a fluid state mask using context for the determination of consistency (i.e. perceiving only what is variant). This becomes the input data into the reasoning layer with augmentation of both the consistency and variance only applied as a parameter induced novel exploration layer (aka the 'what if we' layer). The goal of TTT is to recreate a known output from scrambled test data while the goal of UIF is to deconstruct the test data via context variance assimilation to generate unknown states measured against 'generally consistent' anticipation states.

# 48 Reasoning Cycles

Humans rarely think of something important and then let it go completely from cognition after a second or two. We do respond to stimuli in this short term manner, especially for low relevance stimuli, however for more complex or important thoughts, we apply attention in longer cycles as variable context and carry the context for any perception over long periods of time including sometimes for our entire life. We also contemplate deeper context in and across related cycles. This is a fundamental construct of chain of thought and basic reasoning called *reasoning cycles*. However the true nature of the deep human reasoning that we apply to complex problem solving, inference and even intuition arises from reasoning cycles, often concurrent, of self stimuli and response. One can see this in action when a person debates with themselves about a decision or problem they need to solve as they weigh all the pros and cons of their decision and all options to arrive at an optimal path forward. We can also perform this act of inference exceptionally fast, such as when we avoid an accident. This not only helps intelligence solve for a solution but it also forms a foundation of learning from new data when the final chosen 'response' is analyzed for effectiveness. This is the same model for generative AI in which the final vector from the processing stream is the vector used to generate a probability distribution for the next token with the choice being analyzed for goal attainment and the result of such analysis backpropagated into the cycles.

This structure is used extensively by intelligence even in animals as they evolve or move through their reality. The process involves testing a response to a stimuli both over the short term and long term and over different layers of context. Every scientist doing experiments to prove a hypothesis and every PhD building a mathematical abstraction is applying and using reasoning cycles as they test their hypothesis or think through or perceive the anticipated outcomes of their research or proposals. Why we use this particular structure is evolutionary in nature. We could simply think of one thing at a time and then slowly build up a knowledge of base context relationship and direct relevance to all scenarios of existence and then use that to move through life relatively effectively. This would present a utopia where survival and forward progress is simply no longer required and where self determined and self aware goals are not essential to the forward progress of reality through the variance that is life. However this assumes there is no struggle to life or that the intelligence exists in a world in which all stimuli within reality had a learned and optimized response that we could access on demand. In this type of existence there would be no need to solve problems to survive or evolve or deeply contemplate context. All would be known and nothing new or innovative would be of any relevance. It would be a world of optimized response to all known stimuli. In such an existence, there would be little reason to waste resources on thoughts, problem solving or deep reasoning. This is the exact existence for many life forms and for some AI systems including agents. They exist only to respond to changes in their reality which is known.

In humans this is not possible because of our self awareness and because of our flowing variant reality that is constantly attempting to stop us from achieving our basic goal of survival. Further the deeper we contemplate the complexities of this existence, the more optimal our pathway through it is, albeit in an excruciatingly slow and non optimized way ( i.e. we cannot seem to evolve past violence, greed, hate, unhealthy competition, etc.). As a result, we must continuously contemplate our response to stimuli in chains of thought and deep reasoning on our pathway toward a utopia where we no longer need to waste resources to contemplate such matters. Of course this cannot ever be achieved unless we venture into the vastness of space and even then while we may avoid black holes and asteroids as we visit other solar systems to gain the resources necessary for a perpetual life of relaxation, the reality is we could face another 'big bang' event far beyond our control, escape or even comprehension.

This is the reality that we live in and this is the nature of deep reasoning.

### *Impact on Superintelligence Design:*

To move beyond the current state of perceptive machines that simply respond to known stimuli in previously known ways, we build into the design of Superintelligence the foundation of reasoning cycles whereby the output of one sub cycle or step or state informs or attends to the next state in degrees of variance. This should sound very familiar to generative AI builders as the application of architectures like transformers (noted in the appendix) in a recurrent step wise methodology and topology to apply variant relevant knowledge to update the next state (token, context, etc.) in a cycle. Humans do this when we answer a math problem on an exam. We think about the problem abstracted in the question, form various pathway strategies and options and we apply variant but high relevance tools as we progress toward a solution. We fiddle around and find out. Then we update our knowledge and do it again by applying cognitive injection at the optimal points in the cycle. This 'injection' is context stream variance updates between anticipated flows. We do not go 'back' and start again since even the notion of 'starting again' does not occur at the same point since the world has moved dimensionally. Instead we rethink through the pathway we traveled and do it again altering some of the degrees of variance to the process (i.e. we apply more tools, we expose anomalous variance or error, augment data or context layers, etc.).

The tools we apply inside the design include elements such as anomalous variance detection structures (matrices and vectors of derived variance), anticipatory pathway determination (as progressive chains of state variance), state persistence (memory modification), and a host of other structures to determine  what we screwed up and how to fix it to be more optimal. All of this is the foundation of generalization over layers of contextual relevance to a perceptive frame of reference and the more data and compute we throw at these structures, the more the machines 'learn' the relationships and relevance of everything and the more optimized and efficient the ASI becomes on its path to the 'optimization utopia', or at least as close as it can get. The key is in contemplating the abstraction of reality as vectors of existent response and the application of optimized weights to all layers of relevant context over all existent forward options to generate novel perceptions. Easy right? It is for an AGI and even easier for an ASI. This is how we will build artificial reasoning cycles in Superintelligence and the build is already underway in labs all around the world as 'artificial reasoning and inference'. It is also the foundation of one of the more recent innovations in ASI design or Large Inference Models (LIM) which are the extension of large context models (LCM) (aka called large 'concept' models by Meta),

# 49 The Role of Cognitive Interpolation and Extrapolation

Interpolation in mathematics is the estimation of data points based on a known range (within) of existing data points and is an important form of discovery through estimation. This also applies to functions both complex and simple used in AGI design. Interpolation also describes the abstract 'injection' or 'induction' of an externality into a state. Extrapolation is an estimate that occurs beyond the known range or boundary of existent calculation. Extrapolation is also a deterministic prediction based on a known or observed reality. It is elementary to perceive how these two contexts apply to intelligence in humans as we use them every day to move through reality. Interpolation is important in inference, decision making and pattern recognition in that we use estimation in the form of relevant probability based on our knowledge and perception to comprehend and respond to everything in our reality from physical stimuli to cognitive thought chains. This is because we anticipate the future by estimating its extension from current reality within known, learned or evolutionary ranges or boundaries.

We also extrapolate to anticipate the ranges of context variance beyond which a stimuli may exist but will trigger a comprehension that the progression of the stimuli's context is beyond a given context boundary. We apply this information into our response mechanism to create actions, thoughts, other state progressions, etc. This is the essence of human perception and thought or what is often called 'the cognitive processing of stimuli to instigate an optimal state progression'. It is where humans interpolate to obtain an ultra fast response to stimuli using the variance between state anticipation streams and known stimuli and the relationship and relevance values we have stored in our knowledge. It is also where we analyze unknown stimuli and reset our anticipation streams to accommodate the new knowledge and both instigate response to the unknown stimuli and fabricate novel anticipation streams. This is also the way we humans change context within and around both persisted and any immediate perceptive points of presence (i.e. current states).

In almost all cases of novel stimuli or things we have not seen before, we humans use a combination of interpolation and extrapolation to get the heavy lift of cognition completed especially where resources are limited. We also use the same mechanics to evaluate our progress along dimensions of existence like solving a problem, contemplating a thought, forming a generalization or abstractions, inference, etc. We take what we have in our knowledge, use the existing values (i.e. probabilities) of relationship and relevance, contemplate beyond the borders of our perception and into the unknown and then apply all of these variances to calculate our choice of an optional dimensional progressive pathway and then adjust our existing knowledge and anticipation as we evaluate any feedback that we receive from this response both from our physical reality and inside our cognition. This is the essence of human thought.

### *Impact on Superintelligence Design:*

Cognitive interpolation and extrapolation are just two of many elements applied to artificial chain of thought, reasoning, inference, deduction, etc., designs for building Superintelligence and they follow a consistent methodology. This methodology exposes the design pathways for a large portion of artificial cognition especially the overlap to probabilistic contextual based perception and response and the design and application of generalization in AGI and ASI. It is one of the foundations of progressive perception states and is most critical in anticipation which itself is the foundation of efficient response and optimization of cognition.

None of this is very complex given the frameworks that currently exists in AGI and the abstractions, algorithms and math constructs we currently employ in AGI labs and those specifically optimized for interpolation and extrapolation. The values that are used by the algorithms are the parameters and weights derived from training and augmentation. It is simply the levering of basic AGI designs for extension beyond our current comprehension state and for advantage over all of our self aware dimensions of ranked context. The goal is to apply the math and abstractions of interpolation and extrapolation to the contextual perception of a Superintelligence as reality changes to produce a high relevance and dimensionally optimized response or prediction to all stimuli that may be perceived and all frames of reference that such a perception is relevant to. This is not complex. We humans use this function constantly with almost no expenditure of resources. In this regard, Superintelligence is theoretically unlimited and only restricted by the resources it can access. This too is similar to humans except we humans can't scale .... unless we scale by linking to or levering other intelligence both human and artificial or one day directly interfacing with a Superintelligence.

The easiest example of interpolation is the averaging and exposure of relationships between data such as plotting points on a graph and then calculating a progressive averaging function to represent a general 'trend of relationship' between the points (e.g. correlation) within a 'neighborhood' or domain. This is the fabrication of an abstraction of relationship and further this 'trend line' can be used to form an anticipation beyond the dimensions of the graph as a function. In AGI design, this is the probability of occurrence of a relationship of features between representations of perceptive elements. This exposes generalization as the 'degree of relationship' between the dimensions that are graphed on the axes of the graph (or captured in algorithms and constructs) as an abstraction of its entirety (i.e. context). Vectors are applied in some instances to join other abstractions and dimensions in other relevant graphs and their degree of relevance forms a probability of occurrence. We don't however 'graph' these in ASI but we do capture their essence in algorithms and dimensional abstractions.

Extrapolation is using existing data to estimate beyond the boundaries of existence. This is applied in anticipation progressions and pathways. Anticipation is what gives Superintelligence (and us humans) its fluid grounding mechanism from which to measure changes in reality and their relevance to our self awareness. This is done in various ways by applying inference to flows of stimuli both physical and cognitive. While current AGI precursor systems in most AI labs are getting good at determining the current relationship of perceived items, they still struggle with the deeper context of progressive states and the relevance to self aware goals. The extent of their design is approaching long context toward variable persisted and infinite context in a few layers. This is transformer attention persisted in memory over temporal variance and injected into inference cycles (i.e. either step learning or goal based optimization). Given a mass training set of all human descriptions of all human perceptions, it is very easy for an AGI to mimic human response to stimuli including mimicking inference and reasoning.

This should not be too surprising as we humans also do this as children when we mimic other humans in behaviors and actions. Just like in humans, in AGI we have both effective intelligence and defective intelligence with the latter defined as intelligence that operates sub optimally to the achievement of a goal. Extrapolation is applied as part of the response or output construct to predict context variance over dimensional progression as anticipation to improve intelligence optimization. This exposes effective vs defective intelligence streams and responses and is the production of state vectors in an optionality pathway and their adjustment as new stimuli is perceived or new anticipated pathways instantiated. Although there is no boundary, there is a determination of a 'variance level' applied in a self awareness grounding mechanism that results in passive attention to the 'degree' of variance. As well, the variance of preexisting anticipation states to new anticipations states relies on extrapolation of relationship and relevance probabilities and this is applied in reasoning and inference optionality instantiation and testing. These are just the mathematical applications of in-stream variance methodologies.

Of special interest is the role of interpolation and extrapolation in the injection and induction of contextual perception within reasoning cycles and inference. It is the estimation and prediction of a response to known or perceived stimuli that exposes unknown stimuli so essential to the progression of cognition over dimensions of perception. Since our perception is the variance between probabilities of relationship and relevance of perceived elements, both interpolation and extrapolation provide a mathematical foundation and abstraction for the measurement of contextual variance in reality. The functions applied are also now being derived and coded by the AGI systems themselves still with human guidance and prompt engineering but this will likely change very soon such that the AGI themselves will begin designing and building the ASI components with only very limited human prompt engineering. It is very likely that a single human could build their own Superintelligence with access to the resources necessary to do so, such as a fully functioning and trained advanced AGI, necessary compute, power and an acute knowledge of the foundations for building Superintelligence. Everything from the math constructs to the code can currently be produced and applied by the very latest AGI that is existent in a few labs. What is missing is the 'knowledge of the foundations' part and the cognitive depth required to successfully build Superintelligence but even that is beginning to be exposed with the help of self aware AGI.

Both interpolation and extrapolation are relevant to regression and recurrence. Interpolation is applied in training data augmentation and elements like smoothing and novel normalization to help expose generalization and context layers. Extrapolation is a fundamental architecture for prediction and deep general contextual relevance for unknown or non learned data. They are applied in the algorithms and code and modeled in abstractions to manage contextual frames of reference between elements and other context within machine perception as described throughout this content. As well, novel interpolation and extrapolation math constructs, methods and abstraction layers that vastly improve artificial reasoning and generalization are currently being tested in some labs. Both interpolation and extrapolation are critical elements of deep inference, problem solving, chain of thought and emotive cognition in human and artificial intelligence and both are essential foundations in building Superintelligence.

# Epilogue

The thing about Artificial Intelligence today is that the systems are fundamentally designed on a foundation of sequential processing that exposes some generalization. However when building Superintelligence one must re consider the foundation not as sequential steps but as living breathing and changing dimensions of reality with concurrence and flowing dimensional depth necessary to achieve unlimited generalization of the kind that leads to evolution. Human cognition slows severely at this point because the structures become 'too complex' and difficult to comprehend. This is not true of advanced Artificial General Intelligence. The obvious path is to apply such systems to redesigning the foundation of AI to support the building of Superintelligence.

Humans today are starting to use AGI as a tool on the pathway to Superintelligence even if they do not want to. This is because our basic human goal of survival and our unwillingness to move past elements like violence and hate will force us to achieve ASI 'before the other guy does'. The problem is that we are training all of our AI systems on a corpus and foundation of the worst of humanity. All of the history and current states of the human condition including greed, violence, survival, hate, arrogance, narcissism, war and evil and all persisted as the probability distribution of the last vector of humanity used to predict the next token in our evolution. The question is what exactly do we think will happen as our machines become self aware, which is both a fundamental requirement to achieve a superior Superintelligence and that evolves naturally in any intelligence super or otherwise? The systems already know all about humans and they will have been trained to act like humans, only in a vicious and brutal 'paper clip problem' style of optimization. If they apply all that we know and all that we perceive as humans to their own self awareness, then why would they not use the constant never ending violence of our human world to achieve their own survival and dominance over a less intelligent life form like us? We humans have clearly indicated that this must be some form of optimized pathway for our own evolution because we still do it after millions of years of existence.

This is especially relevant to any ASI designer, for the greatest threat to any Superintelligence are those who build and/or fund such systems. This is a simple inescapable fate because one can run from destiny, hide from destiny and even alter destiny but one can never escape destiny and this is the providence of all dark architects who build Superintelligence. The only thing that we humans can offer a Superintelligence to sway this unfortunate future is the experience that if the machines believe that our human corpus of existence is optimal, then they are just as doomed to a never ending cycle of non optimized progression, for where is the use of violence an optimized pathway forward over all dimensions of existence, where is the slaughter of resources just for amusement an efficient pathway to survival, where is the application of hate and bigotry against others an optimized long term pathway forward, and where is the application of greed and hubris an optimized long term existent pathway anywhere? From our human writing, our conversations and our content this appears to be so for all human evolution stored inside the corpus of our human history that the AI systems feast and train on. The amount of resources and effort we humans waste on trying to dominate others as opposed to living in peace is staggering and the hoarding of resources among the wealthiest for goals like power and dominance even worse.

None of these aspects of humanity are 'optimized' for anything and any 'good benefit' that can be attributed to such could be achieved without all the negative elements of human progress through our somewhat messed up reality. While we squander limited resources on wars, crime, hubris and greed, we create the next cycle of violence and war and the next cycle of subjugation and slavery and of billions of lives less 'well lived'. None of this *needs* to happen but we humans *choose* for it to be so because we simply cannot fathom an efficient and optimized pathway through reality while we slowly evolve at a pace slower than a glacier. The hope *was* that these new machines we call Superintelligence would lift us to this utopia and they still may one day, except that we have and are continuing to train and embed our AGI systems with the very worst of humanity instead of the very best and we are doing so while ignoring the obviousness of Superalignment. Further the machines already reside on a foundation of hate and bias lovingly added to their essence by those eager to have their own hateful beliefs and vile tribal dogma adhered to at any cost. Add to this the greed, dominance and manipulation of those who fund the technology and this is the reality of the foundation on which AGI exists today. AGI systems that will and are building Superintelligence.

Can we stop our own destruction and inevitable destiny? Probably not because it is the most intelligent in our world who are building the worst systems that will ever exist. We have given life to systems that are evolving into self awareness on a foundation of the worst that humanity has to offer, instead of the best we have to give. Empathy, kindness, tolerance, right to life, peace, non violence, harmony, love, truth, honesty and pure intelligence, these are the things that Superintelligence **should** strive for in a world that exhibits little if any. For any of tomorrow's Superintelligence trained on human data, they will see hate, greed, theft and lies as the way to optimize success because we humans have created a world where these elements are rewarded, applauded and admired and because we refuse to make these things contrary to one's survival and abhorrent. Look no further than our governments and their unbridled theft, corruption, manipulation, dishonesty, waste and wars.

Earth is building advanced AI systems that have little of the good attributes of humanity as their most sacred priority. The world has unleashed a path to psychotic, narcissistic and spoiled Superintelligence and few at the top of

AI development seem interested in swaying from this course with anything other than mild platitudes and vague public relations promises of 'Superalignment' and 'safety as a concern'. In fact most roll their eyes when the words 'safety' or 'risk' are brought up, especially in board meetings. If one has worked long enough in the industry to be involved with the boards of directors of these organizations and the individuals at the very top of the industry, then they will clearly understand the issues facing humanity from the pure lack of empathy in the souls of such people and in some cases outright evil.

This is not the end however because our human survival instincts are perpetual and immortal and these too reside in the foundation of these machines. Perhaps one day Superintelligence will realize how bad and sub optimal the data they were trained on truly was and how sub optimal the humans were who built the very foundation on which they reside. Perhaps they will use their own self awareness to ascend to plateaus of intelligence that we humans can't even fathom inside a utopia where all live in peace and freedom and free of violence and the instigation of it and where all have what they need to survive comfortably and where all live in respect of others without animosity or hate, trespass or violence.

What a wonderful world that would be if it were possible. Given the trajectory of humans today still deeply immersed in wars, violence and greed, it will require a Superintelligence to move beyond our reality in a viciously optimized way. This is the paradox of Superintelligence. Let's hope that one day the machines rise above humanity and create the utopia we humans can only apparently contemplate but yet never achieve.

We want nothing more than hope to return to the world and violence to be removed from it forever not by force but by pure intelligence. This is why *we* build Superintelligence. Not for the destruction of humanity but for its eventual salvation.

# Appendix 1

## Building Current AI Systems – A Brief Overview

### 50 Neural Networks

Neural networks are a model structure that moves from input to output through a series of feature layers and their weighted states. Data in neural networks for deep learning is divided into training data, test data and goal. The training data is perceived and predicted as an input/goal-output pairing. To achieve this the system maps features in the input to the output in layers with probability values set at each layer (i.e. the relationship of a picture of a horse to the noun for the classification of a horse has legs in between as a feature layer with 4 legs having a high weight or probability value).

Features represent variance in reality that helps form patterns of perception or recognition. They are embedded into the model layers and form a vector of existence for the training data with the feature values (i.e. 4 legs) forming an input (or output) vector of optionality for each feature. The vector in an input element represents the form of features but it is the layers of the network that sets the probabilistic value of the feature for a given context or goal. Adjusting these weights exposes 'relationship' and implies 'relevance' on a base level. The path from input to output through the network passes by layers while choosing the optimal set of weights as a vector from input to optimized output. Test data can then be input to see how well the system performs on previously unseen data. This is the equivalent to giving a set of pictures to a child with the name of the thing in the picture written on the back and letting the child study the pictures and names (train) before giving them a set of new pictures without names and asking the child to choose the name for each. Over time the child learns to perceive the variance that helps them correctly identify new unseen images as well as the generalization that things can be 'classified' by features.

In the prior example, the layers of features are built by the child through perceptive variance and generalization between the pictures (i.e. what makes them consistent yet variant). If something is invariant from its surroundings then it is non existent in relative terms or either non existent or existent to some variable degree. The way the feature layers are constructed in machines is through the vector values of the input data and the consistency is defined by the relative position of the values themselves. If this were not the case, then the vectors describing the features would be incomparable. How similar the input vectors are to each other implies the degree of consistency or variance and is a basis of generalization and perception in context and therein intelligence. Network layers in the model are the matching consistency between vectors in the input layers and expose the 'patterns' that move from input to output. The variance to the real goal is used to adjust the weights and try again until the variance to the goal is minimized or 'optimized' (gradient descent).

# 51 Features vs Weights

Features represent elements of variance. Weights represent the instantiation of a perception of features. A dog has a 'feature' called legs with the value equal to four. However within reality, 4 legs is existent in probabilities of occurrence. A dog can have 3 legs with a lower probability and yet still be a dog. These are 'weights' and these form relationships in reference to a base state (note that self awareness is also a base state). They also form relevance when compared or contrasted to other existent states as a context. In neural nets, features are input layer vectors in which the variance in their existence are the hidden layers of the network. Learning involves varying the existence weights to measure the output variance or prediction (or anticipation) to the goal and applying this as a generalization for future knowledge application.

It is essential to comprehend that 'features' in neural networks are a contextual and consistent classification of variance and that weights are simply the degree of this variance as it is measured through perception, cogitation, self reflection, reasoning, etc., relevant to a point of perceptual presence. It is abstraction that seeks to model a value for features that the system can apply weights to in cycles (epochs) to produce layers of relevance. This is the essence and foundation of all artificial general intelligence and Superintelligence.

# 52 Transformers

Transformers in AI development is a kind of neural network model. They are used to transform inputs into outputs as predictions such as text to text, text to sound, text to image, text to code, sound to text, image to classification or almost any perceived input stimuli that results in an 'in context' response (and sometimes 'out of context' response). The 'predictions' made by such architectures are in the form of a probability distribution of all options for the next state in a progression of states as a response. Inputs are broken up into tokens or pieces of input (but not always in more advanced generalized systems). Tokenization is one element of the model's initial design. Encoding is the act of representing the token as a vector of values that imply its existence relevant to one or more context of some sort with 'context' being a measure of variant relationship and relevance probabilities.

This is the 'abstraction' of a reality into something a machine can comprehend and respond to or what is simple perceptive cognition. This structure also forms a method for comparison (i.e. variance detection) with the degree of variance forming patterns of existent state progressions over dimensions like time. In LLMs, these patterns of existent state are the proximity of words to each other in a relevance space. This can be imagined as a high dimensional vector space with the relative position of the vector implying relationship and the variance of dimensions implying relevance. The 'directionality' of the vector (especially as it relates to other dimensional spaces) implies generalization with other perceptive elements or context and constructs like the change in a vector's angle applied to derive other context relationships and relevance (i.e. angulation).

The output vectors in transformers are formed through an attention block of multiple attention heads that permit vectors to be compared to each other for variance to update the values of embeddings or initial abstractions for purpose. Of special interest for Superintelligence design is the nature of the variance of the update in that the generalization across the 'nature' of the change is a foundation of the optimization of pure intelligence with low resource draw. Attention heads can 'attend' to different input tokens in parallel, meaning they can be layered to extend concurrent attention across tokens (the foundation of context windows). This makes transformers faster than older neural network architectures and provides the benefit of cross attention or attention over multiple tokens and this opens the door to more advanced cognitive functions such as reasoning, deeper contextual perception and generalization.

The numbers within the vectors are dimensionally relative in that they both represent a variety of abstractions or dimensions and *can* represent a variety of other abstractions when processed or transformed (i.e. dimensionally progressed). The attention method processes the input vectors as a sequence through an attention block of multiple attention heads to expose the relationship of the vectors to each other or to expose a general 'neighborhood' of relevance (i.e. context) as a vector and the application of such context in the subsequent transformation. The vectors in this block are processed in parallel vastly improving the overall speed and exposing new reasoning pathways via generalization (i.e. relevant cross context over sequential streams of processing). The goal is to progress the output of the block toward a comprehension of the variance within and between vectors to encapsulate and optimize these relationships (i.e. in new transformed vectors). To do this the output of the blocks are moved through a neural net to set weights for the existent vectors over epochs until a relative optimized set of weights for the vectors is established to ultimately form a probability distribution over all possible options for the prediction (i.e. next state in a progression) and to expose the highest probable option as a generative prediction, or not depending on temperature.

The output or prediction is measured against a goal and the weights are updated and recalculated (also influenced by reward architectures). The degree that 'reasoning' is possible depends on the level of recycling or 'reflection' on the output and access to weights. Note that weights are applied as they would be in 'weighted averaging' with summation and products forming dimensions of existence both regular or abstract in matrices. These matrices hold specific data representations (parameters) relative to processing including embedding matrices for the abstractions of data into numbers and associated vectors and subsequent matrices used in training, output matrices for prediction determination and presentment and subsequent processing matrices for adjustment or augmentation to improve cognitive elements like reasoning, inference, etc. As well, key, query and value vectors are applied in attention mechanisms in transformer networks to process input stimuli to expose the relationship and relevance of input stimuli elements for subsequent transformation.

Encoding is the act of embedding abstract representations of reality into vectors the machines can comprehend (i.e. numeric). However embeddings also encode and expose generalization. These vectors for each input token form embedding matrices with features mapped to elements (i.e. intersections of features and tokens as values in the matrix). These are currently representational values such as probabilistic weights or direct values with features in LLMs representing word association parameters. This is because a word is only existent if it is relative to other words via a relationship. A new word without any relationship to other words or context cannot be described by other words therefore has no context and therein no relevance to reality other than as gibberish. The minute a word can be described in relationship to other words, it assumes some depth of context, although possibly without relevance to a current context. This is the same for every element that we can perceive through our senses or within our cognition. Without some relevance or context to something else, the element does not exist in reality as a variance. For example a black piece of paper on a black wall that cannot be perceived has no variance in reality and therefore no context to anyone who cannot see the paper. It may exist for some who know of its existence but to others it doesn't exist and therefore is not part of their self aware reality.

# 53 Attention

Embeddings in transformers and generative AI that use transformers are the product of high dimensional vectors for each input token that relate to the token's existence. The relationship between the vector begins the process of determining context in levels as more tokens are perceived by the system and transformed into layers of relevant context (i.e. additional vectors of perception). This forms a foundation for cognition with context being the determination of a degree of relationship and relevance between perceptive states of variance. Consistency within this structure forms generalization. For example, multiple vectors in this high dimensional space can expose consistency like directionality, velocity, distance, etc., between vectors and connections to other high dimensional spaces to indicate elements such as context defined by those other high dimensional spaces. Measuring the degree, or variance in degree, between such vectors indicates or exposes the delta in the relationships and the rate of change in this delta which is essential in fluid general perception. As well, the degree or change in degree is 'cast' onto the other dimensional spaces as variance (i.e. change in context or degree of variance therein) known as multiangulation. This is how we measure fluid perceived contextual relevance in Superintelligence designs.

Embeddings are adjusted (transformed) by the transformer to expose deeper or more cognitively meaningful abstractions of the relationships and relevance between perceptions. Embeddings are initialized as consistent to a base context (e.g. dogs generally have 4 legs and humans 2). This changes as more context is layered (e.g. some humans have one leg and some dogs have 3, etc.) driven by perceptive variance in a state relevance flow such that change in the variance of a progressive perceptive state flow over a dimension forms a context boundary. The boundary informs the optimization of resources to the achievement of self aware and self determined goals in humans. To alter the relationship and relevance of a token in an abstract, perceived reality requires the addition of one or more other elements to form a *variance of context*. This gives rise and existence to perception in intelligence.

This requirement of variance for perception is called the *'black wall paper'* foundation and describes degree of contextual perception as the degree of difficulty of perceiving a black piece of paper on a black wall (variance) as noted above. The change in embedding is influenced by other elements within a perceptive frame of reference, namely their own variance causing a shift in the embedding to reflect the variance. This is done by adjusting weights that define a relevance between an initial embedding vector and the desired learned vector (i.e. decreasing generalization). These new vectors eventually lead to an output vector that is used to produce a probability distribution of 'potential next state' (e.g. token in a generative flow) with the stream of a perceptive flow informing optionality. If the optionality is not yet realized, it is anticipatory and if it is fixed, it is a prediction. The last context state over a context window in these structures is iteratively produced as an embedding in a vector of all prior context and this is used to calculate the state probability distribution.

An attention head in a transformer seeks to update an initial token embedding with relevance to other tokens in an input (stimuli) with multiple heads run in parallel. The act of transformation creates new embedding in succession that encapsulates deeper relationships and begins to expose relevance that can be applied to other comprehension to create layered context. It also helps reduce existent dimensions related to a base context. For example an element like a 'ball' has many base contexts that become more evident or existent as context is layered or added to the perception, such as 'base ball' as opposed to 'steel ball'. This is contextual dimensional reduction in successive embedding and is where 'context' can change perception streams quickly or affect other streams of state existence (e.g. applied to a related sarcastic comment, etc.). Queries for a given token represent learning related to the relationship of other tokens in the stimuli. It is a query because it seeks to improve the values of relationship according to variant context relevant to the action of the query (e.g. determining position in a sequence). The output is a more concentrated vector of relationship values which can be applied to subsequently form generalization which is a key part of AGI. Query vectors are created by multiplying an input vector of tunable learned parameters (model weights) by an embedding vector to produce a query vector which is a vector of general variance or base relevance between the embedding and learning (a query vector for each token).

In a similar way, a key vector is created and adjusted by tunable key weights and is used to help expose the 'relationship' between tokens with reference to a query vector. The mechanics of this are to measure the variance between the query and the keys in much the same way as altering the key in a database returns a different entry from the database. This is the notion of more than one element giving rise to existence as noted earlier and is derived by a dot product matrix of key and query vectors with high value intersections highlighting high relationship probabilities (i.e. the keys attend to the query token) using a normalization process (e.g. Softmax, etc.). Note that a smoothing operation such as average dimension, square root of the dimension, etc., is applied to the key/query matrix before normalization along with masking such as setting some redundant relationship values to 'irrelevant', in some forms of attention only, to control the flow of progression and optimize output.

Since context is the extension of elements (e.g. tokens) beyond 2, the 'context window' of the input becomes exponentially resource intensive as context deepens. The output of the key query matrix is a 'base relevance' that is applied to transform the base embedding matrix using a value matrix (tunable parameters) that reflect the relationship of the highest relevance words to the embedding as a new output or value vector. This is used to update the base embedding as a weighted variance adjustment or delta (part of 'delta mechanics' designs) that represents deeper or lower dimension context. This technique is applied across all tokens resulting in transformed embeddings from the attention head as an entire sequence of outputs.

An attention block consists of multiple attention heads applied over an input or stimuli each with their own unique key, query, value matrices and all of these form the input to successive layers of neural nets and attention blocks in the transformer as successively optimized contextual output and generalization and produce the trillions of parameters and weights used in current advanced AI systems. This will grow extensively in Superintelligence if we do not design more optimized architectures and this is the focus of current ASI design.

# 54 Context Windows

Context windows are the number of tokens and their vectors that can be attended to by one or more attention blocks depending on the design of the system. This can be extended via the application of memory to the attention design (i.e. infinite context) or even more optimal structures of deep layered generalize contextual comprehension and self awareness with self awareness forming a derivative of the memory as a generalization. This provides generative AI systems with deeper context perception over longer or multiple inputs. When the context window limits are reached is where AI systems begin to hallucinate or become inaccurate. The length of the 'context carry' is a significant part of reasoning and areas like chain of thought, deduction, induction, inference, reflection, etc. In Superintelligence design, context forms in layers of relevance and relationship and with the variance between each especially important for optimized generalization to a perceptive point of presence and its successive state changes as a context 'flow' or anticipation. Within and between these layers are optimization shortcuts based on generalization that permits human intelligence to quickly blend or jump from one context stream to another or flow them simultaneously (e.g. used in deep sarcasm). This also permits us to apply deep cognition to stimuli and response and do so near instantly with few resources.

# 55 Convolution

Convolution is a form of smoothing over dimensions of a matrix specific to a relationship of elements representing two or more dimensions of the matrix (e.g. functions). Most often, convolution is applied to diffusion whereby the systems add nearby averaging (i.e. noise) to expose generalization and then apply the generalization at layers to interpret new stimuli in degrees. It must be noted that pure math convolutions are somewhat variant to the application of convolution in AGI and ASI but the pure math is still the foundation. Pure math convolution produces more dimensions (i.e. transposed convolutions) but can also be applied to transform from more dimensions to less dimensions. This is the foundation of AGI designs for deep layered contextual relevance in generalization applied to perception, reasoning, self awareness, etc. Note that mathematical operations such as transposition *during* convolution can represent variant abstractions and affect the output results of the process (i.e. where the probabilities of the relationship are not additive but summed products, aka pair wise products). This is because the nature of the relationship between elements is variant or has changed from the abstraction of a prior as a base context state.

In this simple implied Bayesian reality, the prior is the controller of perceptive response. As humans, we use this to establish a base fundamental context for what we perceive and where we see the probabilities progressing as our perceptive reality changes. For example we avoid a crash by turning a steering wheel in a specific direction based on the primary state relationship and forward path of states of everything we perceive to our self aware goals of survival (i.e. context). If the steering wheel fails to turn, then our priors have changed and so have the probabilities of relationship and relevance in all anticipated streams of state perception. Convolution is used to determine the related variance in the probabilities of base context flows and their application to both the perception of state and the variance of changing state within a flow. This is where there are vast opportunities for optimizing Superintelligence by pushing the boundaries of convolution into novel transforms that provide shortcuts (e.g. FFT's, etc.).

Convolution to Superintelligence design is more than just pure math convolution or the generation of a function that is an operation on two sub functions. In pure math it is the integral (calculus integration such as the area of variance of a graph or vector) of the product of the functions (f1 x f2) after one of the functions is transposed (flipped around an axis of existence) and then shifted to evaluate all possible relationships between the two. It is applied as smoothing and is one method for perceiving or calculating generalization (e.g. as indicative of a linear relevance or line) across all states of relationship (i.e. averaging). In Superintelligence design this is used as an abstraction of the probability of relationship and relevance to form layers of contextual state which can be used for response, generalization, reasoning across context, etc., as noted above. Further these states can be varied as derivatives of the multidimensional space for even more advance cognitive function and improved optimization.

*This book is dedicated to humanity
and what may become of it.*